Node Cookbook
Second Edition

Over 50 recipes to master the art of asynchronous server-side JavaScript using Node.js, with coverage of Express 4 and Socket.IO frameworks and the new Streams API

David Mark Clements

BIRMINGHAM - MUMBAI

Node Cookbook
Second Edition

Copyright © 2014 Packt Publishing

All rights reserved. No part of this book may be reproduced, stored in a retrieval system, or transmitted in any form or by any means, without the prior written permission of the publisher, except in the case of brief quotations embedded in critical articles or reviews.

Every effort has been made in the preparation of this book to ensure the accuracy of the information presented. However, the information contained in this book is sold without warranty, either express or implied. Neither the author, nor Packt Publishing, and its dealers and distributors will be held liable for any damages caused or alleged to be caused directly or indirectly by this book.

Packt Publishing has endeavored to provide trademark information about all of the companies and products mentioned in this book by the appropriate use of capitals. However, Packt Publishing cannot guarantee the accuracy of this information.

First published: July 2012

Second edition: April 2014

Production Reference: 1180414

Published by Packt Publishing Ltd.
Livery Place
35 Livery Street
Birmingham B3 2PB, UK.

ISBN 978-1-78328-043-8

www.packtpub.com

Cover Image by Alvaro Dalloz (alvaroff@gmail.com)

Credits

Author
David Mark Clements

Reviewers
Vijay Annadi
Johannes Boyne
Aravind V.S

Commissioning Editor
Grant Mizen

Acquisition Editors
Antony Lowe
Sam Wood

Content Development Editor
Amey Varangaonkar

Technical Editors
Pratik More
Humera Shaikh
Ritika Singh

Copy Editors
Alisha Aranha
Mradula Hegde
Gladson Monteiro
Adithi Shetty

Project Coordinator
Amey Sawant

Proofreaders
Simran Bhogal
Maria Gould
Ameesha Green
Paul Hindle
Jonathan Todd

Indexer
Priya Subramani

Graphics
Sheetal Aute
Ronak Dhruv

Production Coordinator
Saiprasad Kadam

Cover Work
Saiprasad Kadam

About the Author

David Mark Clements is a JavaScript and Node specialist residing in Northern Ireland. From a very early age he was fascinated with programming and computers. He first learned BASIC on one of the many Atari's he had accumulated by the age of 9. David learned JavaScript at age 12, moving into Linux administration and PHP as a teenager.

Now (as a twenty something), he assists multinationals and startups alike with JavaScript solutions and training. Node has become a prominent member of his toolkit due to its versatility, vast ecosystem, and the cognitive ease that comes with full-stack JavaScript.

When he's not tinkering with computers, he's spending time with the love of his life, Maxine, and her Husky-Spitz cross, Jessi.

> Many thanks to the Node community who have caused Node to grow as it has, and the Node Google Group, which has been an immense source of information and inspiration. I cannot conclude without acknowledging Jesus, who makes my life worthwhile and gives me answers to problems when I'm not seeing the solution myself (Jms 1:5, 1 Cor 1:30).

About the Reviewers

Vijay Annadi is a freelance developer/architect with a passion for designing/developing complex yet simple software. Since 1997, he has been developing software applications using a wide array of languages and technologies, including Java, JavaScript, Python, Scala, and many others, with focus on both desktop and web applications.

Johannes Boyne is a full-stack developer, technical consultant, and entrepreneur. He co-founded Archkomm GmbH and is now working at Zweitag GmbH, a software engineering consultancy. His work with Node.js began with Version 0.4 and since then he has supported the Node.js community.

He started as a rich Internet application developer and did consulting work later on till he joined Archkomm for the VIRTUAL TWINS® project as technical lead. He is interested in new technologies such as NoSQL, high-performance and highly-scalable systems, as well as cloud computing. Besides work, he loves sports, reading about new scientific research, watching movies, and travelling.

He has also worked on books such as *Rich Internet Applications mit Adobe Flex 3, Simon Widjaja, Hanser Fachbuchverlag (2008)* and *Adobe Flex 4, Simon Widjaja, Hanser Fachbuchverlag (July 1, 2010)*. He was also a technical reviewer of the book *Node Security, Dominic Barnes, Packt Publishing*.

Aravind V.S is an aspiring mind and a creative brain to look forward to in the field of technology. He is a successful freelance software developer and web designer. His interest in embedded systems and computers paved his way into a programming career at the age of 15. He then developed an inventory management system for a local provision store and it rocketed his programming career sky high. His compassion and curiosity for technological advances and gadgets can be clearly seen on his blog `http://aravindvs.com/blog/`, where he talks about the current tech trends and also provides tutorials. He can be found outdoors focusing his camera or reading books during his leisure time.

> I would like to take this opportunity to thank my friends and my parents for their support in completing the review of this book, especially my best friend Kavya Babu for her undying support and encouragement, without which I wouldn't be what I am today. Special thanks to Ryan Dahl and his team for NodeJS. Above all, I'd like to thank the Almighty for everything.

www.PacktPub.com

Support files, eBooks, discount offers and more

You might want to visit www.PacktPub.com for support files and downloads related to your book.

Did you know that Packt offers eBook versions of every book published, with PDF and ePub files available? You can upgrade to the eBook version at www.PacktPub.com and as a print book customer, you are entitled to a discount on the eBook copy. Get in touch with us at service@packtpub.com for more details.

At www.PacktPub.com, you can also read a collection of free technical articles, sign up for a range of free newsletters and receive exclusive discounts and offers on Packt books and eBooks.

http://PacktLib.PacktPub.com

Do you need instant solutions to your IT questions? PacktLib is Packt's online digital book library. Here, you can access, read and search across Packt's entire library of books.

Why Subscribe?

- Fully searchable across every book published by Packt
- Copy and paste, print and bookmark content
- On demand and accessible via web browser

Free Access for Packt account holders

If you have an account with Packt at www.PacktPub.com, you can use this to access PacktLib today and view nine entirely free books. Simply use your login credentials for immediate access.

Table of Contents

Preface	**1**
Chapter 1: Making a Web Server	**7**
Introduction	7
Setting up a router	7
Serving static files	13
Caching content in memory for immediate delivery	18
Optimizing performance with streaming	22
Securing against filesystem hacking exploits	28
Chapter 2: Exploring the HTTP Object	**35**
Introduction	35
Processing POST data	35
Handling file uploads	40
Using Node as an HTTP client	47
Implementing download throttling	52
Chapter 3: Working with Data Serialization	**59**
Introduction	59
Converting an object to JSON and back	59
Converting an object to XML and back	64
Browser-server transmission via AJAX	70
Working with real data – fetching trending tweets	79
Chapter 4: Interfacing with Databases	**89**
Introduction	89
Writing to a CSV file	90
Connecting and sending SQL to a MySQL server	94
Storing and retrieving data with MongoDB	99
Storing data to CouchDB with Cradle	107
Retrieving data from CouchDB with Cradle	109

Accessing the CouchDB changes stream with Cradle	115
Storing and retrieving data with Redis	118
Implementing PubSub with Redis	121

Chapter 5: Employing Streams — 127

Introduction	127
Consuming streams	128
Playing with pipes	134
Making stream interfaces	137
Streaming across Node processes	144

Chapter 6: Going Real Time — 153

Introduction	153
Creating a WebSocket server	154
Cross-browser real-time logic with Socket.IO	162
Remote Procedure Calls with Socket.IO	167
Creating a real-time widget	171

Chapter 7: Accelerating Development with Express — 179

Introduction	179
Generating Express scaffolding	180
Managing server tier environments	187
Implementing dynamic routing	191
Templating in Express	195
CSS preprocessors with Express	201
Initializing and using a session	211
Making an Express web app	220

Chapter 8: Implementing Security, Encryption, and Authentication — 241

Introduction	241
Implementing Basic Authentication	242
Hashing passwords	245
Implementing Digest Authentication	250
Setting up an HTTPS web server	257
Preventing cross-site request forgery	260

Chapter 9: Integrating Network Paradigms — 269

Introduction	269
Sending an e-mail	270
Sending an SMS	274
Communicating with TCP	280
Creating an SMTP server	285
Implementing a virtual hosting paradigm	291

Chapter 10: Writing Your Own Node Modules — 299
- Introduction — 299
- Creating a test-driven module specification — 300
- Writing a functional module mock-up — 305
- Refactoring with prototypical inheritance — 310
- Extending a module's API — 317
- Deploying a module to npm — 326

Chapter 11: Taking It Live — 331
- Introduction — 331
- Deploying an app to a server environment — 331
- Automatic crash recovery — 337
- Continuous deployment — 341
- Hosting with a Platform as a Service provider — 348

Index — 353

Preface

The principles of asynchronous event-driven programming are perfect for today's Web, where efficient, high-concurrency applications are essential for good user experience and a company's bottom line.

The use of Node for tooling and server-side logic with a browser-based client-side UI leads to a full-stack unilingual experience—everything is JavaScript. This saves developers, architects, project leads, and entire teams the cognitive energy of context-switching between languages, and yields rapid, fluid development cycles.

With a thriving community and success stories from major organizations (such as Groupon, PayPal, and Yahoo), Node.js is relevant to enthusiasts, start-ups, and enterprises alike.

Node Cookbook Second Edition shows you how to transfer your JavaScript skills to server-side programming. With simple examples and supporting code, this book takes you through various server-side scenarios, often saving you time, effort, and trouble by demonstrating best practices and showing you how to avoid security mistakes.

The second edition comes with an additional chapter (*Chapter 5, Employing Streams*) and has been updated for the latest version of Node along with the most recent versions of the modules and frameworks discussed. In particular, the very latest versions of the popular **Express** and **Socket.IO** frameworks have extensive coverage.

Beginning with making your own web server, the practical recipes in this cookbook are designed to smoothly help you progress to make full web applications, command-line applications, and Node modules. *Node Cookbook Second Edition* takes you through interfacing with various database backends, such as **MySQL**, **MongoDB**, and **Redis**, working with web sockets, and interfacing with network protocols, such as **SMTP**. Additionally, there are recipes on handling streams of data, security implementations, writing your own Node modules, and different ways to take your apps live.

What this book covers

Chapter 1, Making a Web Server, covers how to serve dynamic and static content, cache files in memory, stream large files straight from disk over HTTP, and secure your web server.

Chapter 2, Exploring the HTTP Object, explains the process of receiving and processing POST requests and file uploads using Node as an HTTP client. It also discusses how to throttle downloads.

Chapter 3, Working with Data Serialization, explains how to convert data from your apps into XML and JSON formats when sending to the browser or third-party APIs.

Chapter 4, Interfacing with Databases, covers how to implement persistent data stores with Redis, CouchDB, MongoDB, MySQL, or plain CSV files.

Chapter 5, Employing Streams, is included in the second edition. From streaming fundamentals to creating custom stream abstractions, this chapter introduces a powerful API that can boost the speed and memory efficiency of processing large amounts of data.

Chapter 6, Going Real Time, helps you to make real-time web apps with modern browser WebSocket technology, and gracefully degrade to long polling and other methods with Socket.IO.

Chapter 7, Accelerating Development with Express, explains how to leverage the Express framework to achieve rapid web development. It also covers the use of template languages and CSS engines, such as LESS and Stylus.

Chapter 8, Implementing Security, Encryption, and Authentication, explains how to set up an SSL-secured web server, use the crypto module to create strong password hashes, and protect your users from cross-site request forgery attacks.

Chapter 9, Integrating Network Paradigms, discusses how to send e-mails and create your own e-mail server, send SMS text messages, implement virtual hosting, and do fun and interesting things with raw TCP.

Chapter 10, Writing Your Own Node Modules, explains how to create a test suite, write a solution, refactor, improve and extend, and then deploy your own Node module.

Chapter 11, Taking it Live, discusses how to deploy your web apps to a live server, ensure your apps stay live with crash recovery techniques, implement a continuous deployment workflow, or alternatively, simply use a Platform as a Service Provider.

What you need for this book

The following is a list of the software that is required to run the examples in this book:

- Windows, Mac OS X, or Linux
- Node 0.10.x or higher

The content and code will continue to be relevant for Node's 1.x.x releases.

Who this book is for

If you have some knowledge of JavaScript and want to build fast, efficient, scalable client-server solutions, then *Node Cookbook Second Edition* is for you. Experienced users of Node will improve their skills, and even if you have not worked with Node before, these practical recipes will make it easy to get started.

Conventions

In this book, you will find a number of text styles that distinguish between different kinds of information. Here are some examples of these styles, and an explanation of their meaning.

Code words in text, database table names, folder names, filenames, file extensions, pathnames, dummy URLs, user input, and Twitter handles are shown as follows: "We can load a module into our app using Node's built-in `require` function."

A block of code is set as follows:

```
var http = require('http');
http.createServer(function (request, response) {
  response.writeHead(200, {'Content-Type': 'text/html'});
  response.end('Woohoo!');
}).listen(8080);
```

When we wish to draw your attention to a particular part of a code block, the relevant lines or items are set in bold:

```
var http = require('http');
var path = require('path');
http.createServer(function (request, response) {
  var lookup=path.basename(decodeURI(request.url));
```

Any command-line input or output is written as follows:

```
# cp /usr/src/asterisk-addons/configs/cdr_mysql.conf.sample
    /etc/asterisk/cdr_mysql.conf
```

New terms and **important words** are shown in bold. Words that you see on the screen, in menus or dialog boxes for example, appear in the text like this: "The console will say **foo doesn't exist**, because it doesn't."

> Warnings or important notes appear in a box like this.

> Tips and tricks appear like this.

Reader feedback

Feedback from our readers is always welcome. Let us know what you think about this book—what you liked or may have disliked. Reader feedback is important for us to develop titles that you really get the most out of.

To send us general feedback, simply send an e-mail to feedback@packtpub.com, and mention the book title via the subject of your message.

If there is a topic that you have expertise in and you are interested in either writing or contributing to a book, see our author guide on www.packtpub.com/authors.

Customer support

Now that you are the proud owner of a Packt book, we have a number of things to help you to get the most from your purchase.

Downloading the example code

You can download the example code files for all Packt books you have purchased from your account at http://www.packtpub.com. If you purchased this book elsewhere, you can visit http://www.packtpub.com/support and register to have the files e-mailed directly to you.

Errata

Although we have taken every care to ensure the accuracy of our content, mistakes do happen. If you find a mistake in one of our books—maybe a mistake in the text or the code—we would be grateful if you would report this to us. By doing so, you can save other readers from frustration and help us improve subsequent versions of this book. If you find any errata, please report them by visiting http://www.packtpub.com/submit-errata, selecting your book, clicking on the **errata submission form** link, and entering the details of your errata. Once your errata are verified, your submission will be accepted and the errata will be uploaded on our website, or added to any list of existing errata, under the Errata section of that title. Any existing errata can be viewed by selecting your title from http://www.packtpub.com/support.

Piracy

Piracy of copyright material on the Internet is an ongoing problem across all media. At Packt, we take the protection of our copyright and licenses very seriously. If you come across any illegal copies of our works, in any form, on the Internet, please provide us with the location address or website name immediately so that we can pursue a remedy.

Please contact us at copyright@packtpub.com with a link to the suspected pirated material.

We appreciate your help in protecting our authors, and our ability to bring you valuable content.

Questions

You can contact us at questions@packtpub.com if you are having a problem with any aspect of the book, and we will do our best to address it.

1
Making a Web Server

In this chapter, we will cover the following topics:

- Setting up a router
- Serving static files
- Caching content in memory for immediate delivery
- Optimizing performance with streaming
- Securing against filesystem hacking exploits

Introduction

One of the great qualities of Node is its simplicity. Unlike PHP or ASP, there is no separation between the web server and code, nor do we have to customize large configuration files to get the behavior we want. With Node, we can create the web server, customize it, and deliver content. All this can be done at the code level. This chapter demonstrates how to create a web server with Node and feed content through it, while implementing security and performance enhancements to cater for various situations.

If we don't have Node installed yet, we can head to http://nodejs.org and hit the **INSTALL** button appearing on the homepage. This will download the relevant file to install Node on our operating system.

Setting up a router

In order to deliver web content, we need to make a **Uniform Resource Identifier** (**URI**) available. This recipe walks us through the creation of an HTTP server that exposes routes to the user.

Making a Web Server

Getting ready

First let's create our server file. If our main purpose is to expose server functionality, it's a general practice to call the `server.js` file (because the `npm start` command runs the `node server.js` command by default). We could put this new `server.js` file in a new folder.

It's also a good idea to install and use `supervisor`. We use npm (the module downloading and publishing command-line application that ships with Node) to install. On the command-line utility, we write the following command:

`sudo npm -g install supervisor`

Essentially, `sudo` allows administrative privileges for Linux and Mac OS X systems. If we are using Node on Windows, we can drop the `sudo` part in any of our commands.

The `supervisor` module will conveniently autorestart our server when we save our changes. To kick things off, we can start our `server.js` file with the `supervisor` module by executing the following command:

`supervisor server.js`

For more on possible arguments and the configuration of `supervisor`, check out `https://github.com/isaacs/node-supervisor`.

How to do it...

In order to create the server, we need the HTTP module. So let's load it and use the `http.createServer` method as follows:

```
var http = require('http');
http.createServer(function (request, response) {
  response.writeHead(200, {'Content-Type': 'text/html'});
  response.end('Woohoo!');
}).listen(8080);
```

> **Downloading the example code**
>
> You can download the example code files for all Packt books you have purchased from your account at `http://www.packtpub.com`. If you purchased this book elsewhere, you can visit `http://www.packtpub.com/support` and register to have the files e-mailed directly to you.

Now, if we save our file and access `localhost:8080` on a web browser or using curl, our browser (or curl) will exclaim **Woohoo!** But the same will occur at `localhost:8080/foo`. Indeed, any path will render the same behavior. So let's build in some routing. We can use the `path` module to extract the `basename` variable of the path (the final part of the path) and reverse any URI encoding from the client with `decodeURI` as follows:

```
var http = require('http');
var path = require('path');
http.createServer(function (request, response) {
   var lookup=path.basename(decodeURI(request.url));
```

We now need a way to define our routes. One option is to use an array of objects as follows:

```
var pages = [
  {route: '', output: 'Woohoo!'},
  {route: 'about', output: 'A simple routing with Node example'},
  {route: 'another page', output: function() {return 'Here\'s '
    '+this.route;}},
];
```

Our `pages` array should be placed above the `http.createServer` call.

Within our server, we need to loop through our array and see if the lookup variable matches any of our routes. If it does, we can supply the output. We'll also implement some `404` error-related handling as follows:

```
http.createServer(function (request, response) {
   var lookup=path.basename(decodeURI(request.url));
   pages.forEach(function(page) {
     if (page.route === lookup) {
       response.writeHead(200, {'Content-Type': 'text/html'});
       response.end(typeof page.output === 'function'
       ? page.output() : page.output);
     }
   });
   if (!response.finished) {
      response.writeHead(404);
      response.end('Page Not Found!');
   }
}).listen(8080);
```

How it works...

The callback function we provide to `http.createServer` gives us all the functionality we need to interact with our server through the `request` and `response` objects. We use `request` to obtain the requested URL and then we acquire its `basename` with `path`. We also use `decodeURI`, without which another page route would fail as our code would try to match *another%20page* against our `pages` array and return false.

Once we have our basename, we can match it in any way we want. We could send it in a database query to retrieve content, use regular expressions to effectuate partial matches, or we could match it to a filename and load its contents.

We could have used a switch statement to handle routing, but our pages array has several advantages—it's easier to read, easier to extend, and can be seamlessly converted to JSON. We loop through our pages array using forEach.

Node is built on Google's V8 engine, which provides us with a number of **ECMAScript 5 (ES5)** features. These features can't be used in all browsers as they're not yet universally implemented, but using them in Node is no problem! The forEach function is an ES5 implementation; the ES3 way is to use the less convenient for loop.

While looping through each object, we check its route property. If we get a match, we write the 200 OK status and content-type headers, and then we end the response with the object's output property.

The response.end method allows us to pass a parameter to it, which it writes just before finishing the response. In response.end, we have used a ternary operator (?:) to conditionally call page.output as a function or simply pass it as a string. Notice that the another page route contains a function instead of a string. The function has access to its parent object through the this variable, and allows for greater flexibility in assembling the output we want to provide. In the event that there is no match in our forEach loop, response.end would never be called and therefore the client would continue to wait for a response until it times out. To avoid this, we check the response.finished property and if it's false, we write a 404 header and end the response.

The response.finished flag is affected by the forEach callback, yet it's not nested within the callback. Callback functions are mostly used for asynchronous operations, so on the surface this looks like a potential race condition; however, the forEach loop does not operate asynchronously; it blocks until all loops are complete.

There's more...

There are many ways to extend and alter this example. There are also some great non-core modules available that do the leg work for us.

Simple multilevel routing

Our routing so far only deals with a single level path. A multilevel path (for example, /about/node) will simply return a 404 error message. We can alter our object to reflect a subdirectory-like structure, remove path, and use request.url for our routes instead of path.basename as follows:

```
var http=require('http');
var pages = [
  {route: '/', output: 'Woohoo!'},
```

```
    {route: '/about/this', output: 'Multilevel routing with Node'},
    {route: '/about/node', output: 'Evented I/O for V8 JavaScript.'},
    {route: '/another page', output: function () {return 'Here\'s '
       + this.route; }}
];
http.createServer(function (request, response) {
  var lookup = decodeURI(request.url);
```

 When serving static files, `request.url` must be cleaned prior to fetching a given file. Check out the *Securing against filesystem hacking exploits* recipe in this chapter.

Multilevel routing could be taken further; we could build and then traverse a more complex object as follows:

```
{route: 'about', childRoutes: [
   {route: 'node', output: 'Evented I/O for V8 Javascript'},
   {route: 'this', output: 'Complex Multilevel Example'}
]}
```

After the third or fourth level, this object would become a leviathan to look at. We could alternatively create a helper function to define our routes that essentially pieces our object together for us. Alternatively, we could use one of the excellent noncore routing modules provided by the open source Node community. Excellent solutions already exist that provide helper methods to handle the increasing complexity of scalable multilevel routing. (See the *Routing modules* section and *Chapter 7, Accelerating Development with Express*).

Parsing the querystring module

Two other useful core modules are `url` and `querystring`. The `url.parse` method allows two parameters: first the URL string (in our case, this will be `request.url`) and second a Boolean parameter named `parseQueryString`. If the `url.parse` method is set to `true`, it lazy loads the `querystring` module (saving us the need to require it) to parse the query into an object. This makes it easy for us to interact with the query portion of a URL as shown in the following code:

```
var http = require('http');
var url = require('url');
var pages = [
   {id: '1', route: '', output: 'Woohoo!'},
   {id: '2', route: 'about', output: 'A simple routing with Node
     example'},
   {id: '3', route: 'another page', output: function () {
     return 'Here\'s ' +         this.route; }
   },
];
```

```
http.createServer(function (request, response) {
  var id = url.parse(decodeURI(request.url), true).query.id;
  if (id) {
    pages.forEach(function (page) {
      if (page.id === id) {
        response.writeHead(200, {'Content-Type': 'text/html'});
        response.end(typeof page.output === 'function'
        ? page.output() : page.output);
      }
    });
  }
  if (!response.finished) {
    response.writeHead(404);
    response.end('Page Not Found');
  }
}).listen(8080);
```

With the added `id` properties, we can access our object data by, for instance, `localhost:8080?id=2`.

The routing modules

There's an up-to-date list of various routing modules for Node at `https://github.com/joyent/node/wiki/modules#wiki-web-frameworks-routers`. These community-made routers cater to various scenarios. It's important to research the activity and maturity of a module before taking it into a production environment.

NodeZoo (`http://nodezoo.com`) is an excellent tool to research the state of a NODE module.

In *Chapter 7, Accelerating Development with Express*, we will go into greater detail on using the built-in Express/Connect router for more comprehensive routing solutions.

See also

- The *Serving static files* and *Securing against filesystem hacking exploits* recipes
- The *Implementing dynamic routing* recipe discussed in *Chapter 7, Accelerating Development with Express*

Serving static files

If we have information stored on disk that we want to serve as web content, we can use the `fs` (filesystem) module to load our content and pass it through the `http.createServer` callback. This is a basic conceptual starting point to serve static files; as we will learn in the following recipes, there are much more efficient solutions.

Getting ready

We'll need some files to serve. Let's create a directory named `content`, containing the following three files:

- `index.html`
- `styles.css`
- `script.js`

Add the following code to the HTML file `index.html`:

```html
<html>
  <head>
    <title>Yay Node!</title>
    <link rel=stylesheet href=styles.css type=text/css>
    <script src=script.js type=text/javascript></script>
  </head>
  <body>
    <span id=yay>Yay!</span>
  </body>
</html>
```

Add the following code to the `script.js` JavaScript file:

```js
window.onload = function() { alert('Yay Node!'); };
```

And finally, add the following code to the CSS file `style.css`:

```css
#yay {font-size:5em;background:blue;color:yellow;padding:0.5em}
```

How to do it...

As in the previous recipe, we'll be using the core modules `http` and `path`. We'll also need to access the filesystem, so we'll require `fs` as well. With the help of the following code, let's create the server and use the `path` module to check if a file exists:

```js
var http = require('http');
var path = require('path');
```

Making a Web Server

```
var fs = require('fs');
http.createServer(function (request, response) {
  var lookup = path.basename(decodeURI(request.url)) ||
    'index.html';
  var f = 'content/' + lookup;
  fs.exists(f, function (exists) {
    console.log(exists ? lookup + " is there"
      : lookup + " doesn't exist");
  });
}).listen(8080);
```

If we haven't already done it, then we can initialize our `server.js` file by running the following command:

`supervisor server.js`

Try loading `localhost:8080/foo`. The console will say **foo doesn't exist**, because it doesn't. The `localhost:8080/script.js` URL will tell us that `script.js` is there, because it is. Before we can serve a file, we are supposed to let the client know the `content-type` header, which we can determine from the file extension. So let's make a quick map using an object as follows:

```
var mimeTypes = {
  '.js' : 'text/javascript',
  '.html': 'text/html',
  '.css' : 'text/css'
};
```

We could extend our `mimeTypes` map later to support more types.

Modern browsers may be able to interpret certain mime types (like `text/javascript`), without the server sending a `content-type` header, but older browsers or less common mime types will rely upon the correct `content-type` header being sent from the server.

Remember to place `mimeTypes` outside of the server callback, since we don't want to initialize the same object on every client request. If the requested file exists, we can convert our file extension into a `content-type` header by feeding `path.extname` into `mimeTypes` and then pass our retrieved `content-type` to `response.writeHead`. If the requested file doesn't exist, we'll write out a `404` error and end the response as follows:

```
//requires variables, mimeType object...
http.createServer(function (request, response) {

  var lookup = path.basename(decodeURI(request.url)) ||
    'index.html';
  var f = 'content/' + lookup;
  fs.exists(f, function (exists) {
    if (exists) {
```

```
        fs.readFile(f, function (err, data) {
          if (err) {response.writeHead(500); response.end('Server
             Error!'); return; }
          var headers = {'Content-type': mimeTypes[path.extname
             (lookup)]};
          response.writeHead(200, headers);
          response.end(data);
        });
        return;
      }
      response.writeHead(404); //no such file found!
      response.end();
    });
  }).listen(8080);
```

At the moment, there is still no content sent to the client. We have to get this content from our file, so we wrap the response handling in an `fs.readFile` method callback as follows:

```
//http.createServer, inside fs.exists:
if (exists) {
  fs.readFile(f, function(err, data) {
    var headers={'Content-type': mimeTypes[path.extname(lookup)]};
    response.writeHead(200, headers);
    response.end(data);
  });
  return;
}
```

Before we finish, let's apply some error handling to our `fs.readFile` callback as follows:

```
//requires variables, mimeType object...
//http.createServer,  path exists, inside if(exists):
  fs.readFile(f, function(err, data) {
    if (err) {response.writeHead(500); response.end('Server
       Error!');  return; }
    var headers = {'Content-type': mimeTypes[path.extname
       (lookup)]};
    response.writeHead(200, headers);
    response.end(data);
  });
  return;
}
```

Making a Web Server

> Notice that `return` stays outside of the `fs.readFile` callback. We are returning from the `fs.exists` callback to prevent further code execution (for example, sending the `404` error). Placing a `return` statement in an `if` statement is similar to using an `else` branch. However, the pattern of the `return` statement inside the `if` loop is encouraged instead of `if else`, as it eliminates a level of nesting. Nesting can be particularly prevalent in Node due to performing a lot of asynchronous tasks, which tend to use callback functions.

So, now we can navigate to `localhost:8080`, which will serve our `index.html` file. The `index.html` file makes calls to our `script.js` and `styles.css` files, which our server also delivers with appropriate mime types. We can see the result in the following screenshot:

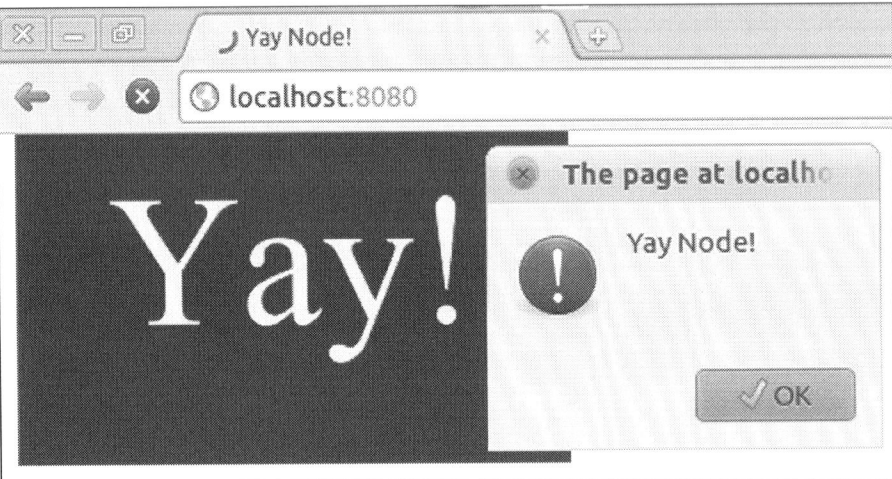

This recipe serves to illustrate the fundamentals of serving static files. Remember, this is not an efficient solution! In a real world situation, we don't want to make an I/O call every time a request hits the server; this is very costly especially with larger files. In the following recipes, we'll learn better ways of serving static files.

How it works...

Our script creates a server and declares a variable called `lookup`. We assign a value to `lookup` using the double pipe || (OR) operator. This defines a default route if `path.basename` is empty. Then we pass `lookup` to a new variable that we named `f` in order to prepend our `content` directory to the intended filename. Next, we run `f` through the `fs.exists` method and check the `exist` parameter in our callback to see if the file is there. If the file does exist, we read it asynchronously using `fs.readFile`. If there is a problem accessing the file, we write a `500` server error, end the response, and return from the `fs.readFile` callback. We can test the error-handling functionality by removing read permissions from `index.html` as follows:

```
chmod -r index.html
```

Doing so will cause the server to throw the `500` server error status code. To set things right again, run the following command:

```
chmod +r index.html
```

 `chmod` is a Unix-type system-specific command. If we are using Windows, there's no need to set file permissions in this case.

As long as we can access the file, we grab the `content-type` header using our handy `mimeTypes` mapping object, write the headers, end the response with data loaded from the file, and finally return from the function. If the requested file does not exist, we bypass all this logic, write a `404` error message, and end the response.

There's more...

The favicon icon file is something to watch out for. We will explore the file in this section.

The favicon gotcha

When using a browser to test our server, sometimes an unexpected server hit can be observed. This is the browser requesting the default `favicon.ico` icon file that servers can provide. Apart from the initial confusion of seeing additional hits, this is usually not a problem. If the favicon request does begin to interfere, we can handle it as follows:

```
if (request.url === '/favicon.ico') {
  console.log('Not found: ' + f);
  response.end();
  return;
}
```

If we wanted to be more polite to the client, we could also inform it of a `404` error by using `response.writeHead(404)` before issuing `response.end`.

See also

- The *Caching content in memory for immediate delivery* recipe
- The *Optimizing performance with streaming* recipe
- The *Securing against filesystem hacking exploits* recipe

Making a Web Server

Caching content in memory for immediate delivery

Directly accessing storage on each client request is not ideal. For this task, we will explore how to enhance server efficiency by accessing the disk only on the first request, caching the data from file for that first request, and serving all further requests out of the process memory.

Getting ready

We are going to improve upon the code from the previous task, so we'll be working with `server.js` and in the `content` directory, with `index.html`, `styles.css`, and `script.js`.

How to do it...

Let's begin by looking at our following script from the previous recipe *Serving static files*:

```
var http = require('http');
var path = require('path');
var fs = require('fs');

var mimeTypes = {
  '.js' : 'text/javascript',
  '.html': 'text/html',
  '.css' : 'text/css'
};

http.createServer(function (request, response) {
  var lookup = path.basename(decodeURI(request.url)) ||
    'index.html';
  var f = 'content/'+lookup;
  fs.exists(f, function (exists) {
    if (exists) {
      fs.readFile(f, function(err,data) {
        if (err) {
          response.writeHead(500); response.end('Server Error!');
          return;
        }
        var headers = {'Content-type': mimeTypes[path.extname
          (lookup)]};
        response.writeHead(200, headers);
        response.end(data);
      });
      return;
    }
    response.writeHead(404); //no such file found!
```

```
      response.end('Page Not Found');
   });
}
```

We need to modify this code to only read the file once, load its contents into memory, and respond to all requests for that file from memory afterwards. To keep things simple and preserve maintainability, we'll extract our cache handling and content delivery into a separate function. So above `http.createServer`, and below `mimeTypes`, we'll add the following:

```
var cache = {};
function cacheAndDeliver(f, cb) {
   if (!cache[f]) {
      fs.readFile(f, function(err, data) {
         if (!err) {
            cache[f] = {content: data} ;
         }
         cb(err, data);
      });
      return;
   }
   console.log('loading ' + f + ' from cache');
   cb(null, cache[f].content);
}
//http.createServer
```

A new `cache` object and a new function called `cacheAndDeliver` have been added to store our files in memory. Our function takes the same parameters as `fs.readFile` so we can replace `fs.readFile` in the `http.createServer` callback while leaving the rest of the code intact as follows:

```
//...inside http.createServer:

fs.exists(f, function (exists) {
   if (exists) {
      cacheAndDeliver(f, function(err, data) {
         if (err) {
            response.writeHead(500);
            response.end('Server Error!');
            return; }
         var headers = {'Content-type': mimeTypes[path.extname(f)]};
         response.writeHead(200, headers);
         response.end(data);
      });
   return;
   }
//rest of path exists code (404 handling)...
```

Making a Web Server

When we execute our `server.js` file and access `localhost:8080` twice, consecutively, the second request causes the console to display the following output:

```
loading content/index.html from cache
loading content/styles.css from cache
loading content/script.js from cache
```

How it works...

We defined a function called `cacheAndDeliver`, which like `fs.readFile`, takes a filename and callback as parameters. This is great because we can pass the exact same callback of `fs.readFile` to `cacheAndDeliver`, padding the server out with caching logic without adding any extra complexity visually to the inside of the `http.createServer` callback.

As it stands, the worth of abstracting our caching logic into an external function is arguable, but the more we build on the server's caching abilities, the more feasible and useful this abstraction becomes. Our `cacheAndDeliver` function checks to see if the requested content is already cached. If not, we call `fs.readFile` and load the data from disk.

Once we have this data, we may as well hold onto it, so it's placed into the `cache` object referenced by its file path (the `f` variable). The next time anyone requests the file, `cacheAndDeliver` will see that we have the file stored in the `cache` object and will issue an alternative callback containing the cached data. Notice that we fill the `cache[f]` property with another new object containing a content property. This makes it easier to extend the caching functionality in the future as we would just have to place extra properties into our `cache[f]` object and supply logic that interfaces with these properties accordingly.

There's more...

If we were to modify the files we are serving, the changes wouldn't be reflected until we restart the server. We can do something about that.

Reflecting content changes

To detect whether a requested file has changed since we last cached it, we must know when the file was cached and when it was last modified. To record when the file was last cached, let's extend the `cache[f]` object as follows:

```
cache[f] = {content: data,timestamp: Date.now() //store a Unix
  time stamp
};
```

That was easy! Now let's find out when the file was updated last. The `fs.stat` method returns an object as the second parameter of its callback. This object contains the same useful information as the command-line GNU (GNU's Not Unix!) coreutils `stat`. The `fs.stat` function supplies three time-related properties: last accessed (`atime`), last modified (`mtime`), and last changed (`ctime`). The difference between `mtime` and `ctime` is that `ctime` will reflect any alterations to the file, whereas `mtime` will only reflect alterations to the content of the file. Consequently, if we changed the permissions of a file, `ctime` would be updated but `mtime` would stay the same. We want to pay attention to permission changes as they happen so let's use the `ctime` property as shown in the following code:

```
//requires and mimeType object....
var cache = {};
function cacheAndDeliver(f, cb) {
  fs.stat(f, function (err, stats) {
    if (err) { return console.log('Oh no!, Eror', err); }
    var lastChanged = Date.parse(stats.ctime),
    isUpdated = (cache[f]) && lastChanged  > cache[f].timestamp;
    if (!cache[f] || isUpdated) {
      fs.readFile(f, function (err, data) {
        console.log('loading ' + f + ' from file');
        //rest of cacheAndDeliver
  }); //end of fs.stat
}
```

 If we're using Node on Windows, we may have to substitute `ctime` with `mtime`, since `ctime` supports at least Version 0.10.12.

The contents of `cacheAndDeliver` have been wrapped in an `fs.stat` callback, two variables have been added, and the `if(!cache[f])` statement has been modified. We parse the `ctime` property of the second parameter dubbed `stats` using `Date.parse` to convert it to milliseconds since midnight, January 1st, 1970 (the Unix epoch) and assign it to our `lastChanged` variable. Then we check whether the requested file's last changed time is greater than when we cached the file (provided the file is indeed cached) and assign the result to our `isUpdated` variable. After that, its merely a case of adding the `isUpdated` Boolean to the conditional `if(!cache[f])` statement via the `||` (or) operator. If the file is newer than our cached version (or if it isn't yet cached), we load the file from disk into the `cache` object.

See also

- The *Optimizing performance with streaming* recipe
- The *Browser-server transmission via AJAX* recipe in *Chapter 3, Working with Data Serialization*
- *Chapter 4, Interfacing with Databases*

Making a Web Server

Optimizing performance with streaming

Caching content certainly improves upon reading a file from disk for every request. However, with `fs.readFile`, we are reading the whole file into memory before sending it out in a `response` object. For better performance, we can stream a file from disk and pipe it directly to the `response` object, sending data straight to the network socket a piece at a time.

Getting ready

We are building on our code from the last example, so let's get `server.js`, `index.html`, `styles.css`, and `script.js` ready.

How to do it...

We will be using `fs.createReadStream` to initialize a stream, which can be piped to the `response` object.

> If streaming and piping are new concepts, don't worry! We'll be covering streams in depth in *Chapter 5, Employing Streams*.

In this case, implementing `fs.createReadStream` within our `cacheAndDeliver` function isn't ideal because the event listeners of `fs.createReadStream` will need to interface with the `request` and `response` objects, which for the sake of simplicity would preferably be dealt with in the `http.createServer` callback. For brevity's sake, we will discard our `cacheAndDeliver` function and implement basic caching within the server callback as follows:

```
//...snip... requires, mime types, createServer, lookup and f
  vars...

fs.exists(f, function (exists) {
  if (exists) {
    var headers = {'Content-type': mimeTypes[path.extname(f)]};
    if (cache[f]) {
      response.writeHead(200, headers);
      response.end(cache[f].content);
      return;
    } //...snip... rest of server code...
```

Later on, we will fill `cache[f].content` while we are interfacing with the `readStream` object. The following code shows how we use `fs.createReadStream`:

```
var s = fs.createReadStream(f);
```

The preceding code will return a `readStream` object that streams the file, which is pointed at by variable `f`. The `readStream` object emits events that we need to listen to. We can listen with `addEventListener` or use the shorthand `on` method as follows:

```
var s = fs.createReadStream(f).on('open', function () {
  //do stuff when the readStream opens
});
```

Because `createReadStream` returns the `readStream` object, we can latch our event listener straight onto it using method chaining with dot notation. Each stream is only going to open once; we don't need to keep listening to it. Therefore, we can use the `once` method instead of `on` to automatically stop listening after the first event occurrence as follows:

```
var s = fs.createReadStream(f).once('open', function () {
  //do stuff when the readStream opens
});
```

Before we fill out the `open` event callback, let's implement some error handling as follows:

```
var s = fs.createReadStream(f).once('open', function () {
  //do stuff when the readStream opens
}).once('error', function (e) {
  console.log(e);
  response.writeHead(500);
  response.end('Server Error!');
});
```

The key to this whole endeavor is the `stream.pipe` method. This is what enables us to take our file straight from disk and stream it directly to the network socket via our `response` object as follows:

```
var s = fs.createReadStream(f).once('open', function () {
  response.writeHead(200, headers);
  this.pipe(response);
}).once('error', function (e) {
  console.log(e);
  response.writeHead(500);
  response.end('Server Error!');
});
```

But what about ending the response? Conveniently, `stream.pipe` detects when the stream has ended and calls `response.end` for us. There's one other event we need to listen to, for caching purposes. Within our `fs.exists` callback, underneath the `createReadStream` code block, we write the following code:

```
fs.stat(f, function(err, stats) {
  var bufferOffset = 0;
  cache[f] = {content: new Buffer(stats.size)};
```

Making a Web Server

```
    s.on('data', function (chunk) {
      chunk.copy(cache[f].content, bufferOffset);
      bufferOffset += chunk.length;
    });
  }); //end of createReadStream
```

We've used the `data` event to capture the buffer as it's being streamed, and copied it into a buffer that we supplied to `cache[f].content`, using `fs.stat` to obtain the file size for the file's cache buffer.

> For this case, we're using the classic mode `data` event instead of the `readable` event coupled with `stream.read()` (see http://nodejs.org/api/stream.html#stream_readable_read_size_1) because it best suits our aim, which is to grab data from the stream as soon as possible. In *Chapter 5, Employing Streams*, we'll learn how to use the `stream.read` method.

How it works...

Instead of the client waiting for the server to load the entire file from disk prior to sending it to the client, we use a stream to load the file in small ordered pieces and promptly send them to the client. With larger files, this is especially useful as there is minimal delay between the file being requested and the client starting to receive the file.

We did this by using `fs.createReadStream` to start streaming our file from disk. The `fs.createReadStream` method creates a `readStream` object, which inherits from the `EventEmitter` class.

The `EventEmitter` class accomplishes the *evented* part of the *Node Cookbook Second Edition* tagline: *Evented I/O for V8 JavaScript*. Due to this, we'll be using listeners instead of callbacks to control the flow of stream logic.

We then added an `open` event listener using the `once` method since we want to stop listening to the `open` event once it is triggered. We respond to the `open` event by writing the headers and using the `stream.pipe` method to shuffle the incoming data straight to the client. If the client becomes overwhelmed with processing, `stream.pipe` applies *backpressure*, which means that the incoming stream is paused until the backlog of data is handled (we'll find out more about this in *Chapter 5, Employing Streams*).

While the response is being piped to the client, the content cache is simultaneously being filled. To achieve this, we had to create an instance of the `Buffer` class for our `cache[f].content` property.

A `Buffer` class must be supplied with a size (or array or string), which in our case is the size of the file. To get the size, we used the asynchronous `fs.stat` method and captured the `size` property in the callback. The `data` event returns a `Buffer` variable as its only callback parameter.

The default value of `bufferSize` for a stream is 64 KB; any file whose size is less than the value of the `bufferSize` property will only trigger one `data` event because the whole file will fit into the first chunk of data. But for files that are greater than the value of the `bufferSize` property, we have to fill our `cache[f].content` property one piece at a time.

> **Changing the default readStream buffer size**
>
> We can change the buffer size of our `readStream` object by passing an `options` object with a `bufferSize` property as the second parameter of `fs.createReadStream`.
>
> For instance, to double the buffer, you could use `fs.createReadStream (f,{bufferSize: 128 * 1024});`.

We cannot simply concatenate each chunk with `cache[f].content` because this will coerce binary data into string format, which, though no longer in binary format, will later be interpreted as binary. Instead, we have to copy all the little binary buffer chunks into our binary `cache[f].content` buffer.

We created a `bufferOffset` variable to assist us with this. Each time we add another chunk to our `cache[f].content` buffer, we update our new `bufferOffset` property by adding the length of the chunk buffer to it. When we call the `Buffer.copy` method on the chunk buffer, we pass `bufferOffset` as the second parameter, so our `cache[f].content` buffer is filled correctly.

Moreover, operating with the `Buffer` class renders performance enhancements with larger files because it bypasses the V8 garbage-collection methods, which tend to fragment a large amount of data, thus slowing down Node's ability to process them.

There's more...

While streaming has solved the problem of waiting for files to be loaded into memory before delivering them, we are nevertheless still loading files into memory via our `cache` object. With larger files or a large number of files, this could have potential ramifications.

Protecting against process memory overruns

Streaming allows for intelligent and minimal use of memory for processing large memory items. But even with well-written code, some apps may require significant memory.

Making a Web Server

There is a limited amount of heap memory. By default, V8's memory is set to 1400 MB on 64-bit systems and 700 MB on 32-bit systems. This can be altered by running node with `--max-old-space-size=N`, where `N` is the amount of megabytes (the actual maximum amount that it can be set to depends upon the OS, whether we're running on a 32-bit or 64-bit architecture—a 32-bit may peak out around 2 GB and of course the amount of physical RAM available).

> The `--max-old-space-size` method doesn't apply to buffers, since it applies to the v8 heap (memory allocated for JavaScript objects and primitives) and buffers are allocated outside of the v8 heap.

If we absolutely had to be memory intensive, we could run our server on a large cloud platform, divide up the logic, and start new instances of node using the `child_process` class, or better still the higher level `cluster` module.

> There are other more advanced ways to increase the usable memory, including editing and recompiling the v8 code base. The http://blog.caustik.com/2012/04/11/escape-the-1-4gb-v8-heap-limit-in-node-js link has some tips along these lines.

In this case, high memory usage isn't necessarily required and we can optimize our code to significantly reduce the potential for memory overruns. There is less benefit to caching larger files because the slight speed improvement relative to the total download time is negligible, while the cost of caching them is quite significant in ratio to our available process memory. We can also improve cache efficiency by implementing an expiration time on `cache` objects, which can then be used to clean the cache, consequently removing files in low demand and prioritizing high demand files for faster delivery. Let's rearrange our `cache` object slightly as follows:

```
var cache = {
  store: {},
  maxSize : 26214400, //(bytes) 25mb
}
```

For a clearer mental model, we're making a distinction between the `cache` object as a functioning entity and the `cache` object as a store (which is a part of the broader `cache` entity). Our first goal is to only cache files under a certain size; we've defined `cache.maxSize` for this purpose. All we have to do now is insert an `if` condition within the `fs.stat` callback as follows:

```
fs.stat(f, function (err, stats) {
  if (stats.size<cache.maxSize) {
    var bufferOffset = 0;
    cache.store[f] = {content: new Buffer(stats.size),
      timestamp: Date.now() };
```

```
    s.on('data', function (data) {
      data.copy(cache.store[f].content, bufferOffset);
      bufferOffset += data.length;
    });
  }
});
```

Notice that we also slipped in a new `timestamp` property into our `cache.store[f]` method. This is for our second goal—cleaning the cache. Let's extend `cache` as follows:

```
var cache = {
  store: {},
  maxSize: 26214400, //(bytes) 25mb
  maxAge: 5400 * 1000, //(ms) 1 and a half hours
  clean: function(now) {
    var that = this;
    Object.keys(this.store).forEach(function (file) {
      if (now > that.store[file].timestamp + that.maxAge) {
        delete that.store[file];
      }
    });
  }
};
```

So in addition to `maxSize`, we've created a `maxAge` property and added a `clean` method. We call `cache.clean` at the bottom of the server with the help of the following code:

```
//all of our code prior
  cache.clean(Date.now());
}).listen(8080); //end of the http.createServer
```

The `cache.clean` method loops through the `cache.store` function and checks to see if it has exceeded its specified lifetime. If it has, we remove it from the store. One further improvement and then we're done. The `cache.clean` method is called on each request. This means the `cache.store` function is going to be looped through on every server hit, which is neither necessary nor efficient. It would be better if we clean the cache, say, every two hours or so. We'll add two more properties to cache—`cleanAfter` to specify the time between cache cleans, and `cleanedAt` to determine how long it has been since the cache was last cleaned, as follows:

```
var cache = {
  store: {},
  maxSize: 26214400, //(bytes) 25mb
  maxAge : 5400 * 1000, //(ms) 1 and a half hours
  cleanAfter: 7200 * 1000,//(ms) two hours
  cleanedAt: 0, //to be set dynamically
```

```
      clean: function (now) {
        if (now - this.cleanAfter>this.cleanedAt) {
          this.cleanedAt = now;
          that = this;
          Object.keys(this.store).forEach(function (file) {
            if (now > that.store[file].timestamp + that.maxAge) {
              delete that.store[file];
            }
          });
        }
      }
    };
```

So we wrap our `cache.clean` method in an `if` statement, which will allow a loop through `cache.store` only if it has been longer than two hours (or whatever `cleanAfter` is set to) since the last clean.

See also

- The *Handling file uploads* recipe discussed in *Chapter 2, Exploring the HTTP Object*
- *Chapter 2, Exploring the HTTP Object*
- The *Securing against filesystem hacking exploits* recipe
- *Chapter 5, Employing Streams*

Securing against filesystem hacking exploits

For a Node app to be insecure, there must be something an attacker can interact with for exploitation purposes. Due to Node's minimalist approach, the onus is on the programmer to ensure that their implementation doesn't expose security flaws. This recipe will help identify some security risk anti-patterns that could occur when working with the filesystem.

Getting ready

We'll be working with the same `content` directory as we did in the previous recipes. But we'll start a new `insecure_server.js` file (there's a clue in the name!) from scratch to demonstrate mistaken techniques.

How to do it...

Our previous static file recipes tend to use `path.basename` to acquire a route, but this ignores intermediate paths. If we accessed `localhost:8080/foo/bar/styles.css`, our code would take `styles.css` as the `basename` property and deliver `content/styles.css` to us. How about we make a subdirectory in our `content` folder? Call it `subcontent` and move our `script.js` and `styles.css` files into it. We'd have to alter our script and link tags in `index.html` as follows:

```
<link rel=stylesheet type=text/css href=subcontent/styles.css>
<script src=subcontent/script.js type=text/javascript></script>
```

We can use the `url` module to grab the entire `pathname` property. So let's include the `url` module in our new `insecure_server.js` file, create our HTTP server, and use `pathname` to get the whole requested path as follows:

```
var http = require('http');
var url = require('url');
var fs = require('fs');

http.createServer(function (request, response) {
  var lookup = url.parse(decodeURI(request.url)).pathname;
  lookup = (lookup === "/") ? '/index.html' : lookup;
  var f = 'content' + lookup;
  console.log(f);
  fs.readFile(f, function (err, data) {
    response.end(data);
  });
}).listen(8080);
```

If we navigate to `localhost:8080`, everything works great! We've gone multilevel, hooray! For demonstration purposes, a few things have been stripped out from the previous recipes (such as `fs.exists`); but even with them, this code presents the same security hazards if we type the following:

```
curl localhost:8080/../insecure_server.js
```

Now we have our server's code. An attacker could also access `/etc/passwd` with a few attempts at guessing its relative path as follows:

```
curl localhost:8080/..//../../../../../etc/passwd
```

> If we're using Windows, we can download and install `curl` from http://curl.haxx.se/download.html.

Making a Web Server

In order to test these attacks, we have to use `curl` or another equivalent because modern browsers will filter these sort of requests. As a solution, what if we added a unique suffix to each file we wanted to serve and made it mandatory for the suffix to exist before the server coughs it up? That way, an attacker could request /etc/passwd or our `insecure_server.js` file because they wouldn't have the unique suffix. To try this, let's copy the `content` folder and call it `content-pseudosafe`, and rename our files to `index.html-serve`, `script.js-serve`, and `styles.css-serve`. Let's create a new server file and name it `pseudosafe_server.js`. Now all we have to do is make the `-serve` suffix mandatory as follows:

```
//requires section ...snip...
http.createServer(function (request, response) {
  var lookup = url.parse(decodeURI(request.url)).pathname;
  lookup = (lookup === "/") ? '/index.html-serve'
    : lookup + '-serve';
  var f = 'content-pseudosafe' + lookup;
//...snip... rest of the server code...
```

For feedback purposes, we'll also include some `404` handling with the help of `fs.exists` as follows:

```
//requires, create server etc
fs.exists(f, function (exists) {
  if (!exists) {
    response.writeHead(404);
    response.end('Page Not Found!');
    return;
  }
//read file etc
```

So, let's start our `pseudosafe_server.js` file and try out the same exploit by executing the following command:

```
curl -i localhost:8080/../insecure_server.js
```

We've used the `-i` argument so that `curl` will output the headers. The result? A `404`, because the file it's actually looking for is `../insecure_server.js-serve`, which doesn't exist. So what's wrong with this method? Well it's inconvenient and prone to error. But more importantly, an attacker can still work around it! Try this by typing the following:

```
curl localhost:8080/../insecure_server.js%00/index.html
```

And voilà! There's our server code again. The solution to our problem is `path.normalize`, which cleans up our `pathname` before it gets to `fs.readFile` as shown in the following code:

```
http.createServer(function (request, response) {
  var lookup = url.parse(decodeURI(request.url)).pathname;
  lookup = path.normalize(lookup);
  lookup = (lookup === "/") ? '/index.html' : lookup;
  var f = 'content' + lookup
```

> Prior recipes haven't used `path.normalize` and yet they're still relatively safe. The `path.basename` method gives us the last part of the path, thus removing any preceding double dot paths (`../`) that would take an attacker higher up the directory hierarchy than should be allowed.

How it works...

Here we have two filesystem exploitation techniques: the **relative directory traversal** and **poison null byte attacks**. These attacks can take different forms, such as in a POST request or from an external file. They can have different effects—if we were writing to files instead of reading them, an attacker could potentially start making changes to our server. The key to security in all cases is to validate and clean any data that comes from the user. In `insecure_server.js`, we pass whatever the user requests to our `fs.readFile` method. This is foolish because it allows an attacker to take advantage of the relative path functionality in our operating system by using `../`, thus gaining access to areas that should be off limits. By adding the `-serve` suffix, we didn't solve the problem, we put a plaster on it, which can be circumvented by the poison null byte.

The key to this attack is the `%00` value, which is a URL hex code for the null byte. In this case, the null byte blinds Node to the `../insecure_server.js` portion, but when the same null byte is sent through to our `fs.readFile` method, it has to interface with the kernel. But the kernel gets blinded to the `index.html` part. So our code sees `index.html` but the read operation sees `../insecure_server.js`. This is known as null byte poisoning. To protect ourselves, we could use a `regex` statement to remove the `../` parts of the path. We could also check for the null byte and spit out a `400 Bad Request` statement. But we don't have to, because `path.normalize` filters out the null byte and relative parts for us.

There's more...

Let's further delve into how we can protect our servers when it comes to serving static files.

Whitelisting

If security was an extreme priority, we could adopt a strict whitelisting approach. In this approach, we would create a manual route for each file we are willing to deliver. Anything not on our whitelist would return a `404` error. We can place a whitelist array above `http.createServer` as follows:

```
var whitelist = [
  '/index.html',
  '/subcontent/styles.css',
  '/subcontent/script.js'
];
```

Making a Web Server

And inside our `http.createServer` callback, we'll put an `if` statement to check if the requested path is in the whitelist array, as follows:

```
if (whitelist.indexOf(lookup) === -1) {
  response.writeHead(404);
  response.end('Page Not Found!');
  return;
}
```

And that's it! We can test this by placing a file `non-whitelisted.html` in our content directory and then executing the following command:

```
curl -i localhost:8080/non-whitelisted.html
```

This will return a `404` error because `non-whitelisted.html` isn't on the whitelist.

Node static

The module's wiki page (https://github.com/joyent/node/wiki/modules#wiki-web-frameworks-static) has a list of static file server modules available for different purposes. It's a good idea to ensure that a project is mature and active before relying upon it to serve your content. The `node-static` module is a well-developed module with built-in caching. It's also compliant with the RFC2616 HTTP standards specification, which defines how files should be delivered over HTTP. The `node-static` module implements all the essentials discussed in this chapter and more.

For the next example, we'll need the `node-static` module. You could install it by executing the following command:

npm install node-static

The following piece of code is slightly adapted from the `node-static` module's GitHub page at https://github.com/cloudhead/node-static:

```
var static = require('node-static');
var fileServer = new static.Server('./content');
require('http').createServer(function (request, response) {
  request.addListener('end', function () {
    fileServer.serve(request, response);
  });
}).listen(8080);
```

The preceding code will interface with the `node-static` module to handle server-side and client-side caching, use streams to deliver content, and filter out relative requests and null bytes, among other things.

See also

- The *Preventing cross-site request forgery* recipe discussed in *Chapter 8, Implementing Security, Encryption, and Authentication*
- The *Setting up an HTTPS web server* recipe in *Chapter 8, Implementing Security, Encryption, and Authentication*
- The *Hashing passwords* recipe discussed in *Chapter 8, Implementing Security, Encryption, and Authentication*
- The *Deploying an app to a server environment* recipe discussed in *Chapter 11, Taking It Live*

2
Exploring the HTTP Object

In this chapter, we will cover:

- Processing POST data
- Handling file uploads
- Using Node as an HTTP client
- Implementing download throttling

Introduction

In the previous chapter, we used the `http` module to create a web server. Now, we're going to look into some associated use cases beyond simply pushing content from the server to client. The first three recipes will explore how to receive data via client-initiated HTTP POST (and PUT) requests and in the final recipe, we'll demonstrate how to throttle a stream of outbound data.

Processing POST data

If we want to be able to receive POST data, we have to instruct our server how to accept and handle a POST request. In PHP, we could access our POST values seamlessly with `$_POST['fieldname']`, because it would block until an array value was filled. Contrariwise, Node provides low-level interaction with the flow of HTTP data, allowing us to interface with the incoming message body as a stream, leaving it entirely up to the developer to turn that stream into usable data

Exploring the HTTP Object

Getting ready

Let's create a `server.js` file ready for our code, and an HTML file called `form.html`, that contains the following:

```
<form method=post>
   <input type=text name=userinput1><br>
   <input type=text name=userinput2><br>
   <input type=submit>
</form>
```

For our purposes, we'll place `form.html` in the same folder as `server.js`. Though this is not generally a recommended practice, we should usually place our public code in a separate folder from our server code.

How to do it...

We'll provision our server for both GET and POST requests. Let's start with GET by requiring the `http` module and loading `form.html` to serve through `createServer`, as follows:

```
var http = require('http');
var form = require('fs').readFileSync('form.html');
http.createServer(function (request, response) {
   if (request.method === "GET") {
      response.writeHead(200, {'Content-Type': 'text/html'});
      response.end(form);
   }
}).listen(8080);
```

We are synchronously loading `form.html` at initialization time instead of accessing the disk on each request. If we navigate to `localhost:8080`, we'll be presented with a form. But if we fill out our form, nothing happens because we need to handle POST requests, as follows:

```
if (request.method === "POST") {
   var postData = '';
   request.on('data', function (chunk) {
      postData += chunk;
   }).on('end', function () {
      console.log('User Posted:\n' + postData);
      response.end('You Posted:\n' + postData);
   });
}
```

Once the form is completed and submitted, the browser and console will output the raw query string sent from the client. Converting our `postData` variable into an object provides an easy way to interact with and manipulate the submitted information. The `querystring` module has a `parse` method, which transforms query strings into objects, and since form submission arrives in query string format, we can use it to objectify our data as follows:

```
var http = require('http');
var querystring = require('querystring');
var util = require('util');
var form = require('fs').readFileSync('form.html');

http.createServer(function (request, response) {
  if (request.method === "POST") {
    var postData = '';
    request.on('data', function (chunk) {
      postData += chunk;
    }).on('end', function () {
      var postDataObject = querystring.parse(postData);
      console.log('User Posted:\n', postData);
      response.end('You Posted:\n' + util.inspect(postDataObject));
    });
  }
  if (request.method === "GET") {
    response.writeHead(200, {'Content-Type': 'text/html'});
    response.end(form);
  }
}).listen(8080);
```

Notice the `util` module—we require it to use its `inspect` method for a simple way to output our `postDataObject` to the browser.

Finally, we're going to protect our server from memory overload exploits.

> **Protecting a POST server**
>
> V8 (and therefore Node) has virtual memory limitations based upon the processor architecture and operating system constraints. If we don't restrict the amount of data our POST server accepts, we could leave ourselves open for a type of denial-of-service attack. Without protection, an extremely large POST request could cause our server to slow down significantly or even crash.

To achieve this, we'll set a variable for the maximum acceptable data size and check it against the growing length of our `postData` variable as follows:

```
var http = require('http');
var querystring = require('querystring');
```

Exploring the HTTP Object

```javascript
var util = require('util');
var form = require('fs').readFileSync('form.html');
var maxData = 2 * 1024 * 1024; //2mb
http.createServer(function (request, response) {
  if (request.method === "POST") {
    var postData = '';
    request.on('data', function (chunk) {
      postData += chunk;
      if (postData.length > maxData) {
        postData = '';
        this.destroy();
        response.writeHead(413); // Request Entity Too Large
        response.end('Too large');
      }
    }).on('end', function () {
      if (!postData) { response.end(); return; } // prevents empty post
      // requests from
      // crashing the server
      var postDataObject = querystring.parse(postData);
      console.log('User Posted:\n', postData);
      response.end('You Posted:\n' + util.inspect
        (postDataObject));
    });
//rest of our code....
```

How it works...

Once we know that a `POST` request has been made for our server (by checking `request.method`), we aggregate our incoming data into our `postData` variable via the `data` event listener on the `request` object. However, if we find that the submitted data exceeds our `maxData` limit, we clear our `postData` variable and pause the incoming stream, preventing any further data arriving from the client (using `stream.destroy` instead of `stream.pause` seems to interfere with our response mechanism. Once a stream has been paused for a while, it is automatically removed from memory by V8's garbage collector).

We then send a `413 Request Entity Too Large` HTTP header. In the `end` event listener, as long as `postData` hasn't been cleared for exceeding `maxData` (or wasn't blank in the first place), we use `querystring.parse` to turn our POST message body into an object. From this point on, we can perform any number of interesting activities, such as manipulate, analyze, and pass it to a database. However, for the example, we simply output `postDataObject` to the browser and `postData` to the console.

In *Chapter 5, Employing Streams*, we'll look into ways to constrain the actual stream input to a maximum size and abort if that size is exceeded by using the post-Node 0.8 extra stream API's.

There's more...

If we want our code to look a little more elegant and we're not so concerned about handling POST data as a stream, we can employ a user land (non-core) module to get a little sugar on our syntax.

Accessing POST data with connect and body-parser

Connect is an excellent middleware framework for Node, providing a method framework that assimilates a higher level of abstraction for common server tasks. The **body-parser** module is actually part of the Express web framework (which was inspired by, and originally built on top of Connect). We will be discussing Express in detail in *Chapter 7, Accelerating Development with Express*.

By chaining `body-parser` to a normal callback function, we suddenly have access to the POST data via `request.body` (when data is sent by the POST request, it is held in the message body). The `request.body` object turns out to be exactly the same object as the `postDataObject` we generated in our recipe.

First, let's make sure we have Connect and body-parser installed by executing the following commands:

npm install connect

npm install body-parser

We can require `connect` in place of `http`, since it provides us with `createServer` capabilities. To access the `createServer` method, we can use `connect.createServer`, or the shorthand version, which is simply `connect`. Connect allows us to combine multiple pieces of middleware together, by passing them as parameters to the `createServer` method. The following code shows how to implement similar behavior to what is as seen in the recipe, using Connect:

```
var connect = require('connect');
var bodyParser = require('body-parser');
var util = require('util');
var form = require('fs').readFileSync('form.html');
connect(connect.limit('2mb'), bodyParser(),function (request,
  response) {
  if (request.method === "POST") {
    console.log('User Posted:\n', request.body);
    response.end('You Posted:\n' + util.inspect(request.body));
  }
  if (request.method === "GET") {
```

Exploring the HTTP Object

```
        response.writeHead(200, {'Content-Type': 'text/html'});
        response.end(form);
    }
}).listen(8080);
```

Notice that we are no longer using the `http` module directly. We pass `connect.limit` as our first parameter to achieve the same `maxData` restriction implemented in the main example.

Next, we pass in the `bodyParser` method, allowing `connect` to retrieve our POST data for us, objectifying the data into `request.body`. Finally, there's our callback function, with all the former POST functionality stripped out except the code to echo our data object (which is now `request.body`) to the console and browser. This is where we deviate slightly from our original recipe.

In the recipe, we return the raw `postData` variable to the console, but, here we return the `request.body` object. To output raw data with Connect would either take pointless deconstruction of our object to reassemble the raw query string or an extension of the `bodyParser` function. This is the trade off with using third-party modules; we can only easily interact with information the module author expects us to interact with.

Let's look under the hood for a moment. If we fire up an instance of `node` without any arguments, we can access **Read-Eval-Print-Loop** (**REPL**), which is the Node command-line environment. In REPL, we can write the following:

```
console.log(require('body-parser').toString());
```

If we look at the output, we'll see its `connect.bodyParser` function code and should be able to easily identify the similarities between the `connect.bodyParser` code and our main recipe's code.

See also

- The *Handling file uploads* recipe
- The *Browser-server transmission via AJAX* recipe discussed in *Chapter 3, Working with Data Serialization*
- The *Initializing and using a session* recipe discussed in *Chapter 7, Accelerating Development with Express*

Handling file uploads

We cannot process an uploaded file in the same way we process other POST data. When a file input is submitted in a form, the browser processes the file into a multipart message.

Multipart was originally developed as an e-mail format allowing multiple pieces of mixed content to be combined into one message. If we attempted to receive the upload as a stream and write it to a file, we would have a file filled with multipart data instead of the file or files themselves. We need a multipart parser, the writing of which is more than a recipe can cover. So, we'll be using the well-known and battle-tested `formidable` module to convert our upload data into files.

Getting ready

Let's create a new `uploads` directory to store the uploaded files and get ready to make modifications to our `server.js` file from the previous recipe.

> If the owner of the Node process (for example, the user of the system that runs the `node` executable) isn't also the creator (and therefore owner) of the `uploads` directory, then on some systems (such as Linux and Mac OS X) we'd also have to run `chown` and/or `chmod`, and `chgrp`.

We'll also need to install `formidable` by executing the following command:

npm install formidable@1.x.x

> Notice how we can control the version we install from `npm` by using an at (@) symbol, and specifying a version range using the character `x` as a wildcard to specify the latest subversion number. In this case, we're installing formidable major Version 1, the latest minor version, and the latest patch number.

We run the preceding command in the folder that contains the `uploads` directory.

Finally, we'll make some changes to our `form.html` file from the last recipe, as follows:

```
<form method=POST enctype=multipart/form-data>
  <input type=file name=userfile1><br>
  <input type=file name=userfile2><br>
  <input type=submit>
</form>
```

We included an `enctype` attribute of `multipart/form-data` to signify to the browser that the form will contain upload data and we've replaced the text inputs with file inputs.

Exploring the HTTP Object

How to do it...

Let's see what happens when we use our modified form to upload a file to the server from the last recipe. Let's upload `form.html` itself as our file, as shown in the following screenshot:

```
Node Server
File Edit View Search Terminal Help
        server.js changed
        Node.js process restarted
        server.js changed
        Node.js process restarted
User Posted:
------WebKitFormBoundaryw9lhsJW9CK5SaaRA
Content-Disposition: form-data; name="userfile1"; filename="form.html"
Content-Type: text/html

<form method=POST enctype=multipart/form-data>
<input type=file name=userfile1><br>
<input type=file name=userfile2><br>
<input type=submit>
</form>

------WebKitFormBoundaryw9lhsJW9CK5SaaRA
Content-Disposition: form-data; name="userfile2"; filename=""
Content-Type: application/octet-stream


------WebKitFormBoundaryw9lhsJW9CK5SaaRA--
```

Our POST server simply logs the raw HTTP message body to the console, which in this case is multipart data. We had two file inputs on the form. Though we only uploaded one file, the second input is still included in the multipart request. Each file is separated by a predefined boundary that is set in a secondary attribute of the `content-type` HTTP headers. We'll need to use `formidable` to parse this data, extracting each file contained therein. We'll do this with the help of the following code:

```
var http = require('http');
var formidable = require('formidable');
var form = require('fs').readFileSync('form.html');

http.createServer(function (request, response) {
  if (request.method === "POST") {
    var incoming = new formidable.IncomingForm();
    incoming.uploadDir = 'uploads';
```

```
      incoming.on('file', function (field, file) {
        if (!file.size) { return; }
        response.write(file.name + ' received\n');
      }).on('end', function () {
        response.end('All files received');
      });
      incoming.parse(request);
    }
    if (request.method === "GET") {
      response.writeHead(200, {'Content-Type': 'text/html'});
      response.end(form);
    }
  }).listen(8080);
```

Our POST server has now become an upload server.

How it works...

We create a new instance of the `formidable IncomingForm` class and tell it where to upload files. In order to provide feedback to the user, we can listen to our incoming instance. The `IncomingForm` class emits its own higher level events, so rather than listening to the `request` object for events and processing data as it comes, we wait for `formidable` to parse the files out of the multipart message and then notify us through its custom `file` event.

The `file` event callback provides us with two parameters: `field` and `file`. We don't use the `field` parameter in our recipe; each `field` parameter holds the name of the file input element in our HTML done. The `file` parameter is an object that contains information about the uploaded file. We use this to filter out empty files (usually caused by empty input fields) and grab the filename, which we show to users as confirmation. When `formidable` has finished parsing the multipart message, it sends an `end` event in which we end the response.

There's more...

We can POST more than simple form fields and values from a browser. Let's take a look at transferring files from the browser to server.

Using formidable to accept all POST data

Formidable doesn't just handle uploaded files, it will also process general POST data. All we have to do is add a listener for the `field` event to process forms that contain both files and user data, as follows:

```
    incoming.on('file', function (field, file) {
      response.write(file.name + ' received\n');
    }).on('field', function (field, value) {
```

```
      response.write(field + ' : ' + value + '\n');
   }).on('end', function () {
      response.end('All files received');
   });
});
```

There's no need to manually implement field data size limits as `formidable` takes care of this for us, although we can change the defaults with `incoming.maxFieldsSize`, which allows us to limit the total byte count for the sum of all fields. This limit doesn't apply to file uploads.

Preserving filenames with formidable

When `formidable` places our files in the `uploads` directory, it assigns them a name that consists of a randomly generated hexadecimal number. This prevents files of the same name from being overwritten. However, what if we want to know which files are which and still retain the unique filename advantage? We can alter the way `formidable` names each file during its `fileBegin` event with the help of the following code:

```
if (request.method === "POST") {
   var incoming = new formidable.IncomingForm();
   incoming.uploadDir = 'uploads';
   incoming.on('fileBegin', function (field, file) {
      if (file.name){
         file.path += "-" + file.name;
      } //...rest of the code
   }).on('file', function (field, file) {
//...rest of the code
```

We've appended the original filename onto the end of the random filename assigned by `formidable`, separating them with a dash. Now we can easily identify our files, though for many scenarios this may not be necessary as we would likely be outputting file information to a database and cross-referencing it to randomly generated names.

Uploading files via PUT

It's also possible to upload files via an HTTP `PUT` request. While we can only send one file per request, we don't need to do any parsing on the server side since the file will simply stream directly to our server, which means less server-side processing overhead. It would be magnificent if we could achieve this by changing our form's `method` attribute from `POST` to `PUT`, but alas, no. However, thanks to the up and coming XMLHttpRequest Level 2 (xhr2) request, we can now transfer binary data via JavaScript in some browsers (see http://caniuse.com). We grab a file pointer using a `change` event listener on the input file element, and then we open a `PUT` request and send the file. The following is for use in our `form.html` file, which we'll save as `put_upload_form.html`:

```
<form id=frm>
   <input type=file id=userfile name=userfile><br>
   <input type=submit>
```

```
</form>
<script>
(function () {
  var userfile = document.getElementById('userfile'),
  frm = document.getElementById('frm'),
  file;
  userfile.addEventListener('change', function () {
    file = this.files[0];
  });
  frm.addEventListener('submit', function (e) {
    e.preventDefault();
    if (file) {
      var xhr = new XMLHttpRequest();
      xhr.file = file;
      xhr.open('put', window.location, true);
      xhr.setRequestHeader("x-uploadedfilename", file.fileName ||
        file.name);
      xhr.send(file);
      file = '';
      frm.reset();
    }
  });
}());
</script>
```

> The id attribute is added to the form and the file input. method and enctype attributes have been removed. We're using just one file element because we can only send one file per request, although the example could be extended to asynchronously stream multiple files to our server at once.

Our script attaches a change listener to the file input element. When the user selects a file, we are able to capture a pointer to the file. As the form is submitted, we prevent default behavior, check whether a file is selected, initialize an xhr object, open a PUT request to our server, and set a custom header (which we'll be calling X-UPLOADEDFILENAME), so we can grab the filename later and send the file to our server. Our server code looks like the following:

```
var http = require('http');
var fs = require('fs');
var form = fs.readFileSync('put_upload.html');
http.createServer(function (request, response) {
  if (request.method === "PUT") {
    var fileData = new Buffer(+request.headers['content-length']);
    var bufferOffset = 0;
    request.on('data', function(chunk) {
```

```
        chunk.copy(fileData, bufferOffset);
        bufferOffset += chunk.length;
      }).on('end', function() {
        var rand = (Math.random()*Math.random())
          .toString(16).replace('.','');
        var to = 'uploads/' + rand + "-" +
        request.headers['x-uploadedfilename'];

        fs.writeFile(to, fileData, function(err) {
          if (err) { throw err; }
          console.log('Saved file to ' + to);
          response.end();
        });
      });
    }
    if (request.method === "GET") {
      response.writeHead(200, {'Content-Type': 'text/html'});
      response.end(form);
    }
  }).listen(8080);
```

Our PUT server follows a similar pattern to the simple POST server in the *Processing POST data* recipe; we listen to the `data` event and piece the chunks together. However, rather than a string concatenating our data, we must pass our chunks into a buffer because a buffer can handle any data type including binary, whereas a `String` object will always coerce non-string data into string format—this changes the underlying binary, resulting in corrupted files. Once the `end` event is triggered, we generate a random filename similar to the naming convention of `formidable` and write the file to our `uploads` folder.

This uploading via PUT demonstration will not work in older browsers, so an alternative fallback should be provided in a production environment. Browsers that will support this method are IE10 and above, Firefox, Chrome, Safari, iOS 5+ Safari, and Android browsers. However, due to browser vendors' differing implementations of the same functionality, the example may need some tweaking for cross-browser compatibility.

See also

- The *Sending e-mail* recipe discussed in *Chapter 9, Integrating Network Paradigms*
- The *Using Node as an HTTP client* recipe
- *Chapter 5, Employing Streams*

Using Node as an HTTP client

The HTTP object doesn't just provide server capabilities, it also affords us with client functionality. We might want to use this functionality for a myriad of purposes: HTTP-based API's (such as a REST-based interface), website scraping for statistical processing or in the absence of an API, or the first step in automated UI testing. In this task, we're going to use `http.get` with `process` to fetch external web pages dynamically via the command line.

Getting ready

We are not creating a server. So in the name of convention, we should use a different name for our new file. Let's call it `fetch.js`.

How to do it...

The `http.request` method allows us to make requests of any kind (for example, GET, POST, DELETE, OPTION, and so on), but for GET requests, we can use the shorthand `http.get` method as shown in the following code:

```
var http = require('http');
var urlOpts = {host: 'www.nodejs.org', path: '/', port: '80'};
http.get(urlOpts, function (response) {
  response.on('data', function (chunk) {
    console.log(chunk.toString());
  });
});
```

Essentially, we're done! Try to run the following command:

node fetch.js

Our console will output the HTML of `nodejs.org`. However, let's pad it out a bit with some interactivity and error handling, as follows:

```
var http = require('http');
var url = require('url');
var urlOpts = {host: 'www.nodejs.org', path: '/', port: '80'};
if (process.argv[2]) {
  if (!process.argv[2].match('http://')) {
    process.argv[2] = 'http://' + process.argv[2];
  }
  urlOpts = url.parse(process.argv[2]);
}
http.get(urlOpts, function (response) {
  response.on('data', function (chunk) {
```

```
      console.log(chunk.toString());
    });
  }).on('error', function (e) {
    console.log('error:' + e.message);
  });
```

Now we can use our script with the help of the following command:

`node fetch.js www.google.com`

How it works...

The `http.get` method takes an object that defines the criteria of our desired request. We defined a variable called `urlOpts` for this purpose and set our host to `www.nodejs.org`. We use the `process.argv` property to check whether a web address has been specified via the command line.

Just like the `console` object, the `process` object is a global variable that is always available within Node's runtime environment. The `process.argv[2]` argument is the third command-line argument, with `node` and `fetch.js` being allocated to `[0]` and `[1]`, respectively.

If `process.argv[2]` exists (that is, if an address has been specified), we append `http://`; if it isn't there (`url.parse` requires it), then replace the object in our default `urlOpts` with the output from `url.parse`. An object is returned by `url.parse` happily with the same properties that `http.get` requires.

As a client, we are interacting with the server's response to us, rather than the client's request from us. So inside the `http.get` callback, we listen for the `data` event on `response` instead of (as with our server examples) `request`. As the `response` data stream arrives, we output the chunks to the console.

> For terser APIs built on top of the HTTP request, check out the third-party module's request (`https://npmjs.org/package/request`) and superagent (`https://npmjs.org/package/superagent`).

There's more...

Let's explore some of the possibilities of the `http.get` method's underlying `http.request` method.

Sending POST requests

We'll need to fire up our `server.js` app from the *Processing POST data* recipe to receive our POST requests. Let's create the following new file and call it `post.js`, which we'll use to send POST requests to our POST server:

```
var http = require('http');
var urlOpts = {host: 'localhost', path: '/', port: '8080', method:
  'POST'};
var request = http.request(urlOpts, function (response) {
  response.on('data', function (chunk) {
    console.log(chunk.toString());
  });
}).on('error', function (e) {
  console.log('error:' + e.stack);
});
process.argv.forEach(function (postItem, index) {
  if (index > 1) { request.write(postItem + '\n'); }
});
request.end();
```

As we're using the more general `http.request` method, we've had to define our HTTP verb in the `urlOpts` variable. Our `urlOpts` variable also specifies the server as `localhost:8080` (we must ensure that our POST server is running in order for this code to work).

As seen before, we set up an event listener in our callback for data on the `response` object. The `http.request` method returns a `clientRequest` object, which we load into a variable called `request`. This is a newly declared variable, which holds the returned `clientRequest` object from our `http.request` method.

After our event listeners, we loop through the command-line arguments using the `forEach` method of Ecmascript 5 (which is safe to use in Node, but not yet in browsers). On running this script, `node` and `post.js` would be the zero and first arguments, so we check that our array index is greater than 1 before sending any arguments as POST data. We use `request.write` to send data, similar to how we would use `response.write` if we were building a server. Even though it uses a callback, `forEach` is not asynchronous (it blocks until completion). So only after every element is processed, our POST data is written and our request ended. The following command shows how we use it:

node post.js foo=bar&x=y&anotherfield=anothervalue

Multipart file upload as a client

We'll use our upload server from the *Handling file uploads* recipe to receive the files from our uploading client. To achieve this, we have to deal with the multipart data format. To inform a server of the client's intentions of sending multipart data, we set the `Content-Type` header to `multipart/form-data` with an additional attribute called `boundary`, which is a custom-named delimiter that separates in the multipart data, as follows:

```
var http = require('http');
var fs = require('fs');
var urlOpts = { host: 'localhost', path: '/', port: '8080',
  method: 'POST'};
```

Exploring the HTTP Object

```
    var boundary = Date.now();
    urlOpts.headers = {
      'Content-Type': 'multipart/form-data; boundary="' +boundary+ '"'
    };
```

We've used the `fs` module here too as we'll require that later to load our files.

We've set our `boundary` parameter to the current Unix time (milliseconds since midnight, January 1, 1970). We won't need `boundary` again in this format, so let's update it with the required multipart double dash (`--`) prefix and set up our `http.request` call, as follows:

```
    boundary = "--" + boundary;
    var request = http.request(urlOpts, function (response) {
      response.on('data', function (chunk) {
        console.log(chunk.toString());
      });
    }).on('error', function (e) {
      console.log('error:' + e.stack);
    });
```

We want to be able to stream multipart data to the server, which may be compiled from multiple files. If we streamed these files simultaneously, attempting to compile them together into the multipart format, the data would likely be mashed together from different file streams in an unpredictable order, becoming impossible to parse. So we need a way to preserve the data order.

We could build it all in one go and send it to the server afterwards. A more efficient (and Node-like) solution is to build the multipart message by progressively assembling each file into the multipart format as the file is streamed in, while instantly streaming the multipart data as it's being built.

To achieve this, we can use a recursively self-invoking function, calling each iteration from within the `end` event callback to ensure each stream is captured separately and in order, as follows:

```
    (function multipartAssembler(files) {
      var f = files.shift(), fSize = fs.statSync(f).size;
      fs.createReadStream(f).on('end', function () {
        if (files.length) {
          multipartAssembler(files);
          return; //early finish
        }
        //any code placed here wont execute until no files are left
        //due to early return from function.
      });
    }(process.argv.splice(2, process.argv.length)));
```

This is also a self-calling function because we've changed it from a declaration to an expression by wrapping parentheses around it. Then we've called it by appending parentheses, also passing in the command-line arguments, which specify what files to upload. We'll see this by executing the following command:

node upload.js file1 file2 fileN

We use `splice` on the `process.argv` array to remove the first two arguments (which would be `node` and `upload.js`). The result is passed into our `multipartAssembler` function as our `files` parameter.

Inside our function, we immediately shift the first file off the `files` array and load it into variable `f`, which is passed into `createReadStream`. Once it's finished reading, we pass any remaining files back through our `multipartAssembler` function and repeat the process until the array is empty. Now, let's flesh our self-iterating function out with multipart goodness, as follows:

```
(function multipartAssembler(files) {
  var f = files.shift(), fSize = fs.statSync(f).size,
  progress = 0;
  fs.createReadStream(f)
  .once('open', function () {
    request.write(boundary + '\r\n' +
      'Content-Disposition: ' +
      'form-data; name="userfile"; filename="' + f + '"\r\n' +
      'Content-Type: application/octet-stream\r\n' +
      'Content-Transfer-Encoding: binary\r\n\r\n');
  }).on('data', function(chunk) {
    request.write(chunk);
    progress += chunk.length;
    console.log(f + ': ' + Math.round((progress / fSize) *
      10000)/100 + '%');
  }).on('end', function () {
    if (files.length) {
      multipartAssembler(files);
      return; //early finish
    }
    request.end('\r\n' + boundary + '--\r\n\r\n\r\n');
  });
}(process.argv.splice(2, process.argv.length)));
```

We specify a part with the predefined boundary initially set in the `content-type` header. Each part has to begin with a header; we latch on to the `open` event to send this header out.

Exploring the HTTP Object

The `Content-Disposition` header has three parts. In this scenario, the first part will always be `form-data`. The remaining two parts define the name of the field (for instance the `name` attribute of a file input), and the original filename. The `Content-Type` header can be set to whatever mime is relevant. However, by setting all files to `application/octet-stream` and `Content-Transfer-Encoding` to `binary`, we can safely treat all files the same way if all we're doing is saving to disk without any interim processing. We finish each multipart header with a double CRLF (`\r\n\r\n`) at the end of our `request.write` method.

Also, notice we've also assigned a new `progress` variable at the top of the `multipartAssembler` function. We use this to determine the relative percent of the upload by dividing the chunks received so far (`progress`) by the total file size (`fSize`). This calculation is performed in our `data` event callback, where we also stream each chunk to the server.

In our `end` event, if there are no more files to process, we end the request with the final multipart boundary, which is the same as other boundary partitions except it has leading and trailing slashes.

See also

- The *Working with real data: fetching trending tweets* recipe discussed in *Chapter 3, Working with Data Serialization*

Implementing download throttling

Node provides `pause` and `resume` methods for incoming streams but not for outbound streams. Essentially, this means we can easily throttle upload speeds in Node, but download throttling requires a more creative solution.

Getting ready

We'll need a new `server.js` file along with a big enough file to serve. With the `dd` command-line program, we can generate a file for testing purposes, as follows:

```
dd if=/dev/zero of=50meg count=50 bs=1048576
```

The preceding command will create a 50 MB file named `50meg`, which we'll be serving.

> For a similar Windows tool that can be used to generate a large file, check out http://www.bertel.de/software/rdfc/index-en.html.

How to do it...

To keep things as simple as possible, our download server will serve just one file, but we'll implement it in a way that allows us to easily plug in some router code to serve multiple files. First, we will require our modules and set up an `options` object for file and speed settings, as follows:

```
var http = require('http');
var fs = require('fs');

var options = {}
options.file = '50meg';
options.fileSize = fs.statSync(options.file).size;
options.kbps = 32;
```

> If we were serving multiple files, our `options` object would be largely redundant; however, we're using it here to emulate the concept of a user-determined file choice. In a multifile situation, we would instead be loading file specifics based upon the requested URL.
>
> To see how this recipe can be configured to serve and throttle more than one file, check out the routing recipes in *Chapter 1, Making a Web Server*.

The `http` module is for the server and the `fs` module is used to create a `readStream` method and grab the size of our file.

We're going to be restricting how much data is sent out at once, but first we need to get the data in. So let's create our server and initialize a `readStream` method as follows:

```
http.createServer(function(request, response) {
  var download = Object.create(options);
  download.chunks = new Buffer(download.fileSize);
  download.bufferOffset = 0;

  response.writeHeader(200, {'Content-Length': options.fileSize});

  fs.createReadStream(options.file)
  .on('data', function(chunk) {
    chunk.copy(download.chunks, download.bufferOffset);
    download.bufferOffset += chunk.length;
  })
  .once('open', function() {
    //this is where the throttling will happen
  });
}).listen(8080);
```

Exploring the HTTP Object

We've created our server and specified a new object called `download`, which inherits from our `options` object. We add two properties to our request-bound `download` object: a `chunks` property that collects the file chunks inside the `readStream data` event listener and a `bufferOffset` property that will be used to keep track of the number of bytes loaded from disk.

All we have to do now is the actual throttling. To achieve this, we simply apportion out the specified number of kilobytes from our buffer every second, thus achieving the specified kilobytes per second. We'll make a function for this, which will be placed outside of `http.createServer` and we'll call our function `throttle`, as follows:

```
function throttle(download, cb) {
   var chunkOutSize = download.kbps * 1024, timer = 0;


   (function loop(bytesSent) {
     var remainingOffset;
     if (!download.aborted) {
       setTimeout(function () {
         var bytesOut = bytesSent + chunkOutSize;
         if (download.bufferOffset>bytesOut) {
           timer = 1000;
           cb(download.chunks.slice(bytesSent,bytesOut));
           loop(bytesOut);
           return;
         }

         if (bytesOut >= download.chunks.length) {
           remainingOffset = download.chunks.length - bytesSent;
           cb(download.chunks.slice(remainingOffset,bytesSent));
           return;
         }

         loop(bytesSent); //continue to loop, wait for enough data
       },timer);
     }
   }(0));

   return function () { //return function to handle abort scenario
     download.aborted = true;
   };

}
```

Chapter 2

The `throttle` function interacts with the `download` object created on each server request to measure out each chunk according to our predetermined `options.kbps` speed. For the second parameter (`cb`), the `throttle` function accepts a functional callback. The `cb` parameter in turn takes one parameter, which is the chunk of data the `throttle` function has determined to send. Our `throttle` function returns a `convenience` function that can be used to end the loop on abort, avoiding infinite looping.

We initialize download throttling by calling our `throttle` function in the server callback when the `readStream` method opens, as follows:

```
//...previous code
  fs.createReadStream(options.file)
  .on('data', function (chunk) {
    chunk.copy(download.chunks,download.bufferOffset);
    download.bufferOffset += chunk.length;
  })
  .once('open', function () {
    var handleAbort = throttle(download, function (send) {
      response.write(send);
    });

    request.on('close', function () {
      handleAbort();
    });
  });

}).listen(8080);
```

How it works...

The key to this recipe is our `throttle` function; let's walk through it. To achieve the specified speed, we send a chunk of data of a certain size every second. The size is determined by the desired number of kilobytes per second. So if `download.kbps` is 32, we'll send 32 KB chunks every second.

Buffers work in bytes, so we set a new variable called `chunkOutSize` and multiply `download.kbps` by 1,024 to realize the appropriate chunk size in bytes. Next, we set a `timer` variable, which is passed into `setTimeout`. It is first set to 0 on two accounts. For one, it eliminates an unnecessary initial 1,000 millisecond overhead, allowing our server the opportunity to immediately send the first chunk of data, if available. Secondly, if the `download.chunks` buffer is not full enough to accommodate the demand of `chunkOutSize`, the embedded `loop` function recurses without changing `timer`. This causes the CPU to cycle in real time until the buffer loads enough data to deliver a whole chunk (a process, which should take less than a second).

Exploring the HTTP Object

Once we have enough data for the first chunk, `timer` is set to `1000` because from here on out, we want to push a chunk every second.

The `loop` function is the gut of our throttling engine; it's a recursive function that calls itself with one parameter—bytesSent. The `bytesSent` parameter allows us to keep track of how much data has been sent so far and we use it to determine which bytes to slice out of our `download.chunks` buffer using `Buffer.slice`. The `Buffer.slice` variable takes two parameters: `start` and `end`. These two parameters are fulfilled with `bytesSent` and `bytesOut`, respectively. The `bytesOut` variable is also used against `download.bufferOffset` to ensure we have enough data loaded for a whole chunk to be sent out.

If there is enough data, we proceed to set the `timer` variable to `1000` to initiate our chunk per second policy, and then pass the result of `download.chunks.slice` into `cb`, which becomes our `send` parameter.

Back inside our server, our `send` parameter is passed to `response.write` within our `throttle` callback so each chunk is streamed to the client. Once we've passed our sliced chunk to `cb`, we call `loop(bytesOut)` for a new iteration (thus `bytesOut` transforms into `bytesSent`). We then return from the function to prevent any further execution.

The third and final place where `bytesOut` appears is in the second conditional statement of the `setTimeout` callback, where we use it against `download.chunks.length`. This is important to handle the last chunk of data. We don't want to loop again after the final chunk has been sent, and if the `options.kbps` callback doesn't divide exactly into the total file size, the final `bytesOut` variable would be larger than the size of the buffer, which if passed into the `slice` method unchecked would cause an **Object Out of Bounds** (**OOB**) error.

So, if `bytesOut` equals or is greater than the memory allocated to the `download.chunks` buffer (that is, the size of our file), we slice the remaining bytes from our `download.chunks` buffer and return from the function without calling `loop`, effectively terminating recursion.

To prevent infinite looping when the connection is closed unexpectedly (for instance on connection failure or client abort), throttle returns another function, which is caught in the `handleAbort` variable and called in the `close` event of `response`. The function simply adds a property to the `download` object to say that the download has been aborted. This is checked on each recursion of the `loop` function. As long as `download.aborted` isn't true, it continues to iterate; otherwise the looping stops short.

> There are (configurable) limits on operating systems that define how many files can be opened at once. We would probably want to implement caching in a production download server to optimize file system access. For file limits on Unix systems, see http://stackoverflow.com/questions/34588/how-do-i-change-the-number-of-open-files-limit-in-linux.

There's more...

What about resuming downloads?

Enabling a resume request from broken downloads

If a connection breaks or a user accidentally aborts a download, the client may initiate a resume request by sending a `Range` HTTP header to the server. A `Range` header would look something like the following:

`Range: bytes=512-1024`

When a server agrees to handle a `Range` header, it sends a `206 Partial Content` status and adds a `Content-Range` header in the response. Where the entire file is 1 MB, a `Content-Range` reply to the above `Range` header might look like the following:

`Content-Range: bytes 512-1024/1024`

Notice that there is no equal sign (=) after `bytes` in a `Content-Range` header. We can pass an object into the second parameter of `fs.createReadStream`, which specifies where to start and end reading. Since we are simply handling a resume request, we only need to set the start property as follows:

```
//requires, options object, throttle function, etc...
download.readStreamOptions = {};
download.headers = {'Content-Length': download.fileSize};
download.statusCode = 200;
if (request.headers.range) {
  download.start = request.headers
  .range.replace('bytes=','').split('-')[0];
  download.readStreamOptions = {start: +download.start};
  download.headers['Content-Range'] = "bytes " + download.start +
  "-" + download.fileSize + "/" + download.fileSize;
  download.statusCode = 206; //partial content
}
response.writeHeader(download.statusCode, download.headers);
fs.createReadStream(download.file, download.readStreamOptions)
//...rest of the code....
```

By adding some properties to `download` and using them to conditionally respond to a `Range` header, we can now handle `resume` requests.

See also

- The *Setting up a router* recipe discussed in *Chapter 1, Making a Web Server*
- The *Caching content in memory for immediate delivery* recipe discussed in *Chapter 1, Making a Web Server*
- The *Communicating via TCP* recipe discussed in *Chapter 9, Integrating Networking Paradigms*

3
Working with Data Serialization

In this chapter, we will cover the following topics:

- Converting an object to JSON and back
- Converting an object to XML and back
- Browser-server transmission via AJAX
- Working with real data – fetching trending tweets

Introduction

The ability to serialize data is fundamental to cross-application and cross-network communication. If we want to give third parties safe access to raw data, we can use serialization to send it in a format that the requester will understand. In this chapter, we'll be working with two well-known standards, JSON and XML, using JavaScript to parse data from and massage data into these formats.

Converting an object to JSON and back

JavaScript Object Notation (**JSON**) is very closely related to JavaScript objects because it's a subset of JavaScript. This task will demonstrate how to use the building blocks of JSON conversion: `JSON.parse` and `JSON.stringify`.

Working with Data Serialization

Getting ready

We'll need to create two new files called `profiles.js`, which will hold the data we'll be converting into JSON and `back.js`, which will be our main file for this recipe.

How to do it...

Let's create the object that we'll later be converting to JSON, in `profiles.js` as follows:

```
module.exports = {
  ryan: {
    name: "Ryan Dahl",
    irc: "ryah",
    twitter: "ryah",
    github: "ry",
    location: "San Francisco, USA",
    description: "Creator of node.js"
  },
  isaac: {
    name: "Isaac Schlueter",
    irc: "isaacs",
    twitter: "izs",
    github: "isaacs",
    location: "San Francisco, USA",
    description: "Former project gatekeeper, CTO npm, Inc."
  },
  timothy: {
    name: "Timothy J Fontaine",
    irc: "tjfontaine",
    twitter: "tjfontaine",
    github: "tjfontaine",
    location: "Alameda, USA",
    description: "Project gatekeeper"
  },
  tj: {
    name: "TJ Holowaychuk",
    irc: "tjholowaychuk",
    twitter: "tjholowaychuk",
    github: "visionmedia",
    location: "Victoria, BC, Canada",
    description: "Author of express, jade and many other modules"
  },
  felix: {
    name: "Felix Geisendorfer",
```

```
        irc: "felixge",
        twitter: "felixge",
        github: "felixge",
        location: "Berlin, Germany",
        description: "Author of formidable, active core developer"
    }
};
```

This object contains profile information on some of the leading members of the Node Community (though it's entirely non-exhaustive and doesn't even contain the entire core development team). One thing to note here is the use of `module.exports`. We'll be seeing more of this in *Chapter 10, Writing Your Own Node Modules*. We're using `module.exports` to modularize our `profiles` object here in a bid to keep our code uncluttered. We can load any expression into `module.exports`, save it as a separate file (which in our case we'll call `profiles.js`), and use `require` in our main file to dynamically load it at initialization, as follows:

```
var profiles = require('./profiles'); // note .js suffix is optional
```

Nice and tidy. To convert our `profiles` object into a JSON representation, we use `JSON.stringify`, which will return a string composed of JSON data. We're going to fundamentally alter our object (which is now a string) using the following statement:

```
replace.profiles = JSON.stringify(profiles).replace(/name/g,
    'fullname');
```

Here we have called `replace`, using a regular expression with the g (global) option, to change every occurrence of name in our JSON string to `fullname`.

But wait! There appears to be some kind of mistake. Felix's last name is missing an umlaut! Let's correct it by converting our JSON data back into an object, and correct his name by altering the value of the redesignated `fullname` property, as follows:

```
profiles = JSON.parse(profiles);
profiles.felix.fullname = "Felix Geisendörfer";
console.log(profiles.felix);
```

When we run our application, `console.log` will output the following:

```
{ fullname: 'Felix Geisendörfer',
  irc: 'felixge',
  twitter: 'felixge',
  github: 'felixge',
  location: 'Berlin, Germany',
  description: 'Author of formidable, active core developer' }
```

The first key is now `fullname`, and Geisendörfer is spelled correctly.

Working with Data Serialization

How it works...

First, we have an everyday JavaScript object that we serialize into a JSON representation. We also call the `String.replace` method on our JSON string, changing every occurrence of name into `fullname`.

Using `replace` in this way and context isn't an advisable practice since any occurrences of name are replaced. There could very easily have been other places in the string where the name may have existed, which would be replaced unintentionally. We used `replace` here to affirm that profiles have become a JSON string, as we couldn't use `replace` on an object.

Then we convert our modified JSON string back into an object, using `JSON.parse`. To test that our keys were indeed transformed from name to `fullname`, and to affirm that we are again working with an object, we correct the `felix` profile via `profiles.felix.fullname`, and then log `profiles.felix` to the console.

There's more...

JSON is a highly versatile and flexible tool for cross-platform communication. Let's look at a more advanced application of the standard.

Constructing JSONP responses

JSON with Padding (JSONP) is a cross-domain policy workaround that allows developers to interface with resources on other domains.

> For more information on JSONP, see `http://www.json-p.org/`.

JSONP responses involve defining a callback function on the client side that handles JSON via its first parameter, and then passing the name of this callback as a query argument in the `src` attribute of a `script` element, which points to a web service on another domain. The web service then returns the JSON data, wrapped in a function named according to the query argument set by the client side. It's possibly easier to illustrate this in code, as follows:

```
<html>
<head>
<script>
  var who = 'ryan';
  function cb(o) {
    alert(o.name + ' : ' + o.description);
  }
  var s = document.createElement('script');
  s.src = 'http://localhost:8080/?callback=cb&who=' + who;
  document.getElementsByTagName("head")[0].appendChild(s);
```

```
    </script>
  </head>
</html>
```

We can name this file `jsonp.html`. It will work fine when opened as a local file (for example, over the `file://` protocol) or via a server.

We define a function called `cb`, which takes an object as its parameter, and then we output the `name` and `description` properties. Prior to this, we set a variable called `who` that will be passed to the server to grab specific data for us. We then dynamically inject a new `script` element, setting `src` to a figurative third-party domain (which for easy demonstration is localhost) and adding `callback` and `who` query arguments. The value of `callback` matches the name of our `cb` function. Our server uses this parameter to wrap JSON in a function invocation.

Let's create our server with the help of the following code. We'll call the following file as `file jsonp_server.js`:

```
var http = require('http');
var url = require('url');
var profiles = require('./profiles');

http.createServer(function (request, response) {
  var urlObj = url.parse(request.url, true),
    cb = urlObj.query.callback, who = urlObj.query.who,
    profile;

  if (cb && who) {
    profile = cb + "(" + JSON.stringify(profiles[who]) + ")";
    response.end(profile);
  }

}).listen(8080);
```

We create a server, extract the `callback` and `who` query parameters, and write a response containing a function call passing our JSON data in as its parameter. This script is loaded by our client, where the `cb` function is called and JSON is received into the function as an object (because it looks like one).

Security and JSONP

Since JSONP uses script injection, any script could be inserted into our page. Therefore, it's highly recommended that this method only be used with trusted sources. An untrusted source could run evil code on the page.

Working with Data Serialization

> A safer alternative to JSONP is **Cross-Origin Resource Sharing** (**CORS**), which is implemented in all modern browsers. The `http://enable-cors.org` link explains in detail and the `corsify` module (`https://npmjs.org/package/corsify`) makes for seamless integration. The CORS (`https://npmjs.org/package/cors`) middleware is also helpful for enabling CORS in Express. We'll be learning more about Express in *Chapter 7, Accelerating Development with Express*.

See also

- The *Browser-server transmission via AJAX* recipe
- The *Working with real data – fetching trending tweets* recipe

Converting an object to XML and back

Since JSON is a string-based representation of a JavaScript object, converting between the two is straightforward. However, XML is less convenient to work with. Nevertheless, there may be times we have to work with it, for instance, if an API works only in XML or if we were contracted with a project that specifies XML support.

There are various non-core XML parsers available. One such parser is the non-core module `xml2js`. The premise of `xml2js` is that working with objects in JavaScript is more suitable than working with XML. The `xml2js` module provides a basis for us to interact with XML by converting it to a JavaScript object.

In this task, we're going to write a function that uses our `profiles` object featured in the previous recipe to create a valid XML string, which we'll then push through `xml2js`, thus converting it back into an object.

Getting ready

Before we start, let's create our file `xml and back.js`, making sure we have our separately modularized `profiles.js` file in the same directory. We should also install `xml2js` by executing the following command:

`npm install xml2js`

How to do it...

To begin with, we'll need to require our `profiles` object along with `xml2js`, as follows:

```
var profiles = require('./profiles');
var xml2js = require('xml2js');
```

Just as XML has a tree-like structure, objects can have objects nested within them. We need a function that can loop through our object and all subobjects, converting all properties into parent XML nodes, and all non-object values into text XML nodes. Fortunately, `xml2js` provides this with its `builder` constructor, as shown in the following code:

```
var builder = new xml2js.Builder({rootName:'profiles'});
profiles = builder.buildObject(profiles);
```

Let's replace all occurrences of name with `fullname` as we did in our *Converting an object to JSON and back* recipe, with the help of the following code:

```
profiles = profiles.replace(/name/g, 'fullname');
console.log(profiles); // <-- show me the XML!
```

Now, with the help of the following code, we'll turn `profiles` back into an object, correct Felix Geisendörfer's name using the renamed `fullname` property, and then log Felix into console to show it has worked:

```
xml2js.parseString(profiles, {
  explicitArray: false,
  explicitRoot: false
}, function (err, obj) {
  profiles = obj;
  profiles.felix.fullname = "Felix Geisendörfer";
  console.log(profiles);
});
```

The `xml2js.parseString` function takes the XML object (which at this point is held in the `profiles` variable) and assembles it into an object, which is passed through as the `obj` parameter in its callback.

How it works...

A JavaScript object is a key-value store, whereas XML is a resource-centric markup language. In XML, keys and values could be represented in two ways: either as a parent node and a child node or as attributes on an XML node. We converted our keys and values to parent and child nodes, mainly because a single XML node is filled with lots of attributes, while valid XML seems to violate the spirit of XML.

We achieved our conversion using the `builder` constructor supplied by `xml2js`, passing in an `options` object to the constructor containing a `rootName` property set to the `profiles` string. This prepares our builder instance to output XML in the following format:

```
<?xml version="1.0" encoding="UTF-8" standalone="yes"?>
<profiles>
    <!-- buildObject Output Here -->
</profiles>
```

Working with Data Serialization

If `rootName` is unspecified, `<root>` is the default, first parent node.

Once we have our `builder` instance, we go ahead and overwrite the `profiles` variable (which contained the `profiles` object exported from `profiles.js`) with the result of `builder.buildObject` (which means build XML from an object, as opposed to building an object) invoked with the original `profiles` object. At this point, the `profiles` variable contains an XML string representing the profile data.

We call `replace` on our `profiles` string, swapping all the name occurrences with `fullname`, and then log out the `profiles` XML.

To turn our XML object back to a JavaScript object, we use the `xml2js` object's `parseString` method. This method takes three arguments: a string of XML (which at this point in our code is represented by the `profiles` variable), an `options` object (which is optional), and a callback function as the third parameter.

To recreate our original object, we set the `explicitArray` option to `false`—this prevents the `parseString` method from creating an array to represent the child nodes of a parent element when there's only one child node. We also set `explicitRoot` to `false`—this stops the returned object from placing the objectified XML within a property named after the root node (`profiles` in our case), and instead just returns the main content in the form of an object.

The callback function is in the form sometimes described as a **continuable**, that is, a Node style callback where the error object is the first argument and the return value is the second. We call the second parameter `obj`, which is the object representation of the converted XML.

> The `xml2js` module depends on the `sax-js` module. **Simple API for XML (SAX)** is an alternative data model to the **Document Object Model (DOM)**—see http://en.wikipedia.org/wiki/Simple_API_for_XML for more information. Instead of seeing the data as a tree all at once, the data is parsed sequentially in an event-driven way (or, if we like, as a stream). Anything event driven in JavaScript and therefore the Node is asynchronous, so this is why `parseString` must use a callback to return the fully parsed object.

We reassign the `profiles` variable again, this time to `obj` (if we hadn't set `explicitRoot` to `false` in the `options` object, we'd be assigning `profiles` to `obj.profiles`), and now we're back to where we started (except that all our name properties are now called `fullname`). So we update the `fullname` property of the `felix` object, ensuring that he has his rightful umlaut.

There's more...

Let's take a look at how we can drive the creation of more intricate XML by using naming conventions on our JavaScript objects, and also discover a technique that when applied to our recipe (and beyond) can increase clarity and maintainability.

Generating XML attributes and text nodes

If we're looking to drive more advanced XML output via an object, we can employ some property naming conventions used by `xml2js` to influence the XML output to present certain values as attributes or text nodes. Let's alter the following `profiles.js` file, saving it as `profiles_enhanced.js`:

```
module.exports = {
  ryan : {
    name: "Ryan Dahl",
    irc: "ryah",
    twitter: "ryah",
    github:["ry","joyent"],
    location:{$: {city: 'San Francisco', country: 'USA'}},
    description: "Creator of node.js"
  },
  isaac : {
    name: "Isaac Schlueter",
    irc: "isaacs",
    twitter: "izs",
    github: "isaacs",
    location: {$: {city: 'San Francisco', country: 'USA'}},
    description: "Author of npm, core contributor"
  },
  timothy: {
    name: "Timothy J Fontaine",
    irc: "tjfontaine",
    twitter: "tjfontaine",
    github: "tjfontaine",
    location: {$: {city: 'San Francisco', country: 'USA'}},
    description: "Project gatekeeper"
  },
  tj : {
    name: "TJ Holowaychuk",
    irc: "tjholowaychuk",
    twitter: "tjholowaychuk",
    github: "visionmedia",
    location:{$: {city: 'Victoria',country: 'Canada'}, region: {_
  :'British Columbia',$:{type:'province'}}},
    description: "Author of express, jade and other popular modules"
  },
  felix : {
    name: "Felix Geisendorfer",
    irc: "felixge",
    twitter: "felixge",
```

```
        github: "felixge",
        location:{$: {city: 'Berlin', country: 'Germany'}},
        description: "Author of formidable, active core developer"
    }
};
```

When parsing an XML string, `xml2js` uses the dollar sign ($) to indicate attributes and the underscore (_) sign to represent text nodes (unless otherwise specified in the options). This convention goes two ways: the `builder` method understands that objects stored under a dollar property are intended as attribute key values, and a string value of an underscore property is meant to be a text node.

Let's copy `xml` and `back.js` to `attributes` and `text.js` respectively, making the following changes:

```
var profiles = require('./profiles_enhanced');
var xml2js = require('xml2js');

var builder = new xml2js.Builder({rootName:'profiles'});
profiles = builder.buildObject(profiles);

console.log(profiles); // <-- show me the XML
```

We changed the first line to require `profiles_enhanced`, rather than just `profiles`, and removed replacement of name with `fullname` and the conversion back with `parseString` (although all that would still work perfectly fine).

Upon running `attributes_and_text.js`, the XML output will contain attributes for everyone's location, and an additional text node for TJ Holowaychuks. For instance, TJ's portion of XML would look like the following code:

```
<tj>
  <name>TJ Holowaychuk</name>
  <irc>tjholowaychuk</irc>
  <twitter>tjholowaychuk</twitter>
  <github>visionmedia</github>
  <location city="Victoria" country="Canada">
    <region type="province">British Columbia</region>
  </location>
  <description>Author of express, jade and other popular
     modules</description>
</tj>
```

Partial application

While partial application has little to do with XML, it's always good to know the ways with which we can make our code cleaner.

If we needed to use `parseString` multiple times, we'd have to continually be passing the same `options` object in. We could break the `options` object out into its own variable and pass it by reference but this demands a level of duplication, which we can avoid with partial application, as shown in the following code:

```
var xml2js = require('xml2js');
var builder = new xml2js.Builder({rootName:'profiles'});
var profiles = {
  normal: builder.buildObject(require('./profiles')),
  enhanced: builder.buildObject(require('./profiles_enhanced'))
};

function apply(options, fn) {
  return function (xml, cb) {
    return fn(xml, options, cb);
  }
}

var parseString = apply({
  explicitArray: false,
  explicitRoot: false
}, xml2js.parseString);

parseString(profiles.normal, console.log);
parseString(profiles.enhanced, console.log);
```

In the adaptation of the main recipe (which we can call `partial_app.js`), we've loaded both, the original `profiles` object and also `profiles_enhanced` (from the previous *Generating XML attributes and text nodes* subsection in the *There's more* section), and immediately converted them to XML, storing them in an all-encompassing `profiles` object declared on the third line.

We create a function called `apply`, which returns a function that calls the second argument (`fn`) of `apply` with the returned function's two arguments (`xml` and `cb`) as the first and third arguments to `fn` and the outer `apply` function's first argument (`options`) as the middle argument of `fn`. Essentially, the `apply` function allows us to capture our `options` object and then map that captured object into the final call of `xml2js.parseString`.

We set up our new `parseString` variable and assign the result of our `apply` call to it, passing in our desired default options, and `xml2js.parseString` as the `fn` argument.

Working with Data Serialization

We now have a customized `parseString` function that we can use to convert our two sets of XML back into objects, without having to supply any options. In this case, we also simply supply `console.log` as the callback function (attempting to do this in most browsers will fail as an illegal invocation. In such a case we would need to pass `console.log.bind(console)`, but a simple `console.log` works fine in Node).

See also

- The *Converting an object to JSON and back* recipe
- The *Browser-server transmission via AJAX* recipe
- The *Working with real data – fetching trending tweets* recipe

Browser-server transmission via AJAX

We can enhance the user's experience by loading new content directly onto the page via AJAX, rather than loading a new page for each content request.

In this recipe, we're going to transfer our serialized data to the browser as the user requests it and then interact with our client-side data. We'll implement a profile viewer in the browser, which retrieves a selected profile in either JSON or XML, outputting the key values or parent-child nodes for that profile.

Getting ready

We're going to continue to work with our `profiles.js` object module (from the first two recipes of this chapter), so let's copy that into a new folder. For XML delivery, we'll be using `xml2js` from the *Converting an object to XML and back* recipe. If we're starting in a new folder, we'll need to install it with the help of the following command:

```
npm install xml2js
```

We'll also create two new files: `server.js` and `index.html`.

How to do it...

Let's start with our `index.html` file. We'll quickly implement a rough layout for our profile viewer consisting of a form with two select elements: a `div` for outputting formatted object data and a `textarea` element for presenting the raw serialized data:

```
<!doctype html>
<html>
  <head>
    <script src=http://ajax.googleapis.com/ajax/libs/jquery
```

```
            /2.1.0/jquery.min.js>
        </script>
        <style>
          #frm, #raw {display:block; float:left; width:210px}
          #raw {height:150px; width:310px; margin-left:0.5em}
        </style>
    </head>
    <body>
      <form id=frm>
        Profile: <select id=profiles>
        <option></option>
        </select><br>
        Format:<select id=formats>
        <option value=json> JSON </option>
        <option value=xml> XML </option>
        </select><br><br>
        <div id=output></div>
      </form>
      <textarea id=raw></textarea>
    </body>
</html>
```

Notice that we've included jQuery to obtain cross-browser benefits, particularly in the area of AJAX requests. We'll be utilizing jQuery in our client-side script shortly, but first let's make our server.

For our modules, we'll need `http`, `path`, and `fs` along with our custom `profiles` object and the third-party `xml2js` modules. For our code to work, we'll need to have `index.html` hosted within our server in order to prevent cross-origin policy errors, as follows:

```
var http = require('http');
var fs = require('fs');
var path = require('path');
var profiles = require('./profiles');
var xml2js = require('xml2js');

var index = fs.readFileSync('index.html');
var routes,
    mimes = {xml: "application/xml", json: "application/json"};
```

Working with Data Serialization

We've also defined `routes` and `mimes` variables so we can answer requests for specific data from the client along with the correct `Content-Type` header. We'll create the following two routes; one will deliver a list of profile names and the other will indicate a request for a particular profile:

```
routes = {
  'profiles': function (format) {
    return output(Object.keys(profiles), format);
  },
  '/profile': function (format, basename) {
    return output(profiles[basename], format, basename);
  }
};
```

Our `output` function, which we just referred to in `routes`, should be placed above the `routes` object and looks like the following code:

```
function output(content, format, rootNode) {
  if (!format || format === 'json') {
    return JSON.stringify(content);
  }
  if (format === 'xml') {
    return (new xml2js.Builder({
      rootName: rootNode
    })).buildObject(content);
  }
}
```

To finish our server, we simply call `http.createServer` and interact with our `routes` object inside the callback, outputting `index.html` where no routes are found, as shown in the following code:

```
http.createServer(function (request, response) {
  var dirname = path.dirname(request.url),
    extname = path.extname(request.url),
    basename = path.basename(request.url, extname);

  extname = extname.replace('.', ''); //remove period

  response.setHeader("Content-Type", mimes[extname] ||
    'text/html');

  if (routes.hasOwnProperty(dirname)) {
    response.end(routes[dirname](extname, basename));
    return;
  }
```

```
        if (routes.hasOwnProperty(basename)) {
          response.end(routes[basename](extname));
          return;
        }

        response.end(index);

    }).listen(8080);
```

Finally, we need to write our client-side code to interface with our server over AJAX, which is to be placed in script tags just underneath our `textarea`, but above the closing `</body>` tag (to ensure the HTML elements have loaded before script execution) of our `index.html` file, as shown in the following code:

```
<script>
$.get('http://localhost:8080/profiles',
  function (profile_names) {
    $.each(profile_names, function (i, pname) {
      $('#profiles').append('<option>' + pname + '</option>');
    });
  }, 'json');
$('#formats, #profiles').change(function () {
  var format = $('#formats').val();
  $.get('http://localhost:8080/profile/' + $('#profiles').val() +
    '.' + format,
    function (profile, stat, jqXHR) {
      var cT = jqXHR.getResponseHeader('Content-Type');
      $('#raw').val(profile);
      $('#output').html('');
      if (cT === 'application/json') {
        $.each($.parseJSON(profile), function (k, v) {
          $('#output').append('<b>' + k + '</b> : ' + v + '<br>');
        });
        return;
      }

      if (cT === 'application/xml') {
        profile = jqXHR.responseXML.firstChild.childNodes;
        $.each(profile,
          function (k, v) {
            if (v && v.nodeType === 1) {
              $('#output').append('<b>' + v.tagName + '</b> : ' +
              v.textContent + '<br>');
            }
```

Working with Data Serialization

```
        });

      }
    }, 'text');

  });
</script>
```

How it works...

Let's begin with the server. Inside our `http.createServer` callback, we set the appropriate header and check to see if the `routes` object has the specified directory name (or sub-route since we're not actually dealing with a filesystem here). If the subroute exists in the `routes` object, we call the method stored at that namespace passing in `basename` and `extname` (we use `extname` to determine the desired format). In cases where there is no directory name match, we check for an existing property matching `basename`. If there is one, we call it and pass in the extension (if any). If both tests turn out to be `false`, we simply output the contents of our `index.html` file.

Our two routes are `profiles` and `/profile`; the latter has a preceding slash, which corresponds to the way `path.dirname` returns the directory name portion of a path. Our `/profile` route also accepts a subroute named after the desired profile and format. For instance, `http://localhost:8080/profile/ryan.json` will return Ryan's profile in the JSON format (if no extension is given, we default to the JSON format).

Both the `profiles` and `/profile` methods utilize our custom output function which, using the format parameter (originally `extname` in the `http.createServer` callback), generates either JSON (using `JSON.stringify`) or XML (with `xml2js`) from the content passed to it. The output function also takes a conditional third parameter (`rootNode`), which is passed into the `builder` constructor to define the `rootName` parameter of the XML generated by the `buildObject` method call.

On the client side, the first thing we do is call the jQuery `$.get` method for `http://localhost:8080/profiles`. This causes the server to call the `profiles` method on the `route` object. This in turn calls our output function with an array of top-level properties from our `profiles.js` object. Since we didn't specify an extension in `$.get`, the output function will default to the JSON format and deliver the result of `JSON.stringify` into `response.end`.

Back on the client side, our third argument in the first `$.get` call is json—this ensures `$.get` interprets the incoming data as JSON, converting it to an object. The object is passed in as the first parameter of the `$.get` function callback (second parameter of `$.get`), which we named `profile_names`. We use jQuery's `$.each` function to loop through the `profile_names`, populating the first select element (#profiles) by applying jQuery's append method to the element, and adding each profile name inside the `<option>` element as we loop through `$.each`.

Next, we apply a listener to our two `select` elements (`change`) whose callback assembles a URL dependent upon the user's selection, passing this URL into another AJAX request using `$.get`.

This time on the server side, the `/profile` route method is invoked, passing in the corresponding profile from our `profiles` object to `output`. This property will contain an object holding the profile information of the requested individual.

In our second `$.get` call, we set the third argument to `text`. This will force jQuery not to automatically interpret incoming data as JSON or XML. This gives us more control and makes it easier to output the raw data into `textarea`. Inside the `$.get` callback, we use the `jqXHR` parameter to determine the `Content-Type` to see if we have JSON or XML. We loop through the returned data according to its type (either Object or XMLObject) and append it to our `#output div` element.

There's more...

We can also convert our objects to JSON and XML in the browser and send them over to our server, where we can interact with them as objects again.

Sending serialized data from the client to the server

Let's extend our example to add new profiles to our `profiles` object on the server using our browser interface.

Starting with `index.html` (which we'll copy to `add_profile_index.html`—we'll also copy `server.js` to `add_profile_server.js`), let's append a form called #add and style it. The following is the form:

```
<form id=add>
  <div><label>profile name</label><input name="profileName"></div>
  <div><label>name</label><input name="name"></div>
  <div><label>irc</label><input name="irc"></div>
  <div><label>twitter</label><input name="twitter"></div>
  <div><label>github</label><input name="github"></div>
  <div><label>location</label><input name="location"></div>
  <div><label>description</label><input name="description"></div>
  <div><button>Add</button></div>
</form>
```

And the following are some additional styles:

```
<style>
  #frm, #raw {display:block; float:left; width:210px}
  #raw {height:150px; width:310px; margin-left:0.5em}
  #add {display:block; float:left; margin-left:1.5em}
  #add div {display:table-row}
```

```
    #add label {float:left; width:5.5em}
    div button {float:right}
</style>
```

We're going to use `xml2js` in the browser as well. In order to do so, we can convert the module into a client-side library using `browserify`, as shown in the following command:

sudo npm -g install browserify #only linux systems will need sudo
browserify node_modules/xml2js -s xml2js -o xml2js.js

The `-s` option tells `browserify` to create a standalone file, which exports the `xml2js` module to the global `xml2js` variable (unless we were to use an AMD or CommonJS module loading framework, which is definitely a best practice rather than polluting global scope as we are). The `-o` flag tells `browserify` to write the resulting generated client code to a file called `xml2js.js`.

Now, we need to expose our client-side code through the server, so we'll read it in the same way as `index.html` in the main recipe, and then expose a route to it via our `routes` object, as follows:

```
var index = fs.readFileSync('add_profile_index.html');
var clientXml2js = fs.readFileSync('./xml2js.js');
var routes,
  mimes = {
    js: "application/javascript",
    json: "application/json",
    xml: "application/xml"
  };
routes = {
  'profiles': function (format) {
    return output(Object.keys(profiles), format);
  },
  '/profile': function (format, basename) {
    return output(profiles[basename], format, basename);
  },
  'xml2js' : function(ext) {
    if (ext === 'js') { return clientXml2js; }
  }
};
```

We also updated our `mimes` object ready to deliver `application/javascript` Content-Type and altered the `index` variable to use our new `add_profile_index.html` file. Back in our client-side code, we fetch our `xml2js` client-side library by including another `<script>` tag in the head section, as follows:

```
<script src=xml2js.js></script>
```

We'll wrap our initial `$.get` call to the server (which fetches all the profile names for the `select` element) in a function called `load`. This allows us to dynamically reload the profile names once a profile has been added, as follows:

```
function load(done) {
$.get('http://localhost:8080/profiles',
  function (profile_names) {
    $.each(profile_names, function (i, pname) {
      $('#profiles').append('<option>' + pname + '</option>');
    });
    done && done();
  }, 'json');
}
load();
```

We added a `done` callback to `load`, but didn't call it in the initial `load` invocation; we will be using it shortly, however.

Next, we define a handler for the `#add` form, as shown in the following code:

```
$('#add').submit(function(e) {
  var output, obj = {}, format = $('#formats').val(), profileName;
  e.preventDefault();
  $.each($(this).serializeArray(), function(i, nameValPair) {
    obj[nameValPair.name] = nameValPair.value; //form an object
  });

  profileName = obj.profileName; delete obj.profileName;
  obj = {_: obj}; obj[profileName] = obj._; delete obj._;

  output = (format === 'json') ? JSON.stringify(obj) :
    (new xml2js.Builder({rootName: profileName}))
      .buildObject(obj);

  $.ajax({ type: 'POST', url: '/', data: output,
    contentType: 'application/' + format, dataType: 'text',
    success: function(response) {
      $('#raw').val(response);
      $('#profiles').html('<option></option>');
      load(function () {
        $('#profiles').val(profileName);
      });
    }
  });
});
```

Working with Data Serialization

Our handler builds an object from the form input using jQuery's `serializeArray` method, and then converts that array to an object resembling our own data structure, with the addition of a `profileName` field. We capture `obj.profileName` into a `profileName` variable, and then remove it from the object. Then, we overwrite the `obj` variable with an object containing our built object stored under a placeholder property (`_`). We then point `obj[profileName]` to our built object referenced via the underscore (`_`) property, removing the temporary placeholder. What we end up with is an object that matches the format of the objects on our `profiles` object. Then, depending on the selected format, we convert `obj` into JSON or XML, and save it to the `output` variable. Once we have our `output` string, we use `jQuery.ajax` to send serialized data to our server. Once the `POST` request is complete, we call the `load` function to reload our data, and use the `load` callback parameter (`done`) function to select our newly added item once it has been reloaded from the server.

On our server, we'll write the following code to handle the `POST` request:

```
function updateProfiles(profile, type, cb) {
  var name = Object.keys(profile).pop();
  profiles[name] = profile[name];
  cb(output(profiles[name], type, name));
}

function addProfile(request, cb) {
  var pD = ''; //post data
  request
    .on('data', function (chunk) { pD += chunk; })
    .on('end',function() {
      var contentType = request.headers['content-type'];

      if (contentType === 'application/json') {
        updateProfiles(JSON.parse(pD), 'json', cb);
      }

      if (contentType === 'application/xml') {
        xml2js.parseString(pD, {
          explicitRoot: false,
          explicitArray: false
        }, function(err, obj) {
          updateProfiles(obj, 'xml', cb);
        });
      }

    });
}
```

As in the first recipe of *Chapter 2, Exploring the HTTP Object*, while handling POST data, `addProfile` compiles all the incoming data together. In the `end` event, we convert the serialized data to an object using a method appropriate to its type. We take this object and add it to our `profiles` object in the `updateProfiles` function using the single root property as the key to add or update our `profiles` object with.

To return data to the client, the `updateProfiles` function invokes the callback (`cb`) parameter (which comes via `addProfile`), passing in our custom `output` function, which will return the serialized data according to the specified format (which is determined by using replace on the `Content-Type` header).

We invoke the `addProfile` function in our server as follows:

```
http.createServer(function (request, response) {
//initial server variables...
  if (request.method === 'POST') {
    addProfile(request, function(output) {
      response.end(output);
    });
    return;
  }
//..rest of the server code (GET handling..)
```

Within our `addProfile` callback function, we simply end the response with the data returned from the `output` function, accessing this data via the `output` parameter as defined in the `addProfile` callback. The new profiles are only saved in operational memory, so they will be lost on server restarts. If we were to store this data on disc, we would ideally want to save it in a database, which we'll talk about in *Chapter 4, Interfacing with Databases*.

See also

- The *Setting up a router* recipe in *Chapter 1, Making a Web Server*
- The *Processing POST data* recipe in *Chapter 2, Exploring the HTTP Object*
- The *Converting an object to JSON and back* recipe
- The *Converting an object to XML and back* recipe

Working with real data – fetching trending tweets

Many online entities format their response data as JSON and XML in their **Application Programmer Interfaces** (**APIs**) to expose pertinent information to third-party developers who can subsequently integrate this data into their applications.

Working with Data Serialization

One such online entity is Twitter. In this recipe, we are going to make a command-line application that makes two requests to Twitter's REST service. The first will retrieve the most popular current topics on Twitter and the second will return the most recent tweets regarding the hottest topic on Twitter.

Getting ready

Let's create a file and name it `twitter_trends.js`. We'll also use the following third-party `colors` module to make our output more beautiful:

`npm install colors`

We'll need to go through some steps to satisfy the authorization requirements of the Twitter API. First, let's go to http://dev.twitter.com/apps, and log in with our Twitter account if need be (or sign up for a Twitter account first). Once logged in, we can press the **Create a new application** button on the top-right corner.

We'll fill out the name field with **ncbtt** (if the name is already taken, we can add a number or our own name to it), and the description as **Node Cookbook Twitter Trends**. For the website, we can simply put http://nodecookbook.com—we won't be needing a site for our implementation but it's a required field.

Once created, we'll see a screen containing OAuth settings. For this recipe, we only need the **Consumer key** and the **Consumer secret** fields from this screen.

To make most API calls, the headers of our HTTP requests made to the Twitter API must contain an `Authorization` field; for our main recipe, we'll need to exchange our consumer key and secret for a "bearer" access token.

Let's write the following quick script (which we'll call `twitter_auth.js`) to grab the access token and save it to a settings file (which we'll name `auth.json`):

```
var https = require('https');
var output = require('fs').createWriteStream('auth.json');
var consumer = {
  key: '<our consumer key>',
  secret: '<our consumer secret>'
};

var request = https.request({
  method: 'POST',
  host: 'api.twitter.com',
  path: '/oauth2/token',
  headers: {
    'User-Agent': 'Node Cookbook: Twitter Trends',
    Authorization: 'Basic ' + Buffer((encodeURIComponent(consumer.key)
 + ':' + encodeURIComponent(consumer.secret))).toString('base64'),
```

```
      'Content-type': 'application/x-www-form-urlencoded;charset=UTF-8',
      'Content-length': 29
  }
});


request.end('grant_type=client_credentials');

request.on('response', function (res) {
    if (res.statusCode !== 200) {
       return console.log('Error, status:' + res.statusCode);
    }

    res.pipe(output);
});
```

Now if we run our script, it will create `auth.json`, ready for us to fetch trending tweets.

How to do it...

We'll need the `https` module (any calls to authenticated API's have to be conducted over SSL) in order to make requests, and the `colors` module to get some color in our console output; the code is as follows:

```
var https = require('https');
var colors = require('colors');
var headers = {
  'User-Agent': 'Node Cookbook: Twitter Trends',
  Authorization: 'Bearer ' + require('./auth.json').access_token
};
```

Notice how we've also defined a `headers` object, in which the `Authorization` property contains the access token from the `auth.json` file we generated in the *Getting ready* section.

We're going to make a GET request inside another GET request. Between these requests, we'll process JSON data to either pass into the subsequent request or output to the console. In the spirit of **Don't Repeat Yourself** (**DRY**), and to demonstrate how to avoid spaghetti code, we'll abstract our GET requests and JSON handling into a function named `makeCall`; the code is as follows:

```
function makeCall(urlOpts, cb) {
  http.get(urlOpts, function (response) { //call the twitter api
    trendingTopics.jsonHandler(response, cb);
  }).on('error', function (e) {
    console.log("Connection Error: " + e.message);
  });
}
```

Working with Data Serialization

Notice the mysterious appearance of `trendingTopics` and its `jsonHandler` method; `trendingTopics` is an object that provides all the settings and methods for our Twitter interactions and `jsonHandler` is a method on the `trendingTopics` object that receives the response stream and converts JSON to an object.

We need to set up options for our calls to the trends and tweet APIs, along with some Twitter interaction-related functionality. So on top of our `makeCall` function, we'll create the `trendingTopics` object as follows:

```
var trendingTopics = module.exports = {
  trends: {
    urlOpts: {
      host: 'api.twitter.com',
      path: '/1.1/trends/place.json?id=1', //1 gives global trends,
      headers: headers
    }
  },
  tweets: {
    maxResults: 3,
    resultsType: 'recent', //choice of mixed, popular or recent
    urlOpts: {
      host: 'api.twitter.com',
      headers: headers,
    }
  },
  jsonHandler: function (response, cb) {
    var json = '';
    response.setEncoding('utf8');
    if (response.statusCode === 200) {
      response.on('data', function (chunk) {
        json += chunk;
      }).on('end', function () {
        cb(JSON.parse(json));
      });
    } else {
      throw ("Server Returned error: " + response.statusCode);
    }
  },
  tweetPath: function (q) {
    var p = '/1.1/search/tweets.json?q=' + q + '&count=' +
      this.tweets.maxResults + '&include_entities=true&result_type=' +
      this.tweets.resultsType;

    this.tweets.urlOpts.path = p;
  }
};
```

While creating the `trendingTopics` variable, we also turn the object into a module by simultaneously loading it into `module.exports`. We can see how to use this in the *There's more...* section of this recipe.

Within our `trendingTopics` object, we have the `trends` and `tweets` objects and two methods: `jsonHandler` and `tweetPath`.

Next up, we'll actually make use of our `makeCall` function but before we do that, we need to add a line to prevent the `makeCall` function from being invoked if the script isn't being run at the top level (that is, being run directly with the node command):

```
if (module.parent) {return;}
```

Finally, let's invoke our `makeCall` function to request the top global trends from the Twitter trends API, convert the returned JSON to an object, and use this object to ascertain the path to request tweets on the highest trending topic for using another embedded `makeCall` invocation. This is shown in the following code:

```
makeCall(trendingTopics.trends.urlOpts, function (trendsArr) {
  trendingTopics.tweetPath(trendsArr[0].trends[0].query)
  makeCall(trendingTopics.tweets.urlOpts, function (tweetsObj) {
    tweetsObj.statuses.forEach(function (tweet) {
      var name = tweet.user.screen_name, text = tweet.text;
      console.log("\n" + name.yellow.bold + ': ' + text);
    });
  });
});
```

How it works...

Let's pick apart the `trendingTopics` object. The `trends` and `tweets` objects provide settings relevant to the Twitter API. For `trends`, this is simply a URL options (`urlOpts`) object that is to be passed on to `https.get`. Within the `tweets` object, we have the URL object along with some other properties pertaining to options we can set within our REST call to the Twitter search API. Both the `urlOpts` objects hold a reference to our `headers` object, which contains the `User-Agent` and `Authorization` properties that are essential HTTP headers for a successful Twitter API request.

Before any actual action can take place, we place a check for `module.parent` and return from the module early if it's set, thus preventing any execution of code after that point. This, along with exporting our `trendingTopics` object, allows `twitter_trends.js` to operate in two capacities: primarily as a command-line app that supplies the currently trending tweets and also as a module that may be required as part of another script without any unwanted side effects (for instance, outputting tweets to the console when we simply want to access the `trendingTopics` functionality).

Working with Data Serialization

Our `jsonHandler` method on the `trendingTopics` object takes `response` and `cb` (callback) as parameters. The `trendingTopics.jsonHandler` uses the `response` object from the `http.get` call to capture the incoming data stream into a variable (`json`). When the stream ends, as detected by the `end` event listener on `response`, `cb` is invoked with an object, which is parsed from the received JSON as its argument. The callback from `trendingTopics.jsonHandler` finds its way up into the `makeCall` callback.

The `makeCall` function abstractly combines the GET request and JSON handling, and provides a callback with a single parameter, which is the data returned by Twitter as parsed JSON (in this case, it is an array of objects).

In the outer `makeCall` invocation, we call the parameter `trendsArr`, because Twitter returns its JSON data in an array wrapper. We use `trendsArr` to locate the query fragment representation of Twitter's top trend and pass it to the final method of our `trendingTopics` object: `trendingTopics.tweetPath`. This method takes a query fragment (`q`) as its single parameter. It then uses this parameter along with the options in `trendingTopics.tweets` to build the final Search API path. It injects this path into the `urlOpts` object of `trendingTopics.tweets`, which is then passed through to the inner `makeCall` invocation.

In the inner `makeCall` invocation, we name the parameter `tweetsArr`. This is an array of objects containing the tweet data as returned from the Twitter Search API in response to a query searching for the top trend discovered via the former (outer) call to the Trend API. We loop through the array using the veritable `forEach` (ES5) looping function, handling each element passed through the loop as a tweet.

The objects contained in the `tweetsArr` array contain a lot of data, such as the time information and amount of retweets. However, we're just interested in the content of the tweet, and who it is tweeted by. So, we log the `user.screen_name` and `text` properties of each tweet to the console, as shown in the following screenshot:

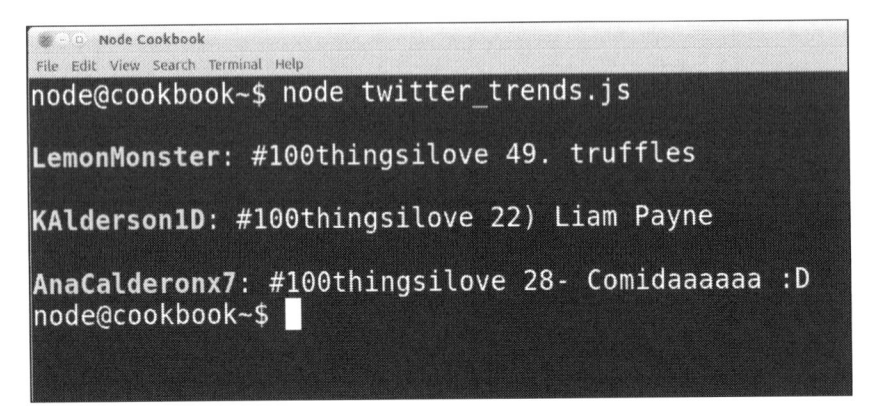

```
node@cookbook~$ node twitter_trends.js

LemonMonster: #100thingsilove 49. truffles

KAlderson1D: #100thingsilove 22) Liam Payne

AnaCalderonx7: #100thingsilove 28- Comidaaaaaa :D
node@cookbook~$
```

This is also where the `colors` module comes in handy, since within `console.log`, we have `name.yellow.bold`. The colors are not properties on the object returned by Twitter, but rather some trickery performed by the `colors` module to provide an easy interface for styling console text.

There's more...

Let's look at working with an XML-based service.

Cross referencing Google Hot Trends with Twitter tweets

Notice that trending tweets tend to have rather fad-like influences generated from within the Twitter community. Google Hot Trends is another source of trending information. It provides hourly updates of the highest trending searches.

We can extend our example to access and process the Google Hot Trends XML atom feed, and then integrate the top result into our Twitter Search API request. To do this, let's create a new file named `google_trends.twitter.js`. It's nice to work with XML data as a JavaScript object, so we'll require the `non-core` `xml2js` file that is featured in the *Converting an object to XML and back* recipe in this chapter, along with `https`, `colors`, and our own `trendingTopics` module from the main recipe. The code is as follows:

```
var https = require('https');
var xml2js = require('xml2js');
var colors = require('colors'); //for prettifying output
var trendingTopics = require('./twitter_trends');
```

Now, we'll extend our `trendingTopics` object by inheriting from it using the EcmaScript 5 `Object.create` method:

```
var hotTrends = Object.create(trendingTopics, {
  trends: {value: {urlOpts: {
    host: 'www.google.com',
    path: '/trends/hottrends/atom/hourly',
    headers: {'User-Agent': 'Node Cookbook: Twitter Trends'}
    }
}}});

hotTrends.xmlHandler = function (response, cb) {
  var hotTrendsfeed = '';
  response.on('data', function (chunk) {
    hotTrendsfeed += chunk;
  }).on('end', function () {
    xml2js.parseString(hotTrendsfeed, function (err, obj) {
      if (err) { throw (err.message); }
      xml2js.parseString(obj.feed.entry[0].content[0]._,
```

Working with Data Serialization

```
          function (err, obj) {
            if (err) { throw (err.message); }
            if (err) { throw (err.message); }
            var query = obj.ol.li[0].span[0].a[0]._;
            cb(encodeURIComponent(query));
          });
        });
      });
    };
```

We declared a variable named `hotTrends`, and used `Object.create` to initialize an instance of `trendingTopics`, resubstantiating the `trends` property via the property declarations object (the second parameter of `Object.create`). This means that instead of `trends` being an inherited property, it now belongs to `hotTrends`, and we haven't overwritten the `trends` property in `trendingTopics` while adding it to our new `hotTrends` object.

We then add a new method: `hotTrends.xmlHandler`. This combines all the incoming chunks into the `hotTrendsfeed` variable. Once the stream has ended, it invokes `xml2js.parseString` and passes the XML contained in `hotTrendsfeed` to it. In the callback of the first `parseString` method, we invoke `xml2js.parseString` again. Why? Because we have to parse two sets of XML, or rather one set of XML and one set of adequately formed HTML. (If we head to http://www.google.com/trends/hottrends/atom/hourly, it will be rendered as HTML. If we view the source, we'll then see an XML document with embedded HTML content.)

The Google Hot Trends XML feed delivers the Hot Trends as HTML inside its content XML node.

The HTML is wrapped within a CDATA section, so it isn't parsed by `xml2js` the first time around. Ergo, we create a new Parser and then parse the HTML via the `obj.feed.entry[0].content[0]._` reference.

Finally, the `hotTrends.xmlHandler` method completes execution in the second embedded `xml2js` callback, where it executes its own callback parameter (`cb`) with a query fragment generated from the top list item element in HTML.

Now, all we have to do is make the following adjustments to `makeCall`:

```
    function makeCall(urlOpts, handler, cb) {
      http.get(urlOpts, function (response) { //make twitter api call
        handler(response, cb);
      }).on('error', function (e) {
        console.log("Connection Error: " + e.message);
      });
    }

    makeCall(hotTopics.trends.urlOpts, hotTopics.xmlHandler,
      function (query) {
```

```
        hotTopics.tweetPath(query);
        makeCall(hotTopics.tweets.urlOpts, hotTopics.jsonHandler,
          function (tweetsObj) {
            tweetsObj.statuses.forEach(function (tweet) {
              var name = tweet.user.screen_name, text = tweet.text;
              console.log("\n" + name.yellow.bold + ': ' + text);
            });
          });
      });
```

As we are now dealing with both JSON and XML, we slipped in another parameter to our `makeCall` function declaration: `handler`. The `handler` parameter allows us to specify whether to use the inherited `jsonHander` method or our supplemented `xmlHandler` method.

When we invoke the outer `makeCall`, we pass in `hotTrends.xmlHandler`, naming the parameter `query`. This is done because we directly pass in the `query` fragment generated by `xmlHandler`, instead of the array returned from Twitter. This is passed directly into the `tweetPath` method, which consequently updates the `path` property of the `hotTrends.tweets.urlOpts` object.

We pass `hotTrends.tweets.urlOpts` into the second `makeCall`, this time setting the `handler` parameter to `hotTrends.jsonHandler`.

The second `makeCall` callback behaves exactly the same as in the main recipe. It outputs the tweets to the console. This time, however, it outputs the tweets based on Google Hot Trends.

See also

- The *Using Node as an HTTP client* recipe in *Chapter 2, Exploring the HTTP Object*
- The *Converting an object to JSON and back* recipe
- The *Converting an object to XML and back* recipe

4
Interfacing with Databases

In this chapter, we will cover:

- Writing to a CSV file
- Connecting and sending SQL to a MySQL server
- Storing and retrieving data with MongoDB
- Storing data to CouchDB with Cradle
- Retrieving data from CouchDB with Cradle
- Accessing the CouchDB changes stream with Cradle
- Storing and retrieving data with Redis
- Implementing PubSub with Redis

Introduction

As the complexity of our code and the demands of our objectives increase, we soon realize the need for a place to store our data.

We then have to ask the question: what is the best way to store our data? The answer depends on the type of data we are working with, as different challenges require different solutions.

If we're doing something very simple, we can save our data as a flat CSV file, which has the added benefit of enabling users to view the CSV file in a spreadsheet application.

If we are working with data that has clearly relational qualities, for instance, accounting data, whereby there are clear, distinct relationships between the two sides of a transaction, then we can choose a relational database, such as the popular MySQL.

Interfacing with Databases

In many cases, relational databases became a de facto standard for nearly all data scenarios. This led to the necessity of imposing relationships on otherwise loosely-related data (such as website content) in an attempt to squeeze it into our relational mental model.

In recent times, though, there has been a movement away from relational databases towards NoSQL, a non-relational paradigm; the driving force being the fact that we tailor our technology to best suit our data, rather than trying to fit our data according to our technology.

In this chapter, we will look at various data storage technologies with examples of their usage in Node.

Writing to a CSV file

A flat file structure is one of the most elementary database models. The columns can either be of a fixed length or used with delimiters. The **Comma Separated Values** (**CSV**) convention conforms to the idea of delimited flat file structure databases. While it's called CSV, the term CSV is also applied as a broad blanket term to any basic delimited structure that consists of one record per line (for example, tab-separated values).

We can follow a brittle approach to construct CSV structures simply by using a multidimensional array and the `join` method, as follows:

```
var data = [['a','b','c','d','e','f','g'],
    ['h','i','j','k','l','m','n']];
var csv = data.join("\r\n");   /* renders:
a,b,c,d,e,f,g,h,i,j,k,l,m,n    */
```

However, the limitations of this technique quickly become apparent. What if one of our fields contains a comma? Now one field becomes two, thus corrupting our data. Furthermore, we are limited to just using commas as delimiters.

In this recipe, we will use the third-party `ya-csv` module to store data in the CSV format.

Getting ready

Let's create a file named `write_to_csv.js`; we'll also need to retrieve the `csv` module.

`npm install csv`

How to do it...

We require the `csv` module, create our `data` array and simply use the language chaining API provided by the `csv` module to generate CSV content from the array. We then save the `data` array to the `./data.csv` path.

```
var csv = require('csv')(),
```

```
data = [
  ['a','b','c,"','d','e','f','g'],
  ['h','i','j','k','l','m','n']
];

csv.from.array(data).to.path('./data.csv');
```

Let's take a look at the file we saved to `data.csv`:

```
a,b,"c,""",d,e,f,g

h,i,j,k,l,m,n
```

Notice that we include a cheeky comma and quote mark in the third item of our first array. The `csv` module handles this seamlessly by wrapping this item in quote marks, and escaping the internal quote with another quote mark. When opened in the likes of LibreOffice Calc or MS Excel, this parses perfectly.

How it works...

The difficulty with writing to and reading from CSV files is the edge cases, such as commas or quotes embedded in text. The `csv` module handles these edge cases for us.

The `csv` module makes writing to CSV files especially easy with its language chaining syntax. For instance, when we use the `to.path` chain combo, the `csv` module creates `writeStream` under the hood. When using the `from.array` method, it processes the array accordingly and streams it onto the internal `writeStream`, which points to our path.

Working with CSV files necessarily depends on using a basic data structure in our code. Multidimensional objects will have to be massaged into an array or string format before being processed by the `csv` module, since CSV, as a structure, has no concept of properties or multilevel structures.

There's more...

Could we easily create this functionality ourselves? Without a doubt. However, `csv` provides an aesthetically pleasing and simple API for us to seamlessly customize the elements of our CSV files and implements the more involved CSV parsing functionality.

Customizing the CSV elements

If we save our recipe file as `write_to_custom_csv.js` and pass an `options` object to `csv.to.options`, we can alter the way our CSV files are constructed as follows:

```
var csv = require('csv')(),
    data = [
```

Interfacing with Databases

```
      ['a','b','c','d','e','f','g'],
      ['h','i','j','k','l','m','n']
   ];

csv.to.options({
  delimiter: '~',
  quote: '|',
  quoted: true
});
csv.from.array(data).to.path('./custom_data.csv');
```

After running our new code, let's take a look at `custom_data.csv`:

```
|a|~|b|~|c|~|d|~|e|~|f|~|g|

|h|~|i|~|j|~|k|~|l|~|m|~|n|
```

Setting `quoted` to `true` enforces quote wrapping around all our values, regardless of whether the values contain a delimiter.

Reading a CSV file

We can also use the `csv` module to read from a CSV file; its built-in parser converts each CSV record back to an array. Let's make `read_from_csv.js`:

```
var csv = require('csv')();

csv.from.path('./data.csv').to.array(function(data){
    console.log(data);
});
```

If we want it to parse alternative delimiters and quotes, we simply pass these through the `options` method of the `from` property:

```
csv.from.options({
  delimiter: '~',
  quote: '|',
  quoted: true
});
```

Manipulating the CSV data stream

The `csv` module interacts with the CSV files as streams. This can reduce operational memory, as streams allow us to process small chunks of information when they are loaded, instead of buffering the entire file into memory first. We can manipulate these streams all the way through using the following `transform` method:

```
var csv = require('csv')();
process.stdin.resume();
```

```
csv.to.options({quoted: true});

csv.from.stream(process.stdin).transform(function (row) {
  return row.map(Function.call, ''.toUpperCase)
}).to.stream(process.stdout);
```

The `transform` function receives each row of CSV as an array. We call `map` on the array to return a new array of uppercase values; this happens as the input stream is being processed.

> On a side note, the arguments passed to `row.map` exploit the fact that the second parameter of `map` sets the context (the `this` object) of the mapping function, which in this case is `Function.call`. So, for each value, we're essentially executing the equivalent of `Function.call.call(String.prototype.toUpperCase, value, ix)`, where `value` is each item of an array as passed in by `map`, and `ix` is the index. There are two calls because we're calling the `call` method. So, this translates to `value.toUpperCase(ix)`. The `ix` value is disregarded since `toUpperCase` doesn't take a parameter, and so we're left with the same result as `value.toUpperCase()`.

We'll call `streaming_csv.js`, so now we can do something like the following:

cat data.csv | node streaming_csv.js

If we're using Windows, we can use the following:

type data.csv | node streaming_csv.js

The `data.csv` file will be piped as a stream into `streaming_csv.js`, which will read it from `process.stdin`, run the `transform` function, and pipe the stream to `process.stdout`. We could pass any other stream in place of `process.stdin` and `process.stdout`, such as a file stream, or the `response` parameter in `createHttpServer`.

See also

- The *Connecting and sending SQL to a MySQL server* recipe
- The *Storing data to CouchDB with Cradle* recipe
- The *Storing and retrieving data with Redis* recipe
- *Chapter 5, Employing Streams*

Interfacing with Databases

Connecting and sending SQL to a MySQL server

Structured Query Language has been a standard since 1986, and it's the prevailing language for relational databases. MySQL is the most popular SQL relational database server around, often appearing in the prevalent **Linux Apache MySQL PHP** (**LAMP**) stack.

If a relational database was conceptually relevant to our goals in a new project, or we were migrating a MySQL-backed project from another framework to Node, the third-party `mysql` module would be particularly useful.

In this task, we will discover how to connect to a MySQL server with Node and execute SQL queries across the wire.

Getting ready

Let's grab `mysql`, which is a pure JavaScript (as opposed to C++ bound) MySQL client module:

```
npm install mysql@2.x
```

We'll need a MySQLserverto connect to. By default, the mysql client module connects to `localhost`, so we'll have MySQL running locally

> Including `@2.x` after `mysql` ensures that we install the most up-to-date minor version of the second major version of the `mysql` module; `mysql@2.x` has a different API than Version 1 (which is covered in the first edition of this book.

On Linux and Mac OS X, we can see if MySQL is already installed with the following command:

```
whereis mysql
```

We can see if it is running using the following command:

```
mysqladmin ping
```

If it is installed but not running, we can use the following command:

```
sudo service mysql start
```

If MySQL isn't installed, we can use the relevant package manager for our system (homebrew, apt-get/synaptic, yum, and so on), or if we're using Node on Windows, we can head to `http://dev.mysql.com/downloads/mysql` and download the installer.

Once we're ready to go, let's create a file and name it `mysql.js`.

How to do it...

First, we require the third-party `mysql` driver. We then create a connection to the server using the following code:

```
var mysql = require('mysql');
var connection = mysql.createConnection({
  user: 'root',
  password: 'OURPASSWORD' ,
//debug: true
});
```

We need a database to connect to. Let's keep things interesting and make a `quotes` database. We can do that by passing SQL to the `query` method as follows:

```
connection.query('CREATE DATABASE quotes');
connection.changeUser({database: 'quotes'});
```

We've also called the `changeUser` method to connect to the database, although we could achieve the same with `connection.query('USE quotes')`.

> The `changeUser` method can also be used to connect as a different user; simply change the user password and current charset.

Now, we'll create a table with the same name:

```
connection.query('CREATE TABLE quotes.quotes (' +
         'id INT NOT NULL AUTO_INCREMENT, ' +
         'author VARCHAR( 128 ) NOT NULL, ' +
         'quote TEXT NOT NULL, PRIMARY KEY ( id )' +
         ')');
```

If we were to run our code more than once, we'd notice that an unhandled error is thrown and the program fails. This is due to the `mysql` driver emitting an error event in reflection of a MySQL server error. It's throwing an unhandled error because the `quotes` database (and table) cannot be created as they already exist.

We want our code to be versatile enough to create a database if necessary, but not throw an error if it's not there. To do this, we're going to catch any errors emitted by our `client` instance, filtering out the database/table errors that exist:

```
var ignore = [mysql.ERROR_DB_CREATE_EXISTS,
              mysql.ERROR_TABLE_EXISTS_ERROR];

connection.on('error', function (err) {
  if (ignore.indexOf(err.number) > -1) { return; }
  throw err;
});
```

Interfacing with Databases

We'll place our error catcher just before the `connection.query` method invocation. Finally, at the end of our code, we'll insert our first quote into the table and send a COM_QUIT packet (using `connection.end`) to the MySQL server. This will only close the connection once all the queued SQL code has been executed.

```
connection.query('INSERT INTO  quotes.quotes (' +
  'author, quote) ' +
  'VALUES ("Bjarne Stroustrup", "Proof by analogy is fraud.");');

connection.end();
```

We can verify its success by running the following on the command line:

`mysql -u root –password=OURPW -D quotes -e "select * from quotes;"`

If we run our script more than once, the quote will be added several times.

How it works...

The `createConnection` method establishes a connection to the server and returns a `connection` instance for us to interact with. We can pass in an `options` object that may contain an assortment of various properties. Other than `user` and `password`, the default options are fine for our purposes. If we uncomment `debug`, we can see the raw data being sent to and from the server.

> Check out the `mysql` module's GitHub page for a list of all the possible options at `https://github.com/felixge/node-mysql`.

The `connection.query` call sends SQL to our database, which is then executed by the MySQL server. With it, we create a database named `quotes` (using CREATE and DATABASE) and also a TABLE named `quotes`. We then insert our first record (using INSERT) into our database.

The `connection.query` invocation queues each piece of SQL passed to it, executing statements asynchronously alongside our other code, but sequentially within the SQL statement queue. When we call `connection.end`, the connection closing task is added to the end of the queue. If we want to disregard the statement queue and immediately end the connection, we can use `connection.destroy`.

Our `ignore` array holds two numbers, 1007 and 1050—we grab these numbers from the `mysql` object, which holds the MySQL error codes. We should ignore the MySQL errors that occur when a table or database already exists, otherwise, we can only run `mysql.js` once. It would crash after the first run, as the database and table would already exist. Ignoring these codes means that we can implicitly set up our database and have just one file rather than a setup app and a separate app to insert code.

In the `error` event listener, we check whether `err.number` is within our `ignore` array. If it is, we simply return early, thus ignoring the error and gracefully continuing with the execution. If the error is of some other nature, we fall through to the usual behavior of throwing the error.

There's more...

We don't just send data to MySQL, we retrieve it. Furthermore, SQL queries are often generated from user input, but this can be open to exploitation if precautions aren't taken.

Using and cleaning user input

As with the other languages that build SQL statements with string concatenation, we must prevent the possibilities of SQL injection attacks to keep our server safe. Essentially, we must clean (that is, escape) any user input to eradicate the potential for unwanted SQL manipulation.

We'll copy `mysql.js` and rename it as `insert_quotes.js`. To implement the concept of user input in a simple way, we'll pull the arguments from the command line, but the principles and methods of data cleaning extend to any input method (for example, via a query string on request).

Our basic API will look like this:

```
node insert_quotes.js "Author Name" "Quote Text Here"
```

Quotation marks are essential to divide the command-line arguments, but for the sake of brevity, we won't be implementing any validation checks.

> **Command-line parsing module – optimist**
>
> For more advanced command-line functionality, check out the excellent `optimist` module, available at `https://www.github.com/substack/node-optimist`.

To receive an author and quote, we'll load the two `quotes` arguments into a new `params` object:

```
var params = {author: process.argv[2], quote: process.argv[3]};
```

Our first argument is at index 2 in the `process.argv` array because 0 and 1 hold `node` and `quotes.js`.

Now, let's slightly modify our `INSERT` statement:

```
if (params.author && params.quote) {
  connection.query('INSERT INTO  quotes.quotes (' +
            'author, quote) ' +
            'VALUES (?, ?);', [ params.author, params.quote ]);
```

Interfacing with Databases

```
    }
    connection.end();
```

We've placed this just before our final `connection.end` call in the main recipe. The `mysql` module can seamlessly clean user input for us. We simply use the question mark (?) as a placeholder and then pass our values (in order) as an array to the second parameter of `connection.query`.

Receiving results from the MySQL server

Let's extend `insert_quotes.js` further by outputting all the quotes for an author, irrespective of whether a quote is provided. We'll save `insert_quotes.js` simply as `quotes.js`.

Underneath our `INSERT` query, but on top of the final `client.end` call, we'll add the following code:

```
    if (params.author) {
      connection.query('SELECT * FROM quotes WHERE ' +
        'author LIKE ' + connection.escape(params.author))
        .on('result', function (rec) {
          console.log('%s: %s \n', rec.author, rec.quote);
        });
    }
    connection.end();
```

On this occasion, we've used an alternative approach to clean user input with `connection.escape`. This has exactly the same effect as the former, but only escapes a single input. Generally, if there's more than one variable, the former method would be preferred.

The results of a `SELECT` statement can be accessed either by passing a callback function or by listening for the `row` event. A `row` event listener allows us to interact with a MySQL server data stream one row at a time.

We can safely call `connection.end` without placing it in the `end` event of our `SELECT` query because `connection.end` only terminates a connection when all the queries are done.

See also

- The *Storing and retrieving data with MongoDB* recipe
- The *Storing and retrieving data with Redis* recipe

Storing and retrieving data with MongoDB

MongoDB is a NoSQL database offering that maintains a philosophy of performance over features. It's designed for speed and scalability. Instead of working relationally, it implements a document-based model that has no need for schemas (column definitions). The document model works well for scenarios where the relationships between data are flexible and where minimal potential data loss is an acceptable cost for speed enhancements (a blog, for instance).

While it is in the NoSQL family, MongoDB attempts to sit between two worlds, providing a syntax reminiscent of SQL but operating nonrelationally.

In this task, we'll implement the same `quotes` database as in the previous recipe, using MongoDB instead of MySQL.

Getting ready

We want to run a MongoDB server locally. It can be downloaded from http://www.mongodb.org/downloads.

Let's start the MongoDB service, `mongod`, in the default `debug` mode:

```
mongod --dbpath [a folder for the database]
```

This allows us to observe the activities of `mongod` as it interacts with our code. If we want to start it as a persistent background service, we can use the following line:

```
mongod --fork --logpath [p] --logappend -dbpath [p]
```

Here, `[p]` is our desired path.

> More information on starting and correctly stopping `mongodb` can be found at http://www.mongodb.org/display/DOCS/Starting+and+Stopping+Mongo.

To interact with MongoDB from Node, we'll need to install the `mongodb` native binding's driver module:

```
npm install mongodb
```

We'll also create a new folder for our MongoDB-based project, with a new `quotes.js` file.

How to do it...

We require the `mongodb` driver, and grab the `MongoClient` instance, which we'll use to connect to our MongoDB server:

Interfacing with Databases

```
var client = require('mongodb').MongoClient,
    params = {author: process.argv[2], quote: process.argv[3]};
```

Notice that we've also inserted our `params` object to read user input from the command line.

Now, we connect to our `quotes` database and load (or create, if necessary) our `quotes` collection (a table would be the closest similar concept in SQL):

```
client.connect('mongodb://localhost:27017/quotes', function (err, db)
{
  if (err) { throw err; }
  var collection = db.collection('quotes');
  db.close();
});
```

The closest similar concept to a collection in a relational database paradigm (such as SQL) would be a table

> The port number (`27017`) is the default port assigned to `mongod` instances. This can be modified when we start a `mongod` service by passing a `--port` flag.

Next, we'll insert a new document (in SQL terms, this would be a **record**) according to the user-defined author and quote. We'll also output any quotes by the specified author to the console as follows:

```
client.connect('mongodb://localhost:27017/quotes', function (err, db)
{
  if (err) { throw err; }

  var collection = db.collection('quotes');

  if (params.author && params.quote) {
    collection.insert({
    author: params.author,
      quote: params.quote}, function (err) {
      if (err) { throw err; }
  });
  }

  if (params.author) {

    collection.find({
    author: params.author
  }).each(function (err, doc) {
      if (err) { throw err; }
```

```
        if (doc) {
    console.log('%s: %s \n', doc.author, doc.quote);
          return;
        }
        db.close();
      });

      return;
    }


    db.close();

  });
```

We can see our MongoDB-backed quotes application in action in the following screenshot:

```
node@cookbook:~$ node quotes.js "Albert Einstein" "Imagination
is more important than knowledge"
Albert Einstein: Imagination is more important than knowledge

node@cookbook:~$ node quotes.js "Ronald Reagan" "You can tell a
lot about a fellow's characters by his way of eating jellybeans
"
Ronald Reagan: You can tell alot about a fellow's characters by
 his way of eating jellybeans

node@cookbook:~$ node quotes.js "Albert Einstein" "It's not tha
t I'm so smart, it's just that I stay with problems longer"
Albert Einstein: Imagination is more important than knowledge

Albert Einstein: It's not that I'm so smart, it's just that I s
tay with problems longer

node@cookbook:~$
```

How it works...

When we call `client.connect`, we pass in a URI with the `mongodb://` protocol as the first parameter. The `mongodb` module will parse this string and attempt to connect to the specified database. MongoDB will intelligently create this database if it doesn't exist, so unlike MySQL, we don't have to plaster over awkward errors.

Once the connection is made, our callback function is executed where we can interact with the database via the `db` parameter.

Interfacing with Databases

We start off by grabbing our `quotes` collection using `db.collection`. A collection is similar to a SQL table which holds all our database fields. However, rather than the field values being grouped by columns, a collection contains multiple documents (such as records) where each field holds both the field name and its value (the documents are very much like JavaScript objects).

If both `quote` and `author` are defined, we invoke the `insert` method of our collection, passing in an object as our document.

Finally, we use `find`, which is comparable to the `SELECT` SQL command, passing in an object that specifies the author field and its desired value. The `mongodb` driver provides a convenience method (`each`) that can be chained to the `find` method. The `each` method executes the callback passed to it for each document as and when it's found. The last loop of `each` passes in doc as `null`, which conveniently signals that MongoDB has returned all the records.

So, as long as `doc` is truthy, we pass the `author` and `quote` properties of every `doc` found. Once `doc` is `null`, we allow the interpreter to discover the last part of the callback, `db.close`, by not returning early from it.

The second and final `db.close` call situated at the end of the `client.connect` callback is invoked only when there are no arguments defined via the command line.

There's more...

Let's check out some other useful MongoDB features.

Indexing and aggregation

Indexing causes MongoDB to create a list of values from a chosen field. Indexed fields accelerate query speeds because a smaller set of data can be used to cross-reference and pull from a larger set. We can apply an index to the author field and see performance benefits, especially as our data grows. Additionally, MongoDB has various commands that allow us to aggregate our data. We can group, count, and return distinct values.

> For more advanced needs or larger sets of data, the `map/reduce` functions can aggregate. CouchDB also uses `map/reduce` to generate views (stored queries); see the *Retrieving data from CouchDB with Cradle* recipe.

Let's create and output a list of authors found in our database and save our code to a file named `authors.js`:

```
var client = require('mongodb').MongoClient;

client.connect('mongodb://localhost:27018/quotes', function (err, db)
{
```

```
    if (err) { throw err; }

    var collection = db.collection('quotes');

    collection.ensureIndex('author', {safe: true}, function (err) {
      if (err) { throw err; }
      collection.distinct('author', function (err, result) {
          if (err) { throw err; }
          console.log(result.join('\n'));
          db.close();
      });
    });

});
```

As usual, we opened up a connection to our `quotes` database, grabbing our `quotes` collection. Using `ensureIndex` creates an index only if one doesn't already exist. We pass in `safe:true` so that MongoDB returns any errors and our callback works as expected. Inside the callback, we invoke the `distinct` method on our collection, passing in `author`. The `result` parameter in our callback function is an array which we join (using `join`) to a string using new lines and output to the console.

Updating modifiers, sort, and limit

We can make it possible for a hypothetical user to indicate if they were inspired by a quote (such as a Like button) and then use the `sort` and `limit` commands to output the top ten most inspiring quotes.

In reality, this would be implemented with some kind of user interface (for example, in a browser), but we'll again emulate user interactions using the command line; let's create a new file named `quotes_votes.js`.

First, in order to vote for a quote, we'll need to reference it. This can be done using the unique `_id` property. So, in `quotes_votes.js`, let's write the following code:

```
var mongodb = require('mongodb'),
  client = mongodb.MongoClient,
  params = {id: process.argv[2]};

client.connect('mongodb://localhost:27018/quotes', function (err, db)
{
  if (err) { throw err; }
  var collection = db.collection('quotes');

//vote handling to go here

    collection.find().each(function (err, doc) {
```

```
            if (err) { throw err; }
            if (doc) { console.log(doc._id, doc.quote); return; }
            db.close();
        });

    });
```

Now, when we run `quotes_votes.js` with `node`, we'll see a list of IDs and quotes. To vote for a quote, we'll simply copy an ID and use it as our command-line parameter. So, let's do our vote handling as shown in the following code:

```
    if (params.id) {
        collection.update({_id : mongodb.ObjectID(params.id)},
            {$inc: {votes: 1}}, {safe: true},
            function (err) {
                if (err) { throw err; }
                console.log('1 vote added to %s by %s', params.id);
                collection.find().sort({votes: -
                    1}).limit(10).each(function (err, doc) {
                    if (err) { throw err; }
                    if (doc) {
                        var votes = (doc.votes) || 0;
                        console.log(doc.author, doc.quote, votes);
                        return;
                    }
                    db.close();
                });
            });

        return;
    }
```

MongoDB IDs must be encoded as a **Binary JSON (BSON)** `ObjectID`. Otherwise, the `update` command will look for `params.id` as a string, failing to find it. So, we convert `params.id` into an `ObjectID` using `mongodb.ObjectID(params.id)`.

The `$inc` property is a MongoDB modifier that performs the incrementing action inside the MongoDB server, essentially allowing us to outsource the calculation. To use it, we pass a document (object) alongside it containing the key to increment and the amount to increase it by. So, we pass `votes` and `1`.

The `$inc` modifier will create the `votes` field if it doesn't exist and increment it by one (we can also decrement using minus figures). Next, we specify the options to be passed to MongoDB. We've set `safe` to `true`, which tells MongoDB to check whether the command was successful and send any errors if it wasn't. For the callback to work correctly, `safe:true` must be passed; otherwise, the errors are not caught and the callback occurs immediately.

> **Upserting**
>
> Another useful option we can set is `upsert:true`. This is a really convenient MongoDB feature that either updates a record or inserts it if it doesn't exist.

Inside the `update` callback, we run a chain of `find.sort.limit.each` methods. A call to `find`, without any parameters, returns every document in a collection. The `sort` callback requires an object whose properties match the keys in our collection. The value of each property can either be `-1` or `+1`, which indicates the ascending and descending order, respectively. The `limit` callback takes integer representing the maximum amount of records, and `each` loops through all our records. Inside the `each` callback, we output every `author`, `quote`, and `votes` of `doc`, closing the connection when no `docs` are left.

MongoDB without MongoDB

If our requirements are simple and we're working on an app that won't be met with high demand, or we're prototyping an app and we don't want to depend on a separate MongoDB process, then we can try the third-party **Node Embedded Database** module (**NeDB**).

The `nedb` module provides a subset of the MongoDB API but it doesn't use MongoDB at all. Instead, all of the data management occurs within Node itself, and this data can simply be saved to a file.

Let's reimplement our main recipe with NeDB; first, we'll need to install it:

```
npm install nedb
```

Next, we'll save `quotes.js` as `quotes_nedb.js` and begin to adapt our code base. We'll then alter our variable declarations at the top of our code:

```
var NeDB = require('nedb'),
  collection = new NeDB('./quotes.db'),
  params = {author: process.argv[2], quote: process.argv[3]};
```

We use `require` to grab `nedb` in our NeDB variable, create a new instance of it, and pass in a path, `./quotes.db`, for our data to be stored. Our NeDB instance is loaded into the `collection` variable because an NeDB variable provides a subset of the API afforded by MongoDB collections.

Now let's load the database and supply the logic to insert and list quotes:

```
collection.loadDatabase(function (err) {
  if (err) { throw err; }

  if (params.author && params.quote) {
    collection.insert({author: params.author, quote:
      params.quote},
```

Interfacing with Databases

```
          function (err) { if (err) { throw err; } }) ;
  }
  if (params.author) {
    collection.find({author: params.author}, function (err, docs) {
      if (err) { throw err; }
      docs.forEach(function(doc) {
        if (doc) { console.log('%s: %s \n', doc.author,
          doc.quote);}
      })
    });
  }

});
```

And that's it! Notice that we didn't need to explicitly close a database as in the main recipe. Since our database logic is completely inside the Node process, our database "connection" will exit with the process.

We have to manually loop through the provided `docs` array in our `collection.find` callback, instead of using the chained `.each` method as in our main recipe. The `mongodb` module provides the `.each` method as a convenience; it's not strictly part of the MongoDB API—nedb doesn't have the same level of convenience.

The fact that NeDB is a subset may mean we have to jump through certain hoops that we wouldn't need when using MongoDB, but this is the trade off for using a familiar API without any dependence on an external process.

> **Migrating from NeDB to MongoDB**
>
> In cases where we need to scale and start using MongoDB instead of NeDB, a tool is available to take an NeDB-generated file and populate a MongoDB database. See `https://github.com/louischatriot/nedb-to-mongodb` for more details.

See also

- The *Connecting and sending SQL to a MySQL server* recipe
- The *Storing data to CouchDB with Cradle* recipe

Storing data to CouchDB with Cradle

In order to achieve stellar performance speeds, MongoDB has a relaxed view towards **Atomicity Consistency Isolation Durability (ACID)** compliance. However, this means there is a (slight) chance that data can become corrupt (especially if there was a power cut in the middle of an operation). CouchDB, on the other hand, is ACID compliant to the extent that when replicated and synchronized, data eventually becomes consistent. Therefore, while slower than MongoDB, it has the added reliability advantage.

CouchDB is entirely administrated via HTTP REST calls, so we could do all of our work with CouchDB using `http.request`. Nevertheless, we can use Cradle to interact with CouchDB in an easy, high-level way, along with the added speed enhancement of automated caching.

In this recipe, we'll use Cradle to store the famous quotes to CouchDB.

Getting ready

We'll need to install and run CouchDB. For this, head on over to `http://wiki.apache.org/couchdb/Installation` for instructions on how to install it for your particular operating system.

After installation, we can check if CouchDB is running by accessing the Futon administration, pointing our browser to `http://localhost:5984/_utils`.

To interact with CouchDB from Node, we'll need the `cradle` module.

npm install cradle

And we will create a new folder with a new `quotes.js` file in it.

How to do it...

First, we require `cradle` and load our `quotes` database, creating it if necessary. We'll also define an error-handling function and our `params` object for easy command-line interaction:

```
var cradle = require('cradle');
var db = new(cradle.Connection)().database('quotes');
var params = {author: process.argv[2], quote: process.argv[3]};
function errorHandler(err) {
   if (err) { console.log(err); process.exit(); }
//checkAndSave function here
```

Before we can write to our database, we need to know whether it exists:

```
db.exists(function (err, exists) {
  errorHandler(err);
```

Interfacing with Databases

```
    if (!exists) { db.create(checkAndSave); return; }
    checkAndSave();
  });
```

Notice that we pass in `checkAndSave` as the callback of `db.create`. The following function is placed above the `db.exists` invocation:

```
function checkAndSave(err) {
  errorHandler(err);

  if (params.author && params.quote) {
     db.save({author: params.author, quote: params.quote},
  errorHandler);

  }

}
```

The `err` parameter that we handle in `checkAndSave` will have to be passed in from `db.create`.

How it works...

CouchDB is administrated via HTTP requests, but Cradle provides an interface to make these requests. When we invoke `db.exists`, Cradle sends a HEAD request to `http://localhost:5984/quotes` and checks whether the reply status is `404 Not Found` or `200 OK`. On Unix-like systems (Mac OS X and Linux), we can perform the same check with the `curl` and `grep` shell commands as follows:

curl -Is http://localhost:5984/quotes | grep -c "200 OK"

This would output `1` if the database exists and `0` if it does not. If our database doesn't exist, we call the `db.create` method of Cradle, which sends an HTTP PUT request to the CouchDB server. Using `curl`, this would be as follows:

curl -X PUT http://localhost:5984/quote

We pass in our `checkAndSave` function as the callback of `db.create`, or we call it from the callback of `db.exists` if the database exists. This is essential. We cannot save data to a database that doesn't exist, and we have to wait for the HTTP response before we know whether it exists (or whether it has been created). The `checkAndSave` function looks for command-line arguments, and then saves the data accordingly.

For instance, let's run the following command line:

node quotes.js "Albert Einstein" "Never lose a holy curiosity."

The `checkAndSave` function will realize that there are two parameters, passing these as `author` and `quote` to `db.save`. Cradle would then post the following, with `Content-Type` set to `application/json`:

```
{"author": "Albert Einstein",  "quote": "Never lose a holy curiosity"}
```

On top of this, Cradle adds a caching layer, which in our example is of little use since the caching data is lost whenever our application exits. However, in a server implementation, caching can prove to be very useful for answering similar requests quickly and efficiently.

There's more...

Couch stands for Cluster Of Unreliable Commodity Hardware. Let's take a brief look at the clustering side of CouchDB.

Scaling CouchDB with BigCouch

Scaling is about making your application responsive to an anticipated demand, but different projects have different characteristics. Therefore, each scaling venture requires an individualized approach.

If a web service was heavily built around database interaction, scaling the database layer would be a priority when responding to the changes in service demand. Scaling CouchDB (or anything else) can be a very in-depth procedure, necessarily so for specialized projects.

However, the open source BigCouch project has the ability to scale CouchDB in a transparent and generic fashion. With BigCouch, we can scale CouchDB across servers, but interact with it as if it was on one server. BigCouch can be found at `https://www.github.com/cloudant/bigcouch`.

See also

- The *Retrieving data from CouchDB with Cradle* recipe
- The *Storing and retrieving data with MongoDB* recipe
- The *Storing and retrieving data with Redis* recipe

Retrieving data from CouchDB with Cradle

CouchDB doesn't use the same query paradigm that MySQL and MongoDB subscribe to. Instead, it uses a precreated view to retrieve the desired data.

In this example, we'll use Cradle to obtain an array of quotes according to the specified author, outputting our quotes to the console.

Interfacing with Databases

Getting ready

As in the previous recipe, *Storing data to CouchDB with Cradle*, we'll need CouchDB installed on our system along with `cradle`. We can also take the `quotes.js` file from that recipe and place it in a new directory.

How to do it...

We're working on the `quotes.js` file from the previous recipe where we called `checkAndSave` if our database existed or we called it from the callback of `db.create` if it didn't exist. Let's modify `checkAndSave` slightly as shown in the following code:

```
function checkAndSave(err) {
  errorHandler(err);
  if (params.author && params.quote) {
    db.save({author: params.author, quote: params.quote},
outputQuotes);
    return;
  }

  outputQuotes();
}
```

We've added a new function invocation, `outputQuotes`, to the end of `checkAndSave` and also as the callback of `db.save`. The `outputQuotes` call is going to access a special CouchDB `_design` document called a **view**.

Before we look at `outputQuotes`, let's look at another new function we'll be creating; let's name it `createQuotesView`. It should be placed just under `errorHandler` but on top of the rest of the code, as follows:

```
function createQuotesView(err) {
  errorHandler(err);
  db.save('_design/quotes', {
    views: { byAuthor: { map: 'function (doc) { emit(doc.author, doc)
}'}}
  }, outputQuotes);
}
```

The `createQuotesView` function also calls the `outputQuotes` function from the `db.save` callback parameter. This `outputQuotes` function is now called from three places: the `db.save` callback of `checkAndSave`, the end of `checkAndSave`, and in the `db.save` callback of `createQuotesView`.

Let's take a look at `outputQuotes`:

```
function outputQuotes(err) {
```

```
      errorHandler(err);

    if (params.author) {
      db.view('quotes/byAuthor', {key: params.author},
      function (err, rowsArray) {
        if (err && err.error === "not_found") {
          createQuotesView();
          return;
        }
        errorHandler(err);

        rowsArray.forEach(function (doc) {
          console.log('%s: %s \n', doc.author, doc.quote); return;
        });
      });
    }
  }
```

The `outputQuotes` function is placed before `checkAndSave` but after `createQuotesView`.

How it works...

The key to querying a CouchDB database is views. There are two types of views: **permanent** and **temporary**. In `createQuotesView`, we define a permanent view using `db.save`, setting the document ID to `_design/quotes`. We then define a `views` field containing an object named `byAuthor`, which holds a key named `map` whose value is a string-formatted function.

Temporary views will be stored with an ID of `quotes/_temp_view`. However, these should only be used for testing. They're very expensive computationally and shouldn't be used for production.

The mapping function is string formatted because it's passed to CouchDB via an HTTP request. CouchDB map functions are not executed with Node; they run within the CouchDB server. A `map` function defines the query we wish to run on the database through the CouchDB server's `emit` function. The first argument of `emit` specifies which field to query (in our case, `doc.author`), and the second argument specifies what to output as a result of the query (we want the whole `doc` object). If we want to search for Albert Einstein, we will make a GET request to `http://localhost:5984/quotes/_design/quotes/_view/byAuthor?key="Albert Einstein"`.

Cradle provides a shorthand method for this request, `db.view`, which appears in our `outputQuotes` function. The `db.view` function allows us to simply pass in `quotes/byAuthor` with a second object containing the `key` parameter (that is, our query), essentially filling in the special underscore routes for us.

Interfacing with Databases

The `db.view` function parses the incoming JSON and provides it via the second parameter of its callback, which we named `rowsArray`. We loop through the array using `forEach` and finish off by outputting `author` and `quote` to the console, as in the previous recipes.

However, before we loop through the array, we need to check whether our view actually exists or not. Views only need to be generated once. After this, they are stored in the CouchDB database. Therefore, we don't want to create a view every time we run our application. So, when we call `db.view`, we look to check whether a `not_found` error occurs in the `db.view` callback. If our view isn't found, we call `createQuotesView`.

In broader terms, the process goes something like this:

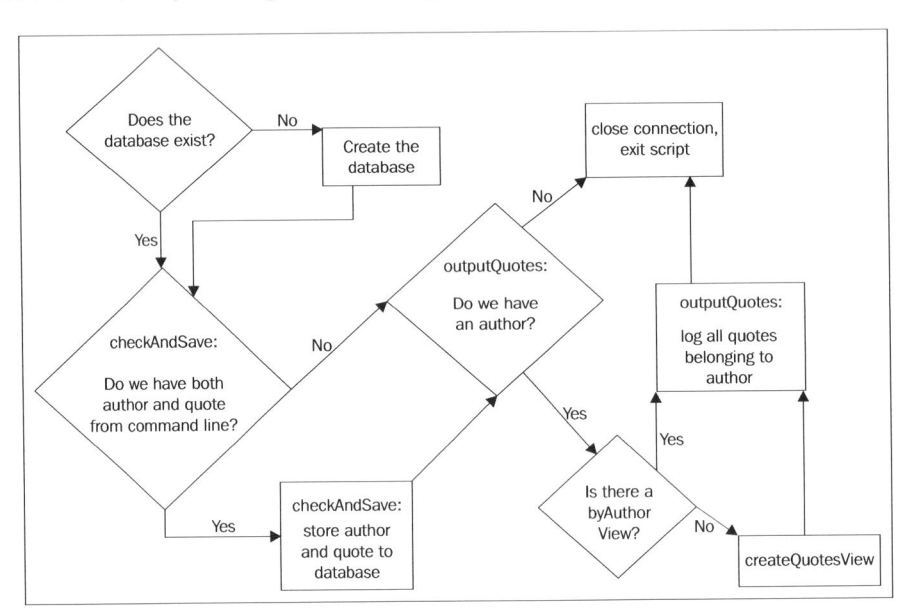

There's more...

CouchDB is easy to get to grips with right out of the box. However, there are certain security considerations we must be attuned to before deploying a CouchDB-backed app to the Web.

Creating an admin user

CouchDB requires no initial authorization settings, which is fine for development. However, as soon as we expose CouchDB to the outside world, anyone on the Internet has permission to edit our entire database: data designs, configuration, users, and so on.

So, before deployment, we want to set a username and password. We can achieve this with the `_config` API:

```
curl -X PUT http://localhost:5984/_config/admins/dave -d '"cookit"'
```

We have created the admin user `dave` and set the password to `cookit`. Now the right to certain calls will be denied without authentication, including the creation or deletion of databases, modification of design documents (for example, for views), or access to the `_config` API.

For instance, if we wanted to view all the admin users, we would use this command:

`curl http://localhost:5984/_config/admins`

CouchDB will reply with the following message:

`{"error":"unauthorized", "reason":"You are not a server admin."}`

Let's include the following authentication information:

`curl http://dave:cookit@localhost:5984/_config/admins`

We will get our only admin user along with a hash of his password:

`{"dave":"-hashed-42e68653895a4c0a5c67baa3cfb9035d01057b0d,44c62ca1bfd4872b773543872d78e950"}`

Using this method to remotely administer a CouchDB database is not without its security flaws. It forces us to send passwords as plaintext over nonsecure HTTP. Ideally, we need to host CouchDB behind an HTTPS proxy, so the password becomes encrypted as it's sent. See the recipe *Setting up an HTTPS server* discussed in *Chapter 8, Implementing Security, Encryption, and Authentication*.

If CouchDB is behind HTTPS, `cradle` can connect to it as follows:

```
var db = new (cradle.Connection)({secure:true,
                  auth: { username: 'dave',
                          password: 'cookit' }})
        .database('quotes');
```

We pass an `options` object when we create our connection. The `secure` property tells `cradle` that we are using SSL, and `auth` contains a subobject with login details.

Alternatively, we create a Node app to authenticate a local CouchDB instance (so that no password is sent to an external HTTP address) and act as a layer between external requests and CouchDB.

Locking all modifying operations to an admin user

Even if an admin user is set, unauthenticated users still have permission to modify existing databases. If we were only writing to the CouchDB server side (but reading from either server or client), we could lock all the write operations for nonadmin users with a validation function.

Interfacing with Databases

A validation function is written in JavaScript and runs on the CouchDB server (like the `map` function). Once a validation function is defined, it's executed against all the user input for the database it is applied to. Three objects appear as parameters in the function: the new document (`newDoc`), the stored document (`savedDoc`), and the user context (`userCtx`) that holds the authenticated user information.

Within a validation function, we can examine and qualify these objects, calling CouchDB's `throw` function to reject the operation requests that fail to meet our requirements.

Let's make a new file named `database_lockdown.js` and begin by connecting to our database:

```
var cradle = require('cradle');
var db = new (cradle.Connection)({auth:
                    { username: 'dave',
                      password: 'cookit' }})
                .database('quotes');
```

We pass in an `options` object to the new `cradle` connection. It contains the authentication information that will now be necessary to create a validation function if we have set a new admin user according to the previous subsection, *Creating an admin user*.

Let's create our validation function and save it as a `_design` document:

```
var admin_lock = function (newDoc, savedDoc, userCtx) {
  if (userCtx.roles.indexOf('_admin') === -1) {
    throw({unauthorized : 'Only for admin users'});
  }
}
  db.save('_design/_auth', {
    views: {},
    validate_doc_update: admin_lock.toString()
  });
```

Let's execute the following command:

node database_lockdown.js

All the write-related operations will now require authorization.

Like views, we store validation functions within a document that has a `_design/` prefixed ID. The other part of the ID can be anything but we named it `_auth`, which reflects conventional practice when a validation function serves this type of purpose. The field name, though, must be named `validate_doc_update`.

By default, Cradle assumes that any `_design` document passed to `db.save` is a view. In order to prevent Cradle from wrapping our `validate_update_doc` field into a view, we specify an empty object to the `views` property.

The `validate_update_doc` field must be passed a string-formatted function, so we define our function under the `admin_lock` variable and call `toString` on it as it's passed into `db.save`.

The `admin_lock` variable is never intended for execution by Node. It's an aesthetic approach to constructing our function before passing it to CouchDB.

When an operation occurs on the database, our `admin_lock` function (which becomes CouchDB's `validate_update_doc` function) asks CouchDB to check whether the user requesting the operation has the `_admin` user role. If not, it tells CouchDB to throw an unauthorized error, thus denying access.

Exposing the CouchDB HTTP interface to remote connections

By default, CouchDB binds to `127.0.0.1`. This ensures that only local connections can be made to the database ensuring safety prior to security enforcements. Once we have CouchDB set up behind HTTPS with at least one admin user set, we can bind CouchDB to `0.0.0.0`, which makes the REST interface accessible via any IP address. This means that remote users can access our CouchDB HTTP interface via our server's public IP address, or more likely via our server's domain name. We can set the bind address with `_config` as follows:

```
curl -X PUT https://u:p@localhost:5984/_config/httpd/bind_address -d '"0.0.0.0"'
```

Here, `u` and `p` are the admin username and password, respectively.

See also

- The *Storing data to CouchDB with Cradle* recipe
- The *Storing and retrieving data with MongoDB* recipe
- The *Setting up an HTTPS web server* recipe discussed in *Chapter 8*, *Implementing Security, Encryption, and Authentication*

Accessing the CouchDB changes stream with Cradle

One of CouchDB's most noteworthy features is the `_changes` API. With it, we can view all the alterations to a database via HTTP.

For instance, to see all the changes made to our `quotes` database, we can make a GET request to `http://localhost:5984/quotes/_changes`. Even better, if we want to hook up to a live stream, we need to add the query parameter `?feed=continuous`.

Cradle provides an attractive interface to the `_changes` API, which we'll explore in this recipe.

Interfacing with Databases

Getting ready

We'll need a functioning CouchDB database and a way to write to it. We can use the `quotes.js` example used in *Storing data to CouchDB with Cradle*, so let's copy that into a new directory and then create a file alongside it named `quotes_stream.js`.

If we followed the *Creating an admin user* and *Locking all modifying operations to an admin user* sections of the previous recipe's *There's more...* section, we will need to modify the second line of `quotes.js` in order to continue to insert quotes in our database:

```
var db = new (cradle.Connection)({ auth: { username: 'dave',
                                            password: 'cookit' }})
        .database('quotes');
```

Here, `dave` and `cookit` are the example username and password, respectively.

How to do it...

We require `cradle` and make a connection to our `quotes` database. Our stream is intended for use with a pre-existing database, so we won't be checking for database existence.

```
var cradle = require('cradle');
var db = new (cradle.Connection)().database('quotes');
```

Next, we call the `changes` method of `cradle` and listen to its `response` event, in turn listening to the passed in `response` emitter's `data` event:

```
db.changes().on('response', function (response) {

  response.on('data', function (change) {
    var changeIsObj = {}.toString.call(change) === '[object Object]';
    if (change.deleted !changeIsObj) { return; }
    db.get(change.id, function (err, doc) {
      if (!doc) {return;}
      if (doc.author && doc.quote) {
        console.log('%s: %s \n', doc.author, doc.quote);
      }
    });
  });

});
```

To test our changes stream implementation, we'll open two terminals. In one, we'll run the following command:

```
node quotes_stream.js
```

In the other terminal window, we can add some quotes using `quotes.js`:

```
node quotes.js "Yogi Berra" "I never said most of the things I said"
node quotes.js "Woody Allen" "I'd call him a sadistic hippophilic necrophile, but that would be beating a dead horse"
node quotes.js "Oliver Wendell Holmes" "Man's mind, once stretched by a new idea, never regains its original dimensions"
```

As each new quote is added to the left-hand terminal, it appears to the right.

The `quotes_stream.js` file was opened up before any new quotes were added and immediately displayed the `Albert Einstein` quote, which was added in the *Storing data to CouchDB with Cradle* recipe. After this, the new quotes appeared in the stream as they were added.

How it works...

The `changes` method can be passed a callback, which simply returns all the changes up to the present and then exits. If we do not pass a callback to `changes`, it adds the `?feed=continuous` parameter to the HTTP CouchDB REST call and returns `EventEmitter`. CouchDB then returns a streamed HTTP response to Cradle, which is sent through as the `response` parameter of the `response` event. The `response` parameter is also `EventEmitter`, and we listen for changes via the `data` event.

Interfacing with Databases

On each `data` event, the callback handles the `change` parameter. Two data events are fired for each change: one is a JSON string and the other is a JavaScript object containing the equivalent JSON data. We check whether the `change` parameter's type is an object (`changeIsObj`) before proceeding. The `change` object holds metadata for our database entries. It has a sequence number (`change.seq`), a revision number (`change.changes[0].rev`), sometimes a deleted property (`changes.deleted`), and always has an `id` property.

If the `deleted` property is found, we need to return early as `db.get` can't fetch a deleted record. Otherwise, we pass `change.id` into `db.get`, which provides access to a document ID. The `doc` is passed into the callback of `db.get`. We only want to output the changes regarding our quotes, so we check for the `author` and `quote` fields and log them to the console.

See also

- The *Storing data to CouchDB with Cradle* recipe
- The *Retrieving data from CouchDB with Cradle* recipe
- The *Implementing PubSub with Redis* recipe

Storing and retrieving data with Redis

Redis is a nontraditional database, dubbed a data structure server, which functions in operational memory with blazingly fast performance.

Redis is excellent for certain tasks, as long as the data model is fairly simple and isn't so large that it swamps your server RAM. Good examples of where Redis shines are in site analytics, server-side session cookies, and providing a list of logged-in users in real time.

In the spirit of our theme, we will reimplement our `quotes` database with Redis.

Getting ready

We'll be using the `redis` module:

`npm install redis`

We also need to install the Redis server, which can be downloaded from `http://www.redis.io/download` along with the installation instructions.

Let's also create a new directory with a new `quotes.js` file.

How to do it...

We'll create the `redis` module, establish a connection, and listen for the `ready` event emitted by the `client`, without forgetting to load the command-line arguments into the `params` object.

```
var redis = require('redis'),
  client = redis.createClient(),
  params = {author: process.argv[2], quote: process.argv[3]};
```

Next, we'll check for `author` and `quote` via the command line. If they're defined, we'll insert these as a hash (an object structure) into Redis:

```
if (params.author && params.quote) {
  var randKey = "Quotes:" + (Math.random() * Math.random())
                            .toString(16).replace('.', '');

  client.hmset(randKey, {"author": params.author,
                         "quote": params.quote});

  client.sadd('Author:' + params.author, randKey);
}
```

Not only did we add our data to Redis, we also constructed a basic index on the fly, enabling us to search for quotes by the author in our next piece of code.

We check for the existence of the first command-line argument, the author, and then output quotes by that author:

```
if (params.author) {
  client.smembers('Author:' + params.author, function (err, keys) {
    keys.forEach(function (key) {
      client.hgetall(key, function (err, hash) {
        console.log('%s: %s \n', hash.author, hash.quote);
      });
    });
    client.quit();
  });
  return;
}
client.quit();
```

How it works...

If both `author` and `quote` are specified via the command line, we go ahead and generate a random key prefixed with `Quote:`. So, each key will look something like `Quote:08d780a57b035f`. It's a common convention to prefix the Redis keys with names delimited by a colon, as this helps us to identify keys when debugging.

Interfacing with Databases

We pass our key into `client.hmset`, a wrapper for the Redis `HMSET` command, which allows us to create multiple hashes. Unlike the raw `HMSET` command, `client.hmset` also accepts a JavaScript object (not just an array) to create multiple key assignments. With the standard Redis command-line client, `redis-cli`, we will use the following command:

```
HMSET author "Steve Jobs" quote "Stay hungry, stay foolish."
```

We could hold on to this format by passing in an array containing the keys next to the values, but in this author's opinion, an object is nicer on the eyes in this case.

Every time we store a new quote with `client.hmset`, we add the `randKey` for that quote to the relevant author set via the second parameter of `client.sadd`. The `client.sadd` method allows us to add a member to a Redis set (a set is like an array of strings). The key for our `SADD` command is based on the intended author. So, in the preceding Steve Jobs quote, the key to pass into `client.sadd` would be `Author:Steve Jobs`.

Next, if an author is specified, we perform the `SMEMBERS` command using `client.smembers`. This returns all the values we stored to a specific author's set, being the keys for all the quotes related to that author.

We loop through these keys using `forEach`, passing every key into `client.hgetall`. Redis `HGETALL` returns a hash (object) that we passed into `client.hmset` earlier. Each author and quote is then logged to the console, and `client.quit` gracefully exits our script once all the Redis commands have been executed.

A final `client.quit` callback is also included for when no command-line arguments are specified. This ensures that our app ends the process correctly.

There's more...

Redis is a speed freak's dream, but we can still make optimizations.

Speeding up the Node Redis module

By default, the `redis` module uses a pure JavaScript parser. However, the Redis project provides a Node `hiredis` module—a C bindings module, which binds to the official Redis client, Hiredis. Hiredis is faster (being written in C) than the JavaScript parser.

The `redis` module will interface with the `hiredis` module if it is installed. Therefore, we can achieve performance benefits simply by installing `hiredis`:

```
npm install hiredis
```

Overcoming network latency by pipelining commands

Redis can receive multiple commands at once. The `redis` module has a `multi` method, which sends collated commands en masse. If the latency (time taken for data to travel) was 20ms per command, for 10 combined commands, we save 180ms (10 * 20 - 20 = 180).

If we copy `quotes.js` to `quotes_multi.js`, we can alter it accordingly:

```
//top variables,

if (params.author && params.quote) {
   var randKey = "Quote:" + (Math.random() * Math.random())
                  .toString(16).replace('.', '');

   client.multi()
     .hmset(randKey, {"author": params.author,
                              "quote": params.quote})
     .sadd('Author:' + params.author, randKey)
     .exec(function (err, replies) {
       if (err) { throw err; };
       if (replies[0] == "OK") { console.log('Added...\n'); }
     });
}

//if params.author, client.smembers, client.quit
```

We can see our original Redis commands highlighted, only they have been chained with `client.multi`. Once all the commands have been added to `client.multi`, we invoke its `exec` method. Finally, we use the callback of `exec` to verify that our data was successfully added.

We didn't provision SMEMBERS for pipelining. It must be called after the quote has been added, or else the new quote won't be displayed. If SMEMBERS was combined with HMSET and SADD, it would be executed asynchronously alongside them. There's no guarantee that the new quote will be available to SMEMBERS. In fact, it's unlikely since SMEMBERS is more complex than SADD, so it takes longer to process.

See also

- The *Connecting and sending SQL to a MySQL server* recipe
- The *Implementing PubSub with Redis* recipe

Implementing PubSub with Redis

Redis exposes a Publish-Subscribe messaging pattern (not so dissimilar to the CouchDB `changes` stream), which can be used to listen to specific data change events. Data from these events could be passed between processes to, for instance, instantly update a web app with fresh new data.

Interfacing with Databases

With PubSub, we publish a message to a specific channel; this channel can then be picked up by any amount of subscribers. The publishing mechanism doesn't care who's listening or how many are listening; it chats away regardless.

In this recipe, we will create a publishing process and a subscribing process. For the publishing process, we'll extend our `quotes.js` file from the previous recipe, *Storing and retrieving data with Redis*, and we'll write the code to a new file for the subscription mechanism.

Getting ready

Let's create a new directory; copy `quotes.js` from the previous recipe and rename it to `quotes_publish.js`. We will also create a file named `quotes_subscribe.js`. We'll need to ensure that Redis is running. If it isn't installed and running globally, we can navigate to the directory where Redis was unpacked and run `./redis-server` from the `src` folder.

How to do it...

In `quotes_publish.js`, we add one extra line of code inside our first conditional statement, just after our `client.sadd` call:

```
        if (params.author && params.quote) {
           var randKey = "Quote:" + (Math.random() * Math.random())
                                                 .toString(16).
    replace('.', '');
            client.hmset(randKey, {"author": params.author,
                         "quote": params.quote});

            client.sadd('Author:' + params.author, randKey);

            client.publish(params.author, params.quote);

        }
```

This means that every time we add an author and quote, we publish the quote to a channel named after the author. We subscribe to channels using `quotes_subscribe.js`, so let's code it.

First, it must require the `redis` module and create a client:

```
    var redis = require('redis');
    var client = redis.createClient();
```

We're going to provide the option to subscribe to multiple channels, again using the command line as our elementary input method. To achieve this, we'll loop through `process.argv`:

```
process.argv.slice(2).forEach(function (authorChannel, i) {

    client.subscribe(authorChannel, function () {
      console.log('Subscribing to ' + authorChannel + ' channel');
    });

});
```

Now that we are subscribing to channels, we need to listen to messages:

```
client.on('message', function (channel, msg) {
  console.log("\n%s: %s", channel, msg);
});
```

We can test our PubSub functionality by first running `quotes_subscribe.js` along with some specified authors:

node quotes_subscribe.js "Sun Tzu" "Steve Jobs" "Ronald Reagan"

Then, we open a new terminal and run several authors and quotes through `quotes_publish.js`:

node quotes_publish.js "Ronald Reagan" "One picture is worth 1,000 denials."

node quotes_publish.js "Sun Tzu" "Know thy self, know thy enemy. A thousand battles, a thousand victories."

node quotes_publish.js "David Clements" "Redis is a speed freak's dream"

node quotes_publish.js "Steve Jobs" "Design is not just what it looks like and feels like. Design is how it works."

Interfacing with Databases

Let's see it in action:

```
Subscribing to Sun Tzu channel
Subscribing to Steve Jobs channel
Subscribing to Ronald Reagan channel

Ronald Reagan: One picture is worth 1,000 denials.

Sun Tzu: Know thy self, know thy enemy. A thousand battles, a thousand victories.

Steve Jobs: Design is not just what it looks like and feels like. Design is how it works.
```

```
node@cookbook~$ node quotes_publish.js "Ronald Reagan" "One picture is worth 1,000 denials."
Ronald Reagan: One picture is worth 1,000 denials.

node@cookbook~$ node quotes_publish.js "Sun Tzu" "Know thy self, know thy enemy. A thousand battles, a thousand victories."
Sun Tzu: Know thy self, know thy enemy. A thousand battles, a thousand victories.

node@cookbook~$ node quotes_publish.js "David Clements" "Redis is a speed freak's dream"
David Clements: Redis is a speed freak's dream

node@cookbook~$ node quotes_publish.js "Steve Jobs" "Design is not just what it looks like and feels like. Design is how it works."
Steve Jobs: Design is not just what it looks like and feels like. Design is how it works.

node@cookbook~$
```

Only the channels we subscribed to appear on the `quotes_subscribe.js` terminal.

How it works...

We access the Redis `PUBLISH` command in `quotes_publish.js` using `client.publish`, setting the channel name as the author name.

In `quotes_subscribe.js`, we loop through any arguments given via the command line (applying `forEach` to `process.argv.slice(2)`). The `process.argv.slice(2)` line removes the first two elements of the `process.argv` array, which would hold the command (`node`) and path to our script. Each relevant argument is passed to `client.subscribe`, telling Redis we wish to subscribe (using `SUBSCRIBE`) to that channel.

When a message arrives over a channel that has been subscribed to, the `client` will emit a `message` event. We listen for this event and pass the incoming `channel` and `msg` (which will be `author` and `quote` accordingly) to `console.log`.

There's more...

Finally, we'll take a look at Redis security.

Redis authentication

We can set the authentication for Redis with the `redis.conf` file, found in the directory we installed Redis to. To set a password in `redis.conf`, we simply add (or uncomment) `requirepass` and `ourpassword`.

Then, we make sure that our Redis server points to the configuration file. If we are running it from the `src` directory, we will initiate with the following command:

```
./redis-server ../redis.conf
```

If we want to set a password quickly, we can use the command that follows:

```
echo "requirepass ourpassword" | ./redis-server -
```

We can set a password from within Node with the `CONFIG SET` Redis command:

```
client.config('SET', 'requirepass', 'ourpassword');
```

To authenticate a Redis server within Node, we can use the `redis` module's `auth` method before any other calls (that is, prior to `client.ready`):

```
client.auth('ourpassword');
```

The password has to be sent before any other commands. The `redis` module's `auth` function takes care of things such as reconnections by pushing the password into the `redis` module's internal operations. Essentially, we can call `auth` at the top of our code and never concern ourselves with the authentication for that script again.

Securing Redis from external connections

If there was no need for any external connections to Redis, we could bind it to `127.0.0.1`, inhibiting all the external traffic.

We can achieve this with a configuration file, such as `redis.conf`, and add the following (or uncomment):

```
bind 127.0.0.1
```

Then, if running the connection from the `src` folder, initialize our Redis server with the command that follows:

```
./redis-server ../redis.conf
```

Alternatively, we could do it as follows:

```
echo "bind 127.0.0.1" | ./redis-server -
```

Interfacing with Databases

The Redis server can be initialized in Node with the `redis` module's `config` method:

```
client.config('set', 'bind', '127.0.0.1');
```

> If we installed Redis via a package manager, it may already be configured to block external connections.

See also

- The *Accessing the CouchDB changes stream with Cradle* recipe
- The *Storing and retrieving data with Redis* recipe

5
Employing Streams

In this chapter, we will cover the following topics:

- Consuming streams
- Playing with pipes
- Making stream interfaces
- Streaming across Node processes

Introduction

To quote Dominic Tarr, the Streams API is Node's "*best and most misunderstood idea*". Throughout this book, recipes often touch on the Streams API. Streams are fundamental to the Node platform and are utilized in many of the core modules.

A **stream** is basically an object with some formalized methods and functionality, which is geared towards receiving, sending, and processing data in small pieces called chunks. The type of stream, that is, whether it's readable, writable, or both, determines these methods and functionality. This is known as a **duplex stream**.

There are many advantages of streams over the more traditional buffering method, whereby all data is read into memory prior to processing. Primarily, we use less memory this way—once a chunk is processed and sent somewhere else, to a client for instance, and we no longer need that data, we can simply discard it. This allows the data to be garbage collected.

In addition, we can deliver this first chunk (and the subsequent chunks) of processed data to the end point (a browser, for instance), which renders a faster time-to-screen interval as opposed to processing everything at once and then pushing it to the client.

Employing Streams

The streaming pattern is distinctively recognizable—it's geared towards interoperability (piping streams together) and often leads to cleaner code. We don't even need to use loops to process the data since we're processing it as it comes through.

In this chapter, we're going to zoom in on streams to see how we can apply them to various situations, which will demonstrate just how powerful and useful a pattern they can be.

> Since we've been using Streams throughout this book, it is assumed that you have some (minimal) familiarity with Streams. It may be worth scanning the Node documentation on Streams (http://nodejs.org/api/stream.html) before embarking upon the recipes that we're going to discuss.

Consuming streams

As of Node v0.10.x, every readable stream has a `read` method that can be used to access data that's loaded into our read stream. Prior to Node v0.10.x, chunks of data were captured by listening to a data event; we can still do this when it is suitable (see the *There's More...* section) but this depends on the use case; therefore using the `read` method instead can be cleaner.

In this recipe, we're going to receive a stream from the Couch database that backs the npm registry and simply log out everything we get.

Getting ready

All we need to do is create a file named `npm_stream_receiver.js`.

How to do it...

We're going use the `response` object returned from an `http.get` call as our readable stream and set up some initial variables, so we'll require the `http` module as shown in the following code:

```
var http = require('http'),
  feed =
  'http://isaacs.iriscouch.com/registry/_changes?feed=continuous',
  ready = false;
```

We'll pass the `feed` variable to `http.get`.

The `ready` variable is being used to introduce some jeopardy. To make things interesting, we're going to give our program the ability to choose whether it wants to obey (a Skynet fetus, if you will).

So, let's declare a `decide` function as shown in the following code:

```
function decide(cb) {
  console.log('deciding');
  setTimeout(function () {
    if (Date.now()%2) { return console.log('rejected'); }
    ready = true;
    cb();
  }, 2000));
}
```

What we're emulating here is a sense of conditional logic that takes time to compute. A real-world equivalent could be some form of validation or waiting on a user confirmation (or both).

Now, let's get the npm registry feed and output the stream to the console (that is, when or if the program is good and ready), as shown in the following code:

```
http.get(feed, function (res) {

  res.on('readable', function log() {

    if (!ready) { return decide(log); }

    console.log(res.read()+'');

  });

});
```

How it works...

In our `http.get` callback, we listened to the `readable` event. This lets us know that the `res` stream can be read from. We named the callback passed to the `readable` event listener `log`. This is because we need to recall the `readable` callback (in its own context) arbitrarily, as the `readable` event will (by design) fire before the `decide` function.

In the `readable` callback, the first thing we check is whether `ready` is falsey. If it is, we let the user know that the program is deciding. We then call the `decide` function and pass the `log` function to it for its supplied callback (`cb`) parameter, and then immediately return from the function before it can begin reading.

The `decide` function waits two seconds, then checks whether the current time (in milliseconds) is odd or even (our primitive decision process) by using the modulus operator (`%`). This means we divide the current time by two and return the integer remainder (which when divided by two can only be 0 or 1). The conditional statement would then coerce our `0` to `false` and `1` to `true`. Hence, in the event of an odd number (where we would have a remainder of `1`), the program declines to obey by returning early from the `setTimeout` callback and also notifying us of its rejection.

Employing Streams

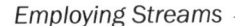

If the current time happens to be an even number, we set `ready` to `true` and call `cb`, which happens to be the `log` function and is, of course, our readable callback. Essentially, we will refire the first callback but without going through the event system.

This time the `log` function recognized that `ready` is `true`, so it goes straight to logging out the result of `res.read`.

When we call `read` without any arguments, all the data currently contained in the buffer is returned and the buffer is flushed.

If more data is loaded into the buffer, another `readable` event is fired and we again read and output everything the buffer has.

We concatenate an empty string with the `res.read` call in order to force a `toString` operation; this converts it from a buffer to a string, so we can read it as text in the console.

There's more...

Not only can we control how much data we read from a stream, but there's also more than one way to access a stream's readable data.

Using read's size argument

Let's save `npm_stream_receiver.js` to `npm_stream_receiver_with_size_arg.js` and navigate to the following line:

```
console.log(res.read()+'');
```

The preceding line needs to be changed to the following:

```
console.log(res.read(20)+'');
```

So now we're going to read 20 bytes at a time. Let's run this file and see what happens.

Providing the program proceeds as far as the GET request, we'll see the first 20 bytes of the request and the program will exit.

This is because no more `readable` events will be fired as there's still data in the streams buffer (it has to be emptied to fire a `readable` event again), and since nothing else is happening, the program exits.

The `read` method will return `null` whenever the buffer is empty. So, we need to continuously read from the stream until its buffer is empty. Once this occurs, a new readable event can happen when more data arrives.

So, let's modify our code accordingly:

```
http.get(feed, function (res) {

  res.on('readable', function log() {
    var chunk;

    if (!ready) { return decide(log); }

    while( (chunk = res.read(20)) !== null) {
        console.log(chunk+'');
    }

  });

});
```

Whenever an assignment is made in JavaScript, the result of the expression assigned to the variable is returned. This allows us to both assign the result of the `res.read` call to the `chunk` variable and check to see whether that result is not `null` within the `while` conditional section.

As long as `res.read` isn't returning `null`, we will continue to read 20 bytes at a time, and log those bytes out (after stringifying them using the string concatenation shorthand).

Assignments within conditionals sometimes break house style rules or our own sense of taste. Another way to read and log the bytes out is with a recursive function that's moderated using `setImmediate` (to avoid maximum stack violations).

The following is an alternative to the preceding code snippet:

```
http.get(feed, function (res) {

  res.on('readable', function log() {

    if (!ready) { return decide(log); }

    (function output () {
      var chunk = res.read(20);
      if (chunk === null) {return;}
      console.log(chunk+'');
      setImmediate(output);
    }());

  });

});
```

Employing Streams

This time, we will use a named self-invoking function expression. We will check whether each `chunk` is `null`; if it is, we return early thus breaking the recursion. If it isn't `null`, we log out the `chunk` variable and then call `output` using `setImmediate`, which is the fastest way to execute the code on the next tick (next tick means the next time around the event loop). If we were to call `output` directly, that is, in the current tick, we would exceed call stack limitations and receive a `RangeError`.

The advantage of using this method is that it's slightly more conventional and is more likely to pass linters such as JSHint or ESLint and conform to code style guides. The disadvantages are that it's a few extra lines of code and may therefore be less performant. Performance would take a hit because we're creating an inner function on each readable event, iteratively calling functions instead of using a simple loop, and separating each recursion into its own tick.

Another method would be to combine the two approaches, where the `output` function returns a Boolean that represents the `null` check on `res.read` and instead of self-recursion is iterated inside a blockless `while` statement, as seen in the following code:

```
function output(res) {
  var chunk = res.read(20);
  if (chunk === null) {return false;}
  console.log(chunk+'');
  return true;
}

http.get(feed, function (res) {

  res.on('readable', function log() {

    if (!ready) { return decide(log); }

    while(output(res));

  });

});
```

This way, we only define the function once, and there's no assignment inside the `while` conditional section. On the other hand, using blockless `while` statements may also be a code style taboo. Also, we're still calling a function instead of the more simple assignment plus `null` check, and this adds even more code (well, one line more but we had to refactor too).

Consuming via the data event

Prior to Node v0.10.x, the data event was the only way to access data from a read stream. While the `read` method is pull oriented, this paradigm is push oriented—it begins to emit data events straightaway, so there's no chance to do any preprocessing before you request the data.

Let's copy our `npm_stream_receiver.js` file to `npm_stream_receiver_data_events.js` and get down to converting our recipe.

We can pause our stream using the `pause` method to stop it from emitting data events before we're ready. Then, we can pass the stream's `resume` method to the `decide` function as the callback argument. After this, it's simply a case of listening to the `data` event and logging to the console.

Let's alter the `http.get` section of our code with the following code:

```
http.get(feed, function (res) {
  res.pause();

  if (!ready) {
    //notice the early return is also removed
    decide(res.resume.bind(res));
  }

  res.on('data', function (data) {
    console.log(data+'');
  });

});
```

When we pass in the callback to the `decide` function call, we use `bind` to bind the `res` object to the `res.resume` method. If we don't, the `cb` function is called in isolation; for example, it is not called as a method on the `res` object, so its context changes and thus an error occurs. This is similar to, though more terse than supplying the `decide` callback argument in the form of an anonymous function, which in turn calls `res.resume`.

In either case, that is, whether we use `bind` or an anonymous function, the call to `resume` causes the `data` events to start emitting because we don't return early from the `!ready` conditional, which allows the `data` listener to be set up.

Choosing between the `read` method or the `data` event can be largely determined by the best fit for our use case. Using the `pause` and `resume` methods seems less contained when compared with the `read` method.

Since our particular case is so simple, it's actually possible to simplify the code further.

Let's modify `http.get` again:

```
http.get(feed, function (res) {

  decide(function () {
    res.on('data', function (data) {
      console.log(data+'');
```

Employing Streams

```
    });
  });

});
```

Now, we have no need for `pause` and `resume` nor for the `ready` Boolean. We only start listening to events once the `decide` function is complete. However, for most cases, this could be over simplification.

There are some potentially confounding factors we need to bear in mind. Firstly, what if (without our knowledge) another piece of code started listening to the events on our stream? Secondly, this method only suits a strictly synchronous and simple logic path; for instance, what if we wanted to execute several operations in parallel before reading from the stream? In more complex cases, `read` may be the better candidate.

See also

- The *Playing with pipes* recipe
- The *Making stream interfaces* recipe
- The *Streaming across Node processes* recipe

Playing with pipes

A pipe is used to connect streams together. DOS and Unix-like shells use the vertical bar (|) to pipe the output of one program to another; we can chain several pipes together to process and massage data in number of ways. Likewise, the Streams API affords us the `pipe` method to channel data through multiple streams. Every readable stream has a `pipe` method that expects a writable stream (the destination) as its first parameter.

As in the *Consuming streams* recipe, we're going to receive a stream from the Couch database, which backs the npm registry, and display it in the terminal; only this time we'll be using pipes instead of the `read` method.

Getting ready

Let's create a file named `npm_stream_piper.js`.

How to do it...

Let's set up some initial variables as shown in the following code:

```
var http = require('http'),
  feed =
'http://isaacs.iriscouch.com/registry/_changes?feed=continuous';
```

Implement the `decide` function (as in the *Consuming streams* recipe) with the following code:

```
function decide(cb) {
  console.log('deciding');
  setTimeout(function () {
    if (Date.now()%2) { return console.log('rejected'); }
    cb();
  }, 2000);
}
```

And finally, let's modify the `http.get` callback:

```
http.get(feed, function (res) {

  decide(function () {
    res.pipe(process.stdout)
  });

});
```

Okay, so this code is smaller than the code required in the *Consuming streams* recipe.

Let's make it smaller by turning our `decide` call into a one liner.

We'll change `http.get` accordingly:

```
http.get(feed, function (res) {

  decide(res.pipe.bind(res, process.stdout));

});
```

We're done! The `pipe` method is highly terse and extremely powerful.

How it works...

We call `pipe` once the `decide` function is complete, that is, from inside its callback argument. From there on, the `pipe` method does all of the hard work for us. Everything read from the `res` stream is written to the `process.stdout` stream. **STDOUT** is the standard output stream of the terminal we use to run our Node script. However, under the hood, it's more sophisticated than just reading and writing.

The `pipe` method also takes care of asserting backpressure. Whenever a stream we're reading from is shunting data to us faster than we can handle, we have to be able to slow it down or stop it, and `pipe` does this for us.

Employing Streams

There's more...

Let's take a peek at a higher functioning piping example and also see how a slight refactor can help us prepare for a more complex code landscape.

Chaining and filtering streams

The npm registry's Couch stream is composed of JSON data. What if we could pipe this data to a stream that was able to extract the properties from the JSON? This is perfectly feasible but it would be a rather large and complex implementation. Fortunately, there's a third-party module available to do just this: `JSONStream`.

We need to install it using the following command:

```
npm install JSONStream
```

Also, let's copy `npm_stream_piper.js` to `npm_stream_piping_filter.js`. We'll slip in `require` at the top of the code:

```
var http = require('http'),
  JSONStream = require('JSONStream'),
  feed =
'http://isaacs.iriscouch.com/registry/_changes?feed=continuous';
```

Then, we finish by altering the `http.get` callback as shown in the following code:

```
http.get(feed, function (res) {

  decide(function () {
    res.pipe(JSONStream.parse('id')).pipe(process.stdout);
  });
});
```

We've gone back to using an anonymous function instead of `bind` because when we start to chain multiple pipes, the one liner becomes inadequate.

All we've done here is slip an extra pipe between `res` and `pipe(process.stdout)`.

The `JSONStream.parse` function generates a write stream using the supplied argument (which is basically a property filter); in this case, we're asking for `id` properties. When we run our code through Node, instead of outputting all the JSON data, only the module `id` values are logged.

Preparing for greater complexity

In the *There's more...* section of the *Consuming streams* recipe, the end of the *Consuming via the data event* subsection discusses the difference between interacting with the stream inside the `decide` callback (as we do in our current recipe) and setting up stream interactions outside of the `decide` callback as well as controlling the stream flow using `pause` and `resume`.

Controlling the stream flow with `pause` and `resume` allows greater flexibility and helps to decouple stream interaction from any preprocessing it may be dependent on. Further, it keeps us interacting with the stream itself instead of slipping into a procedural style that can easily lead to duplicative and messy code.

So, let's refactor the `http.get` callback slightly:

```
http.get(feed, function (res) {

  res.pause();

  decide(res.resume.bind(res));

  res.pipe(process.stdout)

});
```

See also

- The *Consuming streams* recipe
- The *Making stream interfaces* recipe
- The *Streaming across Node processes* recipe

Making stream interfaces

The *Consuming streams* and *Playing with pipes* recipes show us how to initiate and interact with various stream interfaces, such as the `fs` module's read and write streams, the `http` module's `response` object's write stream, and third-party modules, such as `JSONStream` (refer to the *There's More...* section of *Playing with pipes*).

In this recipe, we're going to make our own basic read and write stream interfaces.

Getting ready

Let's create and open a file, which we'll name `basic_streams.js`.

How to do it...

Node's `stream` module contains some base constructors to create streams. So, let's require the `stream` module and instantiate a readable stream as well as a writable stream:

```
var stream = require('stream');
var writable = new stream.Writable();
```

Employing Streams

```
var readable = new stream.Readable();
var store = [];
```

We've also created an empty array named `store`. We'll be writing to `store` via the writable stream and reading from it with the readable stream.

To create streams that we intend to reuse, simply instantiating the base constructor is not the best pattern; we're only using it here for the sake of simplicity. Check out the *There's More...* section to see how we can refactor in order to create the reusable stream code.

Custom streams call special functions whenever data is being written to them or the data is requested for reading. These functions are essentially callbacks in the form of object methods. While creating a stream interface, it's up to us to supply these special callback methods in order to customize how the stream works.

Writable streams expect the special `_write` method, so let's define that with the following code:

```
writable._write = function (chunk, encoding, callback) {
    store.push(chunk);
    callback();
}
```

Likewise, readable streams will call the special `_read` method when a stream user tries to read from them, so let's put it in place:

```
readable._read = function (size, encoding) {
    this.push(store.pop() || null);
}
```

Finally, we'll write some data to the writable stream and read it back from the readable stream:

```
writable.write('fee');
writable.write('fi');
writable.write('fo');
writable.write('fum');

readable.on('data', function (data) {
    console.log(data+'')
});
```

Now if we run our code, the terminal should show the following output:

```
node@cookbook~$ node basic_streams.js
fum
fo
fi
fee
node@cookbook~$
```

How it works...

The `Readable` and `Writable` constructors provided by the `stream` module supply all the functionality we need to create a full-featured stream interface, with proper internal handling of typical streaming challenges such as a read stream being unable to keep up with a write stream and a coverage of edge cases that can arise from using streams.

We use these constructors to instantiate our `readable` and `writable` streams and then supply the `_read` and `_write` methods to them, respectively.

In our `writable._write` method, we customize the stream by pushing each `chunk` (as passed into the first parameter of the `_write` method) written to the stream into the `store` array. Then, since we've nothing else to do in our `_write` method, we call the third parameter that we named `callback`, which tells the writable stream interface that the `chunk` has been handled.

Using a `callback` parameter to signify we're done leaves scope for us to perform asynchronous operations within the `_write` method; for instance, writing to a file or across a TCP socket.

Each `chunk` that comes in through the `_write` function is a `Buffer` object (a special type supplied by the Node platform to store data at a binary level). When instantiating any kind of stream, an encoding parameter can be set; for instance, the parameter could request that the stream delivers UTF8-formatted strings instead of buffers. This encoding setting is passed in as the second parameter of the special `_write` method. In this particular use case, we're ignoring the second `encoding` parameter, choosing to deliver only `Buffer` chunks to the `store`.

The special `_read` method takes two parameters, which we've named `size` and `encoding`. The encoding parameter is much the same as write streams, except that instead of converting the data to a particular code that it's written in, the read stream will convert the data as it's being read out.

Employing Streams

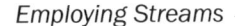

Again, we ignored the `encoding` argument for our purposes. We also ignored the `size` parameter. The public `read` method (the one called by the user of a stream interface, not the private `_read` method as specified by an interface creator) accepts a `size` parameter. This is an advisory argument that requests that each delivered chunk is a minimum of the specified size. The `size` parameter as received by our custom `_read` method reflects what the readable stream is requesting internally, which may or may not be the size specified by the user—it depends upon the internal implementation's assessment of what's best for performance. In many cases, the size passed onto our custom `_read` method will be the `highWaterMark` setting, the data a stream can contain at any given time, which defaults to `16384` (16 KB in bytes).

Since we're popping very small amounts of data from an array, the `size` parameter is meaningless to us.

Streams have been described as "arrays in time", and like an array, the `Readable` stream has a `push` method. Instead of pushing data onto an array, however, it pushes data out through the stream interface.

We call our readable stream instance's `push` method from within the `_read` method to send data out through the stream.

Every time the public `read` method is called, at some point in its logic, it calls our `_read` method. Our `_read` method calls the `push` method and supplies some data to it. Once all the data has been exhausted, we must pass `null` into the `push` method to signal that the stream has ended.

We get our data by popping items off of the `store` array; once the `store` array is empty, the `pop` method will return `undefined`. We use an OR check (`||`) to return `null` in that case, thus signaling that the stream has ended.

> We can get away with a simple OR check in this case because our `store` contains buffer objects that will always be truthy values. If instead, we had an array that contained falsey values (such as `0`, `null`, and `false`), we will need to be more sophisticated in our approach; for instance, checking the array's `length` property and returning `null` if it was `0`, else popping from the array as usual.

Once we've customized our read and write streams, we can use them. We call `writable.write` four times, passing in `fee`, `fi`, and `fo`, and `fum`.

This causes the writable stream to look to the special `_write` method for guidance on how to process the supplied data, passing in each of our original strings a buffer in the form of the `chunk` parameter. We push the buffer (using `push`) to our `store` array, and invoke the `callback` function to allow the write stream to accept the next `write` call. At the end of the four `write` calls, our `store` array contains the first line of the bad giants mantra.

Instead of calling the `read` method directly on the readable stream, we trigger the stream flowing mode by attaching a `data` event listener to it. Internally, this essentially iteratively invokes the `read` method until it returns `null`, at which point it would call the end event listener callback (if we had supplied it). Inside our `data` event listener's callback, we receive each chunk through the `data` parameter and convert the buffer to a string (via an empty string concatenation) as we pass it to `console.log`.

There's more...

So far, our custom read and write streams are very basic. Let's look at some ways to flush them out, starting with making our own constructors that inherit from the base stream classes and finishing by creating a duplex transform stream.

Making reusable streams

So, the main recipe's stream is elementary in its approach. We want to be able to design a stream interface that can be used and reused for many purposes—as is the philosophy behind streams.

So, let's create three files: `stream_to_array.js`, `stream_from_array.js`, and `fee_fi_fo_fum.js`.

The `stream_to_array.js` file will provide our write stream constructor, as shown in the following code:

```
var stream = require('stream');
var util = require('util');

function StreamToArray(store) {
    stream.Writable.call(this);
    this.store = store || [];
}

util.inherits(StreamToArray, stream.Writable);


StreamToArray.prototype._write = function (chunk, encoding, callback)
{
    this.store.push(chunk);
    callback();
}

module.exports = StreamToArray;
```

Employing Streams

The `stream_from_array.js` file is very similar to the `stream_to_array.js` file, except that instead of inheriting from `stream.Writable` we inherit from `stream.Readable`, and instead of implementing the `_write` method, we implement the `_read` method; this is shown in the following code:

```
var stream = require('stream');
var util = require('util');

function StreamFromArray(store) {
    stream.Readable.call(this);
    this.store = store || [];
}

util.inherits(StreamFromArray, stream.Readable);

StreamFromArray.prototype._read = function (size, encoding) {
    this.push(this.store.pop() || null);
}

module.exports = StreamFromArray;
```

In both cases, our Stream constructors are assigned to `module.exports`.

> See *Chapter 10, Writing Your Own Node Modules*, for more information on using `module.exports` and `require`.

This allows us to require our constructors into `fee_fi_fo_fum.js`, as shown in the following block of code:

```
var StreamToArray = require('./stream_to_array.js'),
    StreamFromArray = require('./stream_from_array.js'),
    store = [],
    writable = new StreamToArray(store),
    readable = new StreamFromArray(store);

writable.write('fee');
writable.write('fi');
writable.write('fo');
writable.write('fum');

readable.on('data', function (data) {
    console.log(data+'')
});
```

Both constructors work the same way—they take a `store` parameter, which is then loaded onto the instance via the contextual `this` object in the constructor and later used within the relevant special private method (`_read` or `_write`). Each constructor also invokes JavaScript's `call` method on its relevant stream constructor; for example, `stream.Readable.call(this)`.

Passing our custom constructor's `this` object into the `call` invocation replaces the normal context of `stream.Readable` (or `stream.Writable` in the `StreamToArray` case) with the instance being created via our custom constructor. This causes the constructors to decorate our custom instance with all the properties, methods, and associated logic that would be made available on an object returned from calling the base constructors with new, as in our main recipe.

We also use the core `util` module's `inherit` method, which hooks up our custom constructor's prototype chain with the relevant streams base constructor prototype; for example, `StreamFromArray` has access to all of the prototype methods on the `stream.Readable` constructor.

Finally, in `fee_fi_fo_fum.js`, we require the `StreamToArray` and `StreamFromArray` constructors, create a `store` array, instantiate a new instance of each custom constructor passing in our `store` array, and then call the `write` methods and listen to the `data` event as in the main recipe.

Transform streams

Streaming to and from an array has a fairly limited application, particularly when wanting to handle the amount of data that streams are designed to work with.

When we instantiate a stream, it has its own internal buffer, so there's really no need to store to an array; not even for processing the data that comes through a write stream.

A stream doesn't have to exclusively be a read stream or a write stream, it can be both. This is known as a **duplex stream**. With the power of piping, we can hook up multiple streams together, and the intermittent streams can interact with and convert the data as it's being passed through.

A stream that processes and alters data as it's being passed through is called a **transform stream**, and Node's `stream` module provides a base constructor so that creating fully functioning transform streams is easy.

Let's create a transform stream that uppercases (we'll name the file `uppercase_transform_stream.js`) all content that passes through it, and we'll pipe the `process.stdin` core stream to it, and in turn pipe from our transform stream to the `process.stdout` stream:

```
var stream = require('stream');
var transformable = new stream.Transform();

transformable._transform = function (chunk, encoding, callback) {
    transformable.push(chunk.toString().toUpperCase());
    callback();
}
```

Employing Streams

```
transformable.write('fee');
transformable.write('fi');
transformable.write('fo');
transformable.write('fum');

process.stdin.pipe(transformable).pipe(process.stdout);
```

When we run our code, we'll initially see **FEEFIFOFUM**. If we begin typing, we will generate a stream of data from `process.stdin` to `transformable`. Every time we press return (`process.stdin` and `process.stdout` streams are newline delimited streams), we'll see the data we entered is now in uppercase because our transformable stream will have processed our stream and piped it onto the `process.stdout` stream.

The `Transform` instance expects a `_transform` method to be set instead of the `_read` and `_write` method. Both read and write functionality is defined in this special method. When we call `transformable.push`, we are implementing the read interface, and the `callback` invocation lets the writable side of the transform stream know that we've finished processing the data written to it.

In the case of the `_transform` method, we can actually combine both read and write operations into the `callback` invocation by supplying the argument passed to `transformable.push` as the second parameter, as shown in the following code:

```
transformable._transform = function (chunk, encoding, callback) {
    callback(null, chunk.toString().toUpperCase());
}
```

The first parameter of `callback` indicates that there has been an error in processing `chunk`; in our case, we pass `null` to specify that no error has occurred.

See also

- The *Consuming streams* recipe
- The *Playing with pipes* recipe
- The *Streaming across Node processes* recipe

Streaming across Node processes

Streams are about facilitating efficient, low memory data transfer, and processing; not just to and from the filesystem, but also to other processes and across network sockets.

In this recipe, we're going to write some simple command-line stream apps, then mix and match them with the common stream processing apps written in other languages.

Getting ready

Let's create two files: `text_stream.js` and `uppercaser.js`. Both of these need to be executable files as we're going to run them directly as command-line apps:

```
touch text_stream.js && chmod +x text_stream.js
touch uppercaser.js && chmod + x uppercaser.js
```

How to do it...

Let's start by making a readable stream that randomly pushes lowercase alphabetical letters to its reader and pipes the stream to `process.stdout`. In `text_stream.js`, we will write:

```
#!/usr/bin/env node

var stream = require('stream');
var util = require('util');
var textStream;

function TextStream() {
    stream.Readable.call(this);
}

util.inherits(TextStream, stream.Readable);

TextStream.prototype._read = function (size, encoding) {
    var letter = String.fromCharCode(Math.random() * (123 - 97) + 97);
    this.push(letter === 'z' ? 'z\n' : letter);
}

textStream = new TextStream();

textStream.pipe(process.stdout);
```

Note the **shebang** (the line at the top starting with `#!`) at the top of our code, on the very first line. This tells Unix-like systems, for example, OS X and Linux, to parse and execute this file with Node when we run the file directly from the command line. DOS systems will simply ignore this line.

We use the same shebang technique in our next piece of code `uppercaser.js`, which will be a transform stream that performs a `toUpperCase` conversion on any content read into it, then pipe standard in (`process.stdin`) through our transform stream, which in turn we pipe back to standard out (`process.stdout`):

```
#!/usr/bin/env node

var stream = require('stream');
```

Employing Streams

```
var util = require('util');
var uppercaser;

function Uppercaser() {
    stream.Transform.call(this);
}

util.inherits(Uppercaser, stream.Transform);

Uppercaser.prototype._transform = function (chunk, encoding, callback)
{
    callback(null, chunk.toString().toUpperCase());
}

uppercaser = new Uppercaser();

process.stdin.pipe(uppercaser).pipe(process.stdout);
```

Excellent, now let's play!

We can use `sed` (the stream text editor) to, for instance, wrap every instance of the letters "d", "a", "v", and "e" in parenthesis:

`./text_stream.js | sed 's/[d|a|v|e]/(&)/g'`

We can use `grep` for every instance of the letter "a":

`./text_stream.js | grep a`

We can uppercase anything we like using the following commands:

`echo "foo" | ./uppercaser.js`
`curl http://nodejs.org | ./uppercaser.js`
`./text_stream.js | ./uppercaser.js`

How it works...

Making each of our files executable and including a shebang pointing to Node allows us to create powerful command-line apps in pure JavaScript. The shebang actually points to `/usr/bin/env` and passes `node` as an argument. This allows the host system to have the node binary installed anywhere, and the system will still locate Node, as long as the system has `env` installed in `/usr/bin`, of course.

In `text_stream.js`, we implement a read stream that inherits from the `stream.Readable` interface. We define a `_read` method that loads a random character from a to z into the `letter` variable. We obtain the character using JavaScript's native `String.prototype.fromCharCode` method, which takes an ASCII code and converts it to a character; for instance, `String.fromCharCode(97)` would be the letter a. We get our ASCII code using `Math.random` and apply a calculation to its result to obtain a (pseudo) random number between 97 (the letter "a") and 122 (the letter "z"). We want `text_stream.js` to be compatible with other stream processing apps, such as `sed` and `grep`, which tend to operate on newline-delimited streams—that is, they process a line at a time rather than a character at a time (the `tr` utility would be an exception to this as it processes one character at a time). So, we introduce newlines to our text stream by checking whether the letter is a "z". If it is, we pair it with a newline (`\n`) and push it to our stream instead of the "z" on its own.

We then create an instance of `TextStream` (named `textStream`) and pipe it to `process.stdout` (using `pipe`). As soon as we call `pipe` on our instance, it triggers a read loop on the stream that writes straight to `process.stdout`. Since our stream pushes on every call it never finishes, so it will continuously stream out random characters to standard out.

In a similar fashion, `uppercaser.js` inherits from a stream interface; this time it is `stream.Transform`. The `_transform` method simply pushes an uppercase version of its input onto the output stream by passing the content in uppercase as the second parameter of the `callback` function. Then, we create an instance of `Uppercaser`, (named `uppercaser`) and using pipes, place it between standard in and standard out so that anything coming into the `uppercaser.js` process runs through our `uppercaser` instance straight onto standard out.

By streaming from and to `process.stdin` and `process.stdout` as our ultimate start and end points, we completely decouple our mini apps from their input and output and delegate the management of this to the command line. Coupling this delegation with choosing a nonbinary format for our data (or as streams extraordinaire James Halliday puts it, "Text, the universal interface!") gives us a powerful, flexible paradigm that allows us to mix and match different apps to process our data using the command-line pipe (`|`) to line up our processing stack.

There's more...

Let's work on a more advanced transform stream and see how to stream across a network.

Processing stream chunk buffers efficiently

Let's put together a STDOUT/STDIN transform stream that looks for a sequence of uppercase letters, and when it finds them, it will color the letters in red.

The string that we'll be looking for is DAVE, so let's name the file `daver.js`. You could, if so desired, use your own name for this example:

```
touch daver.js && chmod +x daver.js
```

Employing Streams

We'll be using the third-party module `buffertools` to process our chunks, so let's install this:

npm install buffertools

Working on buffers directly is more efficient than converting them to strings. For one thing, we avoid the overhead of the conversion to strings, and the inevitable conversion back to a buffer once we send our processed chunk back out through the readable side of the transform stream. Further, Node's JavaScript land Buffer constructor is simply the tip of the iceberg. It's backed by C++ code designed for working with binary data. The `buffertools` module operates on the buffer using C++, keeping traversals through the C++ to JavaScript membrane minimal.

We'll put the following code into the `daver.js` file:

```
#!/usr/bin/env node

var stream = require('stream');
var util = require('util');
var buffertools = require('buffertools');

var daver, overspill = new Buffer(0),
  redStart = new Buffer([27, 91, 51, 49, 109]),
  redStop = new Buffer([27, 91, 51, 57, 109]);

function Daver() {
    stream.Transform.call(this);
}

util.inherits(Daver, stream.Transform);


Daver.prototype._transform = function (chunk, encoding, callback){
  chunk = buffertools.concat(overspill, chunk);
  overspill = chunk.slice(chunk.length - 4, chunk.length-1);
  callback(null, colorMatches(chunk));
}

function colorMatches(chunk) {
  var ix = chunk.indexOf('DAVE');
  if (~ix) {
    chunk = buffertools.concat(
      chunk.slice(0 ,ix),
      redStart,
      chunk.slice(ix, ix+4),
      redStop,
      colorMatches(chunk.slice(ix+5, chunk.length-4))
    );
```

```
    }

    return chunk;
}

daver = new Daver();

process.stdin.pipe(daver).pipe(process.stdout);
```

We require the `stream`, `util`, and the third-party `buffertools` modules. We also create three buffers: an empty buffer named `overspill` (we'll be using this as a sort of overlap between chunks), `redStart`, and `redStop`. These two variables (`redStart` and `redStop`) are buffers that contain the necessary bytes, which when printed as characters to a terminal provide the necessary terminal instructions to color a piece of text red. As strings, `redStart` would be `'\u001b[31m'` and `redStop` would be `'\u001b[39m'`. We create them here as buffers because we'll splice them in with chunk buffers whenever we have a pattern match.

As in our main recipe's `uppercaser.js`, we go on to create a reusable transform stream, calling our stream constructor `Daver`. Then, we implement the special `_transform` method.

In `_transform`, we use the `buffertools.concat` function to concatenate the `overspill` buffer with the current `chunk`. The first call to `_transform` will simply concatenate an empty buffer. Then, we redefine `overspill`, taking a `slice` of the last three bytes from the current chunk. The next time `_transform` is called, those three bytes will be concatenated to the beginning of the new chunk. This overlap allows us to match DAVE across two chunks, where, for instance, one chunk might end with DA and the other starts with VE.

Then, we invoke the callback, passing in the second argument as `colorMatches(chunk)`. We defined the `colorMatches` function underneath our `_transform` method.

> `Buffer.prototype.slice` is a a method provided natively by Node's Buffer constructor; however, the next method called (`Buffer.prototype.indexOf`) in the line `var ix = chunk.indexOf('DAVE')` is not provided as standard. The `buffertools` module augments `Buffer.prototype` with this (and other) methods. Refer to https://github.com/bnoordhuis/node-buffertools for more details.

The `colorMatches` function checks to see whether our current `chunk` contains the bytes associated with DAVE, loading any potential index of the chunk into the `ix` variable. If there is a match, we use `buffertools.concat` with `ix` to isolate our match and wrap it with the `redStart` and `redStop` buffers. The last argument to `buffertools.concat` is another call to `colorMatches`, this time supplying any remaining bytes after our DAVE match as the `chunk` argument. This recursive call to `colorMatches` enables us to elegantly match every occurrence of DAVE in our current `chunk`. Finally, we return the processed `chunk` that is fed through the `callback` invocation in `_transform` and subsequently piped onto `process.stdout`.

Employing Streams

Now, let's use it. We can pipe the output of `text_stream.js` through `uppercaser.js` to `daver.js`:

`./text_stream.js | ./uppercaser.js | ./daver.js`

It might be a while before we see a DAVE colored in red. If we want to even the odds a bit, we can remove the new lines and all the letters that aren't D, A, V, or E:

`./text_stream.js | ./uppercaser.js | sed 's/[B-C,F-U,W-Z]//g' | tr -d '\n' | ./daver.js`

Streaming over TCP

Streams are a well-fitting construct for communicating across networks. We can use the `net` module (which utilizes streams) to chain our stream processes over a network socket.

Let's create a file. We'll name it `tcp_pipe_out.js`. We need it to be executable like the other files in this recipe:

`touch tcp_pipe_out.js && chmod +x tcp_pipe_out.js`

Now, we'll write our TCP pipe as follows:

```
#!/usr/bin/env node

var net = require('net'),
    port = 1337;

net.createServer(function (c) {
    process.stdin.pipe(c);
    c.pipe(process.stdout);
}).listen(port);
```

So, we can start streaming through our pipe using the following command:

`./text_stream.js | ./tcp_pipe_out.js`

Then, we can open a new terminal and listen to the socket that we're streaming over:

`nc 127.0.0.1 1337`

We use netcat here to connect to our local loop (the internal network that exists on our own computer), and to the port specified in `tcp_pipe_out.js`. Of course, we could replace `127.0.0.1` with the IP address of our computer, (an example can be `192.168.1.3`) and connect from another computer on our local network. Provided our router is correctly configured, we could access the stream across the Internet through our external IP address (an example can be `109.158.224.190`).

Once connected, we should see the text stream from our main recipe coming through.

Let's create another file named `tcp_pipe_in.js` and make it executable:

touch tcp_pipe_in.js && chmod +x tcp_pipe_in.js

We'll write the following code into our new file:

```
#!/usr/bin/env node

var net = require('net'),
    port = 1337,
    address = '127.0.0.1';

net.connect(port, address, function () {
    process.stdin.pipe(this);
    this.pipe(process.stdout);
});
```

Our `tcp_pipe_in.js` file can now replace netcat.

In the first terminal, we again start our text stream and pipe it through TCP:

./text_stream.js | ./tcp_pipe_out.js

Then, in another terminal, we pipe it using the following command:

./tcp_pipe_in.js

We can pipe our TCP in-stream to other processes as follows:

./tcp_pipe_in.js | ./uppercaser.js

See also

- The *Playing with pipes* recipe
- The *Consuming streams* recipe
- The *Making stream interfaces* recipe

6
Going Real Time

In this chapter, we will cover the following topics:

- Creating a WebSocket server
- Cross-browser real-time logic with Socket.IO
- Remote Procedure Calls with Socket.IO
- Creating a real-time widget

Introduction

HTTP was not made for the kind of real-time web applications that many developers are creating today. As a result, all sorts of workarounds have been discovered to mimic the idea of bi-directional, uninterrupted communication between servers and clients.

WebSockets don't mimic this behavior; they provide it. WebSockets work by stripping down an HTTP connection so it becomes a persistent TCP-like exchange, thus removing all the overhead and restrictions that HTTP introduces.

The HTTP connection is stripped (or rather upgraded) when both the browser and server support WebSockets. The browser discovers this by communicating with the server via GET headers, and only newer browsers (IE10+, Google Chrome 14, Safari 5, and Firefox 6) support WebSockets.

WebSockets is a new protocol. JavaScript combined with the Node platform is often versatile and low-level enough to implement protocols from scratch, or failing that, C/C++ modules can be written to handle a more obscure or revolutionary logic. Thankfully, there's no need to write our own protocol implementation; the open source community has already provided it for us.

In this chapter, we will be using some third-party modules to explore some of the potential of the powerful combination of Node and WebSockets.

Going Real Time

Creating a WebSocket server

For this task, we will use the third-party `ws` module to create a pure WebSocket server that will receive and respond to WebSocket requests from the browser.

Getting ready

We'll create a new folder for our project that will hold two files: `server.js` and `client.html`. The `client.html` file will provide a basic user interface and connect to the WebSocket server while `server.js` supplies the server-side WebSocket functionality and serves up the `client.html` file in response to browser requests. We also need to install the `ws` module. Once we've changed the directory in our new folder on the command line, we can run the following code:

npm install ws

> For more information on the ws module, refer to https://www.github.com/einaros/ws.

How to do it...

Let's use `require` with the `ws` module and create our WebSocket server (we'll call this `wss`):

```
var WSServer = require('ws').Server,
    wss = new WSServer({port:8080});
```

Now that we have our WebSocket server (`wss`) instance, we can listen to its `connection` event which will supply us with a `socket` element for every incoming connection, as shown in the following code:

```
wss.on('connection', function (socket) { });
```

We can interact with the `socket` element inside our `connection` callback by listening and responding to `message` and `close` events:

```
wss.on('connection', function (socket) {

  socket.on('message', function (msg) {
    console.log('Recieved: ', msg, '\n',
      'From IP: ', socket.upgradeReq.connection.remoteAddress);

    if (msg === 'Hello') {   socket.send('Websockets!');   }
  });
```

```
    socket.on('close', function (code, desc) {
      console.log('Disconnect: ' + code + ' - ' + desc);
    });
  });
```

Now, for the client, we'll place the following HTML structure into the `client.html` file:

```
<html>
<head>
</head>
<body>
<input id=msg><button id=send>Send</button>
<div id=output></div>

<script>
//client side JavaScript will go here
</script>

</body>
</html>
```

The content of our `script` tags should look as follows:

```
<script>
(function () {
  var ws = new WebSocket("ws://localhost:8080"),
    output = document.getElementById('output'),
    send = document.getElementById('send');

  function logStr(eventStr, msg) {
    return '<div>' + eventStr + ': ' + msg + '</div>';
  }

  send.addEventListener('click', function () {
      var msg = document.getElementById('msg').value;
      ws.send(msg);
      output.innerHTML += logStr('Sent', msg);
  });

  ws.onmessage = function (e) {
    output.innerHTML += logStr('Recieved', e.data);
  };

  ws.onclose = function (e) {
    output.innerHTML += logStr('Disconnected', e.code + '-' +
      e.type);
```

```
    };

    ws.onerror = function (e) {
       output.innerHTML += logStr('Error', e.data);
    };

}());

</script>
```

If we initialize our server with `node server.js`, we'd need to open the `client.html` file in our (WebSocket-compliant) browser, type `Hello` in the textbox, and click on the **Send** button. The terminal console will then give the following output:

```
Recieved "Hello"
From IP 127.0.0.1
```

Our browser will show that **Hello** was sent and **WebSockets!** was received, as shown in the following screenshot:

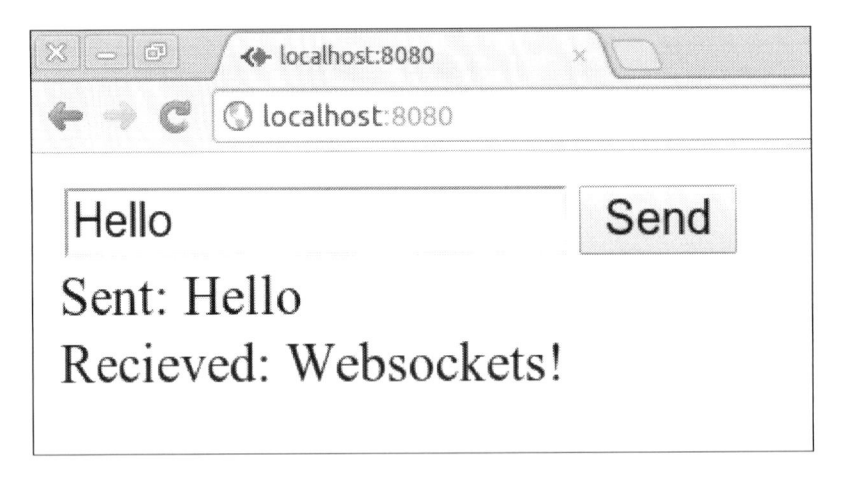

We can use our textbox to send any string we like to our server, but only **Hello** will gain a response.

How it works...

In `server.js`, when we require the `ws` module's `Server` method, we load a constructor function into the `WSServer` variable (which is why we capitalized the first letter). We initialize `WSServer` using the `new` keyword and pass in an object that contains a `port` property set to `8080`.

WebSocket servers start out as HTTP servers, then the browser connects to the HTTP server and asks to upgrade; at this point, the WebSocket logic takes over. When we pass in the options object with `port:8080`, the WSServer constructor creates an HTTP server that listens on port `8080` and accepts WebSocket upgrade requests. We could alternatively supply our own HTTP server to the `server` property instead of providing the `port` property.

As soon as the `client.html` file is loaded in the browser and the inline script is executed, the WebSocket upgrade request is made to our server.

When the server receives this WebSocket upgrade request, `wss` emits a `connection` event that supplies `socket` as the first parameter of the `connection` callback. The `socket` parameter is an instance of `EventEmitter`; we use its `message` and `close` events.

For each message that is received from the client, `socket` emits a `message` event. This is where we log the received data and the client IP address to `console` and check whether the incoming message is `Hello`. If it is, we use the `socket.send` method to respond to the client with **WebSockets!**.

Finally, we listen for the `close` event to inform `console` that the connection has been terminated.

There's more...

WebSockets have so much potential for efficient low latency real-time web apps. Let's take a look at a WebSocket client outside of the browser and then further see how browser APIs can be wrapped in one of Node's fundamental paradigms: streams.

Creating a Node-based WebSocket client

The `ws` module also allows us to create a WebSocket client outside of the browser environment. We may wish to interface Node with a preexisting WebSocket server, which is primarily for browser clients. If not, we are better off creating a simple TCP server; refer to *Chapter 9, Integrating Network Paradigms*.

So let's implement the same functionality in the `client.html` file using Node. We'll create a new file in the same directory, calling it `client.js` as shown in the following code snippet:

```
var WebSocket = require('ws'),
  ws = new WebSocket("ws://localhost:8080");

process.stdin.resume();
process.stdin.setEncoding('utf8');

process.stdin.on('data', function (msg) {
  msg = msg.trim();
  ws.send(msg, console.log.bind(null, 'Sent:', msg));
});
```

```
ws.on('message', function (msg) {
  console.log('Recieved:', msg);
});

ws.on('close', function (code, desc) {
    console.log('Disconnected', code + '-' + desc);
});

ws.on('error', function (e) {
  console.log('Error:', e.code);
});
```

So we run `node server.js` in one terminal and `node client.js` in another; anything we enter into the STDIN of the `client.js` terminal will be sent to our `server.js` terminal. If we type `Hello` and press *Enter*, `client.js` will show the following output:

Sent: Hello

Received: WebSockets!

WebSocket streams

The `websocket-stream` module wraps a streaming interface around the WebSocket interface, both in the browser and Node (by wrapping the `ws` module's API). This allows us to handle WebSockets as streams both on the client and server, resulting in a familiar interface that can be piped into and through other streams.

> Streams are discussed extensively in *Chapter 5, Employing Streams*.

We'll need to install **Browserify** to package `websocket-stream` for browser use:

```
sudo npm -g install browserify
```

> Browserify is a tool that wraps some boilerplate around Node modules to supply an API in keeping with Node idioms. That is, it allows you to use `require` with modules in the browser. Refer to `browserify.org` for more information.

The preceding code will install Browserify as a system-wide executable, which we'll use shortly to package a Node module in a client-side JavaScript library.

We'll also need to install a few dependencies using the following command:

```
npm install ws request JSONStream websocket-stream
```

Once `websocket-stream` is installed, we can package it for browser use:

`browserify -r websocket-stream -o websocket-stream.js`

The `-r` flag allows us to specify modules we wish to have in the browser; the `-o` flag specifies the output file.

We're going to grab npm's registry document to get the last sequential ID. Then, we'll subtract 50 from the ID so that some historical changes will immediately begin to appear when we start piping the changes feed from npm through the `JSONStream` module into our WebSocket stream. We're going to handle the incoming stream with the WebSocket stream in the browser and output the streamed module IDs onto the UI element on our page, as shown in the following diagram:

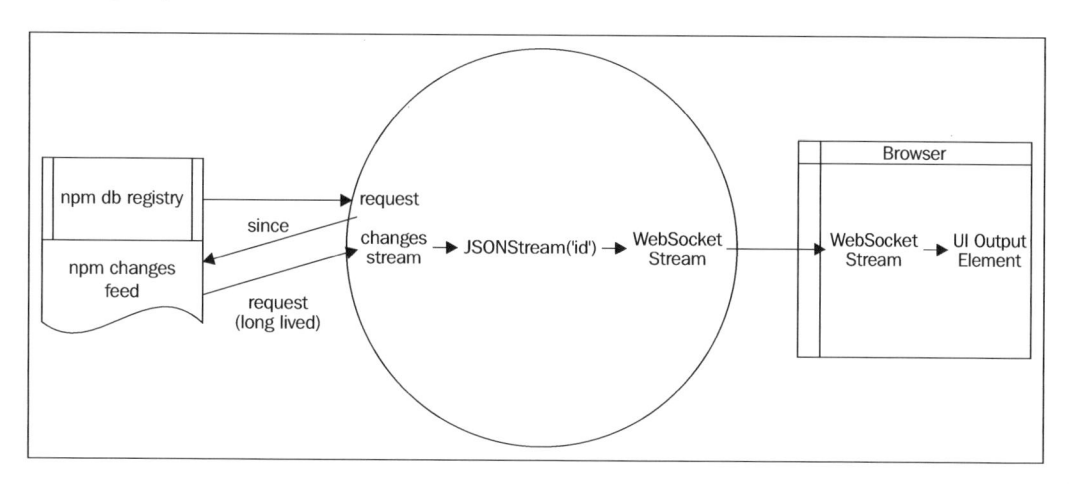

Now that we're all set, let's write the server code; we'll name this file `stream_server.js`:

```
var request = require('request'),
  JSONStream = require('JSONStream'),
  WSServer = require('ws').Server,
  stream = require('websocket-stream'),

  wss = new WSServer({port: 8080}),

  registry = 'http://skimdb.npmjs.com/registry',
  changes = '/_changes?heartbeat=20000&feed=continuous&since=';

wss.on('connection', function(socket) {

  request({url: registry, json:true}, function (err, res, doc) {
    if (err) { return console.log(err); }
```

Going Real Time

```
            var since = doc.committed_update_seq - 50,
              idStream = JSONStream.parse('id');

            request(registry + changes + since)
              .pipe(idStream)
              .pipe(stream(socket));

            socket.on('close', function () { idStream.destroy(); });

      });

    });
```

First, we use `require` with our modules and set up a WebSocket server such as `wss` (just like our main recipe). We also set up two other variables named `registry` and `changes`.

The `npm` command-line app interfaces with a CouchDB store; here, `registry` is the address of the store and `changes` is the path to the `_changes` document along with some parameters that induce a constantly updating feed. We will be streaming the changes feed to the client.

> CouchDB (and the changes feed) is discussed at length in *Chapter 4, Interfacing with Databases*.

The last parameter in the `changes` query string (`since`) does not have a value. This is because we have to ask the CouchDB store for the latest sequence number before we can determine a sensible point to begin streaming changes from.

> With CouchDB 1.3.0, it is possible to supply `since=now` to simply stream from the last change; however, even though the npm CouchDB store is Version 1.3.0r2, it still doesn't seem to support the `now` value (at the time of writing this). Additionally, getting the latest sequence number allows you to load the same number of recent changes by setting `since` to a reasonable subtraction from the latest sequence number.

Whenever our server receives a WebSocket connection, it first makes a request to the registry URL. To do this, we use the `request` module, which we've chosen primarily because it provides a stream interface that can be piped through to the `websocket-stream` interface—we do the piping once a sequence number has been determined.

> The `request` module provides some convenient syntactic sugar on top of Node's core HTTP module's client interfaces (of note is the returning of stream objects). Refer to `https://github.com/mikeal/request` for more information.

The options object passed to `request` has `url` and `json` properties. We set `json` to `true` to ensure that the third parameter of the callback that is passed to `request` (the `doc` argument, which could also be accessed under `res.body`) has been run through `JSON.parse` so that it is ready for us to access as an object.

In our request callback, we use `doc.committed_update_seq` to grab the latest sequence ID in the `npm` CouchDB store, subtract 50 from it, and save it to a variable (`since`).

Having determined a recent starting point, we make the second request and this time to the actual changes feed. We pipe the changes feed to a through-stream (a stream that's both readable and writable) that is generated using `JSONStream`.

This `JSONStream.parse('id')` call takes a stream of JSON, and emits only the values of properties named `id`. We're looking for `id` properties because the changes feed is a line-separated stream of JSON objects that contains `seq`, `id`, and `changes` properties. The `id` property in the context of `npm` is the name of a module that is currently being created or updated via `npm`.

> The `JSONStream` module parses a stream of JSON (string) data and emits JavaScript objects while it's being streamed and parsed. Visit https://github.com/dominictarr/JSONStream for more information.

The `id` attributes emitted from `JSONStream` through the stream parser are piped into `stream(socket)`. When we call `stream`, which is the variable we loaded the `websocket-stream` module into, and pass it the connections `socket`, we wrap the WebSocket connection in a stream interface. This allows other streams to `pipe` directly to a WebSocket client.

So let's quickly create our browser client too; we'll call this file `stream_client.html`:

```
<textarea id='cs' cols=50 rows=20></textarea>
<script src=websocket-stream.js></script>
<script>
  (function () {
    var websocket = require('websocket-stream'),
        ws = websocket('ws://localhost:8080'),
        cs = document.getElementById('cs');

    ws.on('data', function (module) {
      cs.value += module + ' was created/updated\n';
      cs.scrollTop = cs.scrollHeight;
    });
    ws.on('end', function () {
      cs.value = 'disconnected';
    });
  }())
</script>
```

Going Real Time

So we have a `textarea` element with an `id` of `cs` (for changes stream); this provides us with a basic view into the stream data.

We're also loading `websocket-stream.js`, which we generated earlier using `browserify`. Then, in our inline code, we use `require` for the `websocket-stream` module (just like in Node—thanks to Browserify) and set up a WebSocket stream (`ws`) pointed to our server. Then, we get a handle for our `textarea` element (the `cs` variable).

Remember, `ws` is a stream, and we're piping it from the server. We listen for its data event to capture each of the module names being piped to us from the server. We add this module name to the `textarea` element with some supplementary text, and set the `scrollTop` attribute of `textarea` to make sure we'll always be able to see the latest information in `textarea` by keeping the scroll position at the bottom of the text area.

In the `end` event, we simply set the value of the `textarea` element to `'disconnected'`.

If we fire up our `stream_server.js` script and load the `stream_client.html` file in our browser. After a short pause, we should have a live feed of `npm` changes.

> Depending on the time of the day, there can be long gaps between updates. If we want to trigger a `change` event, we could always publish/update our own module; see *Chapter 10, Writing Your Own Modules*, for details.

See also

- The *Cross-browser real-time logic with Socket.IO* recipe
- *Chapter 5, Employing Streams*
- The *Serving static files* recipe discussed in *Chapter 1, Making a Web Server*

Cross-browser real-time logic with Socket.IO

Older browsers don't support WebSockets. In order to provide a similar experience in these browsers, we have to use techniques such as long polling, using the Flash plugin sockets, or proprietary browser-specific options such as ActiveX in Internet Explorer.

Naturally, this is a mine field, requiring hours of browser testing and in some cases highly specific knowledge of proprietary protocols (for example, IE's Active X htmlfile object).

Socket.IO (via the `engine.io` module) provides a WebSocket-like API to the server and client to create the best-case real-time experience across a wide variety of browsers, including old (IE 5.5+) and mobile (iOS Safari and Android) browsers.

> The `engine.io` module has been logically extracted and refactored out from Socket.IO Version 0.9. The `engine.io` module is different in its approach; it uses enhancement instead of degradation. In the original `socket.io`, connections would fallback to the best available method (degradation). This could take a long time (up to 20 seconds), so the `engine.io` module addresses this by starting with the lowest common denominator (long polling) and upgrading to better methods (such as WebSockets) if they are available (enhancement). Generally, we wouldn't use the `engine.io` module directly because in almost every case, we'd want the connection management facilities afforded by Socket.IO. For more information, refer to https://github.com/LearnBoost/engine.io.

In this recipe, we will reimplement the previous task for a highly compatible WebSocket-type application.

> From version 1.0, the `socket.io` module is a simple layer on top of `engine.io` that provides advanced real-time logic such as connection discovery, allowing auto reconnects, custom events, and namespacing. In the next recipe, we'll look into using Socket.IO as an extensive framework for real-time apps. For more information, refer to https://github.com/LearnBoost/socket.io and http://socket.io.

Getting ready

We'll create a new folder with the new `client.html` and `server.js` files. We'll also install the `engine.io` module using the following command:

```
npm install socket.io
```

How to do it...

Like the `websocket` module, `socket.io` can be attached to an HTTP server (though it isn't a necessity with `socket.io`). Let's create the HTTP server and load the `client.html` file. In the `server.js` file, we write the following code:

```
var http = require('http');
var clientHtml = require('fs').readFileSync('client.html');

var plainHttpServer = http.createServer(function (request,
  response) {
    response.writeHead(200, {'Content-type' : 'text/html'});
    response.end(clientHtml);
}).listen(8080);
```

Going Real Time

Now for the `socket.io` part (still in `server.js`), we use the following code:

```
var io = require('socket.io').listen(plainHttpServer);

io.sockets.on('connection', function (socket) {
  socket.on('message', function (msg) {
    if (msg === 'Hello') {
      socket.send('socket.io!');
    }
  });
});
```

Now that the server is set up, let's create our `client.html` file:

```
<html>
<head>
</head>
<body>
<input id=msg><button id=send>Send</button>
<div id=output></div>

<script src="/socket.io/socket.io.js"></script>
<script>
(function () {
  var socket = io.connect('ws://localhost:8080'),
    output = document.getElementById('output'),
    send = document.getElementById('send');

  function logStr(eventStr, msg) {
    return '<div>' + eventStr + ': ' + msg + '</div>';
  }
  socket.on('connect', function () {
    send.addEventListener('click', function () {
      var msg = document.getElementById('msg').value;
      socket.send(msg);
      output.innerHTML += logStr('Sent', msg);
    });

    socket.on('message', function (msg) {
      output.innerHTML += logStr('Recieved', msg);
    });

  });

}());
```

```
            </script>
          </body>
        </html>
```

The final product is essentially the same as in the previous recipe, except that it will also work seamlessly in older browsers that aren't compatible with WebSocket. We type `Hello`, click on the **Send** button, and the server displays **socket.io!**.

How it works...

Instead of passing the HTTP server in an options object, we simply pass it to a `listen` method.

Next, we listen for the connection event on `io.sockets` that provides us with a socket to the client (much like `request.accept` that generates our WebSocket connection in the previous recipe).

Inside `connection`, we listen for the `message` event on the socket, checking that the incoming `msg` is `Hello`. If it is, we respond with **socket.io!**.

When `socket.io` is initialized, it begins to serve the client-side code over HTTP. So in our `client.html` file, we load the `socket.io.js` client script from `/socket.io/socket.io.js`.

The client-side `socket.io.js` provides a global `io` object. By calling its `connect` method with our server's address, we acquire the relevant socket.

We send our `Hello` msg to the server and use the `#output div` element to provide the UI with feedback indicating that we're done.

When the server receives the message `Hello`, it replies to **socket.io!**, which triggers our `message` event callback on the client side.

Now we have the `msg` parameter (different to our `msg Hello` variable) that contains the message from the server, so we output it to our `#output div` element.

There's more...

Let's explore some additional functionality of `socket.io`.

Custom events

The `socket.io` module allows us to define our own events, other than `message`, `connect`, and `disconnect`. We listen to custom events in the same fashion (using `on`) but initiate them using the `emit` method.

Let's use `emit` for a custom event from the server to the client and then have the client respond by emitting another custom event back to the server.

Going Real Time

We can use the same code as in our recipe; the only parts we'll change are the contents of the `connection` event listener callback in `server.js` (which we'll copy as `custom_events_server.js`) and the `connect` event handler in the `client.html` file (which we'll copy as `custom_events_client.html`).

So, for our server code, we will use the following snippet:

```
//require http, load client.html, create plainHttpServer
//require and initialize socket.io, set origin rules

io.sockets.on('connection', function (socket) {
  socket.emit('hello', 'socket.io!');
  socket.on('hollaback', function (from) {
    console.log('Received a hollaback from ' + from);
  });
});
```

Our server emits a `hello` event that will display **socket.io!** to the newly connected client and listens out for a `hollaback` event from the client.

So we modify the JavaScript in the `custom_events_client.html` file accordingly as shown in the following code:

```
//html structure, #output div, script[src=/socket.io/socket.io.js] tag
socket.on('connect', function () {
  socket.on('hello', function (msg) {
    output.innerHTML += '<div>Hello ' + msg + '</div>';
    socket.emit('hollaback', 'the client');
  });
});
```

When we receive a `hello` event, we log in to our `#output div` element (which will say **Hello socket.io!**) and use `emit` with a `hollaback` event to the server, supplying a string (`the client`) as the second argument of `emit`. This will come through as the `from` parameter in the server's `hollaback` listener callback function.

See also

- The *Creating a WebSocket server* recipe discussed
- The *Remote Procedure Calls with Socket.IO* recipe
- The *Creating a real-time widget* recipe

Chapter 6

Remote Procedure Calls with Socket.IO

With `socket.io`, we can execute a callback function over WebSockets (or a relevant alternative). The function is defined client side, yet called server side (and vice versa). This can be a very powerful way to share processing resources and functionalities between clients and servers—it's called **Remote Procedure Calls** (**RPC**).

In this recipe, we'll create a way for the server to call a client-side function that squares a number, and for the client to call a server-side function that sends a Base64 encoded (http://en.wikipedia.org/wiki/Base64) sentence back to the client.

Getting ready

We simply need to create a new folder with the new `client.html` and `server.js` files.

How to do it...

On our server, as before, we load our `http` module and the `client.html` file, create our HTTP server, and attach `socket.io`. Refer to the following code:

```
var http = require('http');
var clientHtml = require('fs').readFileSync('client.html');

var plainHttpServer = http.createServer(function (request,
  response) {
    response.writeHead(200, {'Content-type' : 'text/html'});
    response.end(clientHtml);
}).listen(8080);

var io = require('socket.io').listen(plainHttpServer);
```

Next, in our `connection` event handler, we listen for the custom event `give me a number` from the client, and use `emit` with a custom event `give me a sentence` from the server, as shown in the following code:

```
io.sockets.on('connection', function (socket) {

  socket.on('give me a number', function (cb) {
    cb(4);
  });

  socket.emit('give me a sentence', function (sentence) {
    socket.send(Buffer(sentence).toString('base64'));
  });

});
```

Going Real Time

In our `client.html` file, we write the following code:

```html
<html>
<head> </head>
<body>
<div id=output></div>
<script src="/socket.io/socket.io.js"></script>
<script>
  var socket = io.connect('http://localhost:8080'),
      output = document.getElementById('output');

  function square(num) {
    output.innerHTML = "<div>" + num + " x " + num + " is "
        + (num * num) + "</div>";
  }

  socket.on('connect', function () {
    socket.emit('give me a number', square);

    socket.on('give me a sentence', function (cb) {
      cb('Ok, here is a sentence.');
    });

    socket.on('message', function (msg) {
      output.innerHTML += '<div>Recieved: ' + msg + '</div>';
    });
  });

</script>
</body>
</html>
```

How it works...

Immediately upon connection, both the server and client `emit` a custom `socket.io` event to each other.

> For custom `socket.io` events, see the *There's more...* section of the previous recipe, *Cross-browser real-time logic with Socket.IO*.

For both the client and server, when we pass a function as the second parameter of `emit`, `socket.io` creates a special parameter (`cb`) in the corresponding event listener's callback. The `cb` parameter is not, in this case, the actual function (if it was, it would simply run in the context from which it was called), but an internal `socket.io` function that passes the arguments back to the `emit` method on the other side of the wire. The `emit` method then passes these arguments into its callback, thus executing the function in a local context.

We know that functions run in their own context. If the server-side `give me a sentence` callback was executed on the client, it would fail because there is no `Buffer` object in browsers. If the `give me a number` callback is executed on the server, it would fail since there is no **Document Object Model** (**DOM**) in Node (that is, there is no HTML, hence no document object and no `document.getElementById` method).

There's more...

Let's take a look at an alternative to Socket.IO.

Remote Procedure Calls with SockJS

SockJS is a slimmer multitransport real-time framework with a client-side API that more closely resembles the standards-based WebSocket API. It has less features, but it may be better in cases where prototyping was performed with normal WebSockets and additional features aren't required.

It has a disadvantage compared to Socket.IO Version 1.0 and above in that it still (at the time of writing) uses the fallback approach (trying WebSockets first then degrading to other transport) instead of the upgrade approach (starting with the most supported transport (long polling) and enhancing the connection to WebSockets).

Let's reimplement our recipe with SockJS. First things first, we need to install the `sockjs` module using the following command:

```
npm install sockjs
```

For our client side, we can simply take the code written from the first recipe in this chapter, *Creating a WebSocket server*, and change two lines in it. The first is the script reference. SockJS recommends linking to cdn so we change our `script` loading code to the following line:

```
<script src="http://cdn.sockjs.org/sockjs-0.3.min.js"></script>
```

Then, refer to the following line:

```
var ws = new WebSocket("ws://localhost:8080"),
```

Change it to its SockJS version:

```
var ws = new SockJS("http://localhost:8080/sock"),
```

Let's save this code as `sockjs_client.html`. This is very similar to creating a new WebSocket with a few differences. So we have a `SockJS` constructor instead of a `WebSocket` constructor, we're using the `http://` protocol instead of `ws://`, and we have to point to a route (in this case, `/sock`). We point to a route because a SockJS server is primarily an HTTP server. We can't serve our client-side HTML and provide a SockJS connection from the same URL. With pure WebSockets, however, the two separate protocols are equivalent to two separate roots.

Going Real Time

The rest of our client code can stay the same because SockJS supplies the same API as WebSockets. Now, let's write the code for our server by taking our Socket.IO server from the *Cross-browser real-time logic with Socket.IO* recipe and make some minor changes to it, as shown in the following code:

```
var http = require('http');
var clientHtml = require('fs').readFileSync('sockjs_client.html');

var plainHttpServer = http.createServer(function (req, res) {
    res.writeHead(200, {'Content-type' : 'text/html'});
    res.end(clientHtml);
}).listen(8080);

var sockServer = require('sockjs').listen(plainHttpServer,
    {prefix: '/sock'});

sockServer.on('connection', function (socket) {
  socket.on('data', function (msg) {
    if (msg === 'Hello') {
      socket.write('SockJS!');
    }
  });
});
```

First, we make sure we load the `sockjs_client.html` file instead of `client.html`. We change the `io` variable to `sockServer` for semantic purposes, and when we use `listen`, we pass in an extra options object with a `prefix` property set to `/sock` (because SockJS needs to host its client from a separate route).

On the socket, we listen for data events instead of message events (`socket.io` message events simply mirror data events; listening to a data event would work in `socket.io` as well). Instead of `socket.send` (another `socket.io` abstraction), we use `socket.write`. We'll save this as `sockjs_server.js`. Now if we start our server and navigate to `http://localhost:8080`, type `Hello`, and click on the **Send** button, we'll get a **Hello SockJS!** response.

See also

- The *Cross-browser real-time logic with Socket.IO* recipe
- The *Creating a real-time widget* recipe
- The *Browser-server transmission via AJAX* recipe discussed in *Chapter 3, Working with Data Serialization*

Chapter 6

Creating a real-time widget

The configuration options and well thought out methods of `socket.io` make for a highly versatile library. Let's explore the dexterity of `socket.io` by creating a real-time widget that can be placed on any website and instantly interfacing it with a remote Socket.IO server. We're doing this to begin providing a constantly updated total of all users currently on the site. We'll name it the live online counter (`loc` for short).

Our widget is for public consumption and should require only basic knowledge, so we want a very simple interface. Loading our widget through a `script` tag and then initializing the widget with a prefabricated `init` method would be ideal (this allows us to predefine properties before initialization if necessary).

Getting ready

We'll need to create a new folder with some new files: `widget_server.js`, `widget_client.js`, `server.js`, and `index.html`.

How to do it...

Let's create the `index.html` file to define the kind of interface we want as follows:

```
<html>
<head>
<style>
#_loc {color:blue;} /* widget customization */
</style>
</head>
<body>
<h1> My Web Page </h1>
<script src=http://localhost:8081></script>
<script> locWidget.init(); </script>
</body>
</html>
```

The `localhost:8081` domain is where we'll be serving a concatenated script of both the client-side `socket.io` code and our own widget code.

> By default, Socket.IO hosts its client-side library over HTTP while simultaneously providing a WebSocket server at the same address, in this case `localhost:8081`. See the *There's more...* section for tips on how to configure this behavior.

Going Real Time

Let's create our widget code, saving it as `widget_client.js`:

```javascript
;(function () {
  window.locWidget = {
    style : 'position:absolute;bottom:0;right:0;font-size:3em',
    init : function () {
      var socket = io.connect('http://localhost:8081'),
        style = this.style;
      socket.on('connect', function () {
        var head = document.head,
          body = document.body,
          loc = document.getElementById('_loc_count');
        if (!loc) {
          head.innerHTML += '<style>#_loc{' + style + '}</style>';

          loc = document.createElement('div');
          loc.id = '_loc';
          loc.innerHTML = '<span id=_loc_count></span>';
          body.appendChild(loc);

        }

        socket.on('total', function (total) {
          loc.innerHTML = total;
        });
      });
    }
  }
}());
```

We need to test our widget from multiple domains. We'll just implement a quick HTTP server (`server.js`) to serve `index.html` so we can access it by `http://127.0.0.1:8080` and `http://localhost:8080`, as shown in the following code:

```javascript
var http = require('http');
var fs = require('fs');
var clientHtml = fs.readFileSync('index.html');

http.createServer(function (request, response) {
    response.writeHead(200, {'Content-type' : 'text/html'});
    response.end(clientHtml);
}).listen(8080);
```

Finally, for the server for our widget, we write the following code in the `widget_server.js` file:

```javascript
var io = require('socket.io')(),
  totals = {},
  clientScript = Buffer.concat([
    require('socket.io/node_modules/socket.io-client').source,
    require('fs').readFileSync('widget_client.js')
  ]);

io.static(false);

io.attach(require('http').createServer(function(req, res){
  res.setHeader('Content-Type', 'text/javascript; charset=utf-8');
  res.write(sioclient.source);
  res.write(widgetScript);
  res.end();
}).listen(8081));

io.on('connection', function (socket) {
  var origin = socket.request.socket.domain || 'local';

  totals[origin] = totals[origin] || 0;
  totals[origin] += 1;

  socket.join(origin);

  io.sockets.to(origin).emit('total', totals[origin]);

  socket.on('disconnect', function () {
    totals[origin] -= 1;
    io.sockets.to(origin).emit('total', totals[origin]);
  });
});
```

To test it, we need two terminals; in the first one, we execute the following command:

node widget_server.js

In the other terminal, we execute the following command:

node server.js

We point our browser to `http://localhost:8080` by opening a new tab or window and navigating to `http://localhost:8080`. Again, we will see the counter rise by one. If we close either window, it will drop by one. We can also navigate to `http://127.0.0.1:8080` to emulate a separate origin. The counter at this address is independent from the counter at `http://localhost:8080`.

Going Real Time

How it works...

The `widget_server.js` file is the powerhouse of this recipe. We start by using `require` with `socket.io` and calling it (note the empty parentheses following `require`); this becomes our `io` instance. Under this is our `totals` object; we'll be using this later to store the total number of connected clients for each domain.

Next, we create our `clientScript` variable; it contains both the `socket.io` client code and our `widget_client.js` code. We'll be serving this to all HTTP requests. Both scripts are stored as buffers, not strings. We could simply concatenate them with the plus (+) operator; however, this would force a string conversion first, so we use `Buffer.concat` instead. Anything that is passed to `res.write` or `res.end` is converted to a `Buffer` before being sent across the wire. Using the `Buffer.concat` method means our data stays in buffer format the whole way through instead of being a buffer, then a string then a buffer again.

When we require `socket.io` at the top of `widget_server.js`, we call it to create an `io` instance. Usually, at this point, we would pass in an HTTP server instance or else a port number, and optionally pass in an options object.

To keep our top variables tidy, however, we use some configuration methods available on the `io` instance after all our requires. The `io.static(false)` call prevents `socket.io` from providing its client-side code (because we're providing our own concatenated script file that contains both the `socket.io` client-side code and our widget code).

Then we use the `io.attach` call to hook up our `socket.io` server with an HTTP server. All requests that use the `http://` protocol will be handled by the server we pass to `io.attach`, and all `ws://` protocols will be handled by `socket.io` (whether or not the browser supports the `ws://` protocol).

We're only using the `http` module once, so we require it within the `io.attach` call; we use it's `createServer` method to serve all requests with our `clientScript` variable.

Now, the stage is set for the actual socket action. We wait for a connection by listening for the `connection` event on `io.sockets`. Inside the event handler, we use a few as yet undiscussed `socket.io` qualities.

WebSocket is formed when a client initiates a handshake request over HTTP and the server responds affirmatively. We can access the original request object with `socket.request`. The request object itself has a socket (this is the underlying HTTP socket, not our `socket.io` socket; we can access this via `socket.request.socket`. The socket contains the domain a client request came from. We load `socket.request.socket.domain` into our `origin` object unless it's `null` or `undefined`, in which case we say the origin is `'local'`.

We extract (and simplify) the `origin` object because it allows us to distinguish between websites that use a widget, enabling site-specific counts.

To keep count, we use our `totals` object and add a property for every new `origin` object with an initial value of 0. On each connection, we add 1 to `totals[origin]` while listening to our `socket`; for the `disconnect` event, we subtract 1 from `totals[origin]`.

If these values were exclusively for server use, our solution would be complete. However, we need a way to communicate the total connections to the client, but on a site by site basis.

Socket.IO has had a handy new feature since Socket.IO version 0.7 that allows us to group sockets into rooms by using the `socket.join` method. We cause each socket to join a room named after its `origin`, then we use the `io.sockets.to(origin).emit` method to instruct `socket.io` to only emit to sockets that belongs to the originating `sites` room.

In both the `io.sockets connection` and `socket disconnect` events, we emit our specific totals to corresponding sockets to update each client with the total number of connections to the site the user is on.

The `widget_client.js` file simply creates a `div` element called `#_loc` and updates it with any new `totals` it receives from `widget_server.js`.

There's more...

Let's look at how our app could be made more scalable, as well as looking at another use for WebSockets.

Preparing for scalability

If we were to serve thousands of websites, we would need scalable memory storage, and Redis would be a perfect fit. It operates in memory but also allows us to scale across multiple servers.

> We'll need Redis installed along with the Redis module. For more information, refer to *Chapter 4, Interfacing with Databases*.

We'll alter our `totals` variable so it contains a Redis client instead of a JavaScript object:

```
var io = require('socket.io')(),
  totals = require('redis').createClient(),
  //other variables
```

Now, we modify our `connection` event handler as shown in the following code:

```
io.sockets.on('connection', function (socket) {
  var origin = (socket.handshake.xdomain)
    ? url.parse(socket.handshake.headers.origin).hostname
    : 'local';
  socket.join(origin);
```

```
    totals.incr(origin, function (err, total) {
      io.sockets.to(origin).emit('total', total);
    });
  });

  socket.on('disconnect', function () {
    totals.decr(origin, function (err, total) {
      io.sockets.to(origin).emit('total', total);
    });
  });
});
```

Instead of adding 1 to totals[origin], we use the Redis INCR command to increment a Redis key named after origin. Redis automatically creates the key if it doesn't exist. When a client disconnects, we do the reverse and readjust totals using DECR.

WebSockets as a development tool

When developing a website, we often change something small in our editor, upload our file (if necessary), refresh the browser, and wait to see the results. What if the browser would refresh automatically whenever we saved any file relevant to our site?

We can achieve this with the fs.watch method and WebSockets. The fs.watch method monitors a directory, executing a callback whenever a change to any files in the folder occurs (but it doesn't monitor subfolders).

> The fs.watch method is dependent on the operating system. To date, fs.watch has also been historically buggy (mostly under Mac OS X). Therefore, until further advancements, fs.watch is suited purely to development environments rather than production (you can monitor how fs.watch is doing by viewing the open and closed issues at https://github.com/joyent/node/search?q=fs.watch&ref=cmdform&state=open&type=Issues).

Our development tool could be used alongside any framework, from PHP to static files. For a general server, let's take the *Serving static files* recipe from *Chapter 1, Making a Web Server*, to test our tool. We'll copy the files (including the content folder) from that recipe into a new folder, which we can name watcher.

For the server counterpart of our tool, we'll configure watcher.js:

```
var io = require('socket.io')(),
  fs = require('fs'),
  totals = {},
  watcher = function () {
          var socket = io.connect('ws://localhost:8081');
          socket.on('update', function () {
```

```
            location.reload();
          });
        },
  clientScript = Buffer.concat([
    require('socket.io/node_modules/socket.io-client').source,
    Buffer(';(' + watcher + '());')
  ]);

  io.static(false);

  io.attach(require('http').createServer(function(req, res){
    res.setHeader('Content-Type', 'text/javascript; charset=utf-8');
    res.end(clientScript);
  }).listen(8081));

  fs.watch('content', function (e, f) {
    if (f[0] !== '.') {
      io.sockets.emit('update');
    }
  });
```

Most of this code is familiar. We make a `socket.io` server (on a different port to avoid clashing), generate a concatenated `socket.io.js` plus client-side `watcher` code file, and deliver it via our attached server. Since this is a quick tool for our own development uses, our client-side code is written as a normal JavaScript function (our `watcher` variable), converted to a string while wrapping it in self-calling function code, and then changed to `Buffer` so it's compatible with `Buffer.concat`.

The last piece of code calls the `fs.watch` method where the callback receives the event name (`e`) and the filename (`f`).

We check that the filename isn't a hidden dotfile. During a `save` event, some filesystems or editors will change the hidden files in the directory, thus triggering multiple callbacks and sending several messages at high speed, which can cause issues for the browser.

To use it, we simply place it as a script within every page that is served (probably using server-side templating). However, for demonstration purposes, we simply place the following code into `content/index.html`:

```
<script src=http://localhost:8081/socket.io/watcher.js></script>
```

Once we fire up `server.js` and `watcher.js`, we can point our browser to `http://localhost:8080` and see the familiar excited **Yay!** from *Chapter 1, Making a Web Server*. Any changes we make and save (either to `index.html`, `styles.css`, `script.js`, or the addition of new files) will be almost instantly reflected in the browser. The first change we can make is to get rid of the alert box in the `script.js` file so that the changes can be seen fluidly.

See also

- The *Creating a WebSocket server* recipe
- The *Cross-browser real-time logic with Socket.IO* recipe
- The *Storing and retrieving data with Redis* recipe discussed in *Chapter 4, Interfacing with Databases*

7
Accelerating Development with Express

In this chapter, we will cover the following topics:

- Generating Express scaffolding
- Managing server tier environments
- Implementing dynamic routing
- Templating in Express
- CSS preprocessors with Express
- Initializing and using a session
- Making an Express web app

Introduction

As excellent as Node's HTTP module is, Express repackages and streamlines its functionality to provide us with a fluid interface that makes for almost frictionless rapid web development.

In this chapter, we will progress from generating a vanilla Express project base to a full-fledged Express web-application foundation with MongoDB providing backend data support.

Generating Express scaffolding

Express works both as a Node module and as a command-line executable. The `express-generator` module (part of the Express project) provides an easy way to generate a project skeleton using its command-line tool (`express`).

Getting ready

We need to install `express-generator` using the `-g` flag (install globally) in order to run the subsequently installed `express` executable from any directory:

```
sudo npm -g install express-generator
```

We use `sudo` to ensure that we have appropriate permission to install globally. This doesn't apply with Windows or Mac OS X, so it should be run without `sudo`.

How to do it...

First, we decide upon the name of our app. Let's call it `nca` (Node Cookbook App) and simply run the following command:

```
express nca
```

The preceding command will generate all of our project files under a new directory called `nca`. Before we can run our app, we must ensure that all dependencies are installed. We can find app dependencies at `nca/package.json`. The `package.json` file contains the following code:

```
{
  "name": "application-name",
  "version": "0.0.1",
  "private": true,
  "scripts": {
    "start": "node ./bin/www"
  },
  "dependencies": {
    "express": "~4.0.0",
    "static-favicon": "~1.0.0",
    "morgan": "~1.0.0",
    "cookie-parser": "~1.0.1",
    "body-parser": "~1.0.0",
    "debug": "~0.7.4",
    "jade": "~1.3.0"
  }
}
```

For portability, it's important to have relevant modules installed within the `project` folder. To achieve this, we simply use the command line to change directory (cd) into the `nca` directory and then type the following command:

```
npm install
```

This will create a new `node_modules` directory in our project folder, holding all dependencies.

How it works...

When we run the `express` executable, it creates a folder structure that's suited to Express development. In the `project` root, we have the `app.js` and `package.json` files.

The `package.json` file is a convention established by the CommonJS group (a JavaScript standards community) and has become the established method to describe modules and applications in Node.

The `npm install` command parses the dependencies from `package.json`, installing them locally in the `node_modules` folder.

This is significant because it ensures stability. Node's `require` function looks for the `node_modules` folder in the current working directory before searching for the parent directories. If we upgrade any module in a parent directory, our project will continue to use the same version it was built upon. Installing modules locally allows us to distribute our project along with its dependencies.

The `app.js` files contain the boilerplate for the web app; we'll look at this in closer detail in the following recipes. The `express` executable adds four subdirectories to the project folder: `public`, `routes`, `views`, and `bin`.

In the `package.json` file, the `scripts` object contains a `start` property that points to `./bin/www`. The `www` file initializes our app, listening (by default) on port `3000`. We start our express app with the following command:

```
npm start
```

> The `./bin/www` file contains a hashbang in the form: `#!/usr/bin/env node`.
>
> This allows `www` to also be executed independently. Alternately, we could start our app by running `./bin/www` directly. However, preferred convention is to use `npm start`; in this case, we have no reliance on the actual location or name of the initialization script.

The `public` folder is the default folder that `app.js` passes to the `express.static` method. All of our static files go here. It contains `images`, `javascripts`, and `stylesheets` folders, each for their own self-evident purpose.

Accelerating Development with Express

The `routes` folder holds the `users.js` and `index.js` files and both are required by `app.js`. To define our routes, we push them onto Node's `exports` object (which we'll learn in detail in *Chapter 10, Writing Your Own Node Modules*). Compartmentalizing route logic into separate files in the `routes` directory helps to avoid clutter in `app.js`, dividing the server code from the route code. This way, we can focus purely on our server or on our routes.

Finally, `views` hold template files that can really help with development acceleration. We'll find out how to work with the views in the *Templating in Express* recipe.

There's more...

Let's take a few moments to go deeper into our generated project.

Picking apart app.js

Let's take a look at our generated `app.js` file:

```
var express = require('express');
var http = require('http');
var path = require('path');
var favicon = require('static-favicon');
var logger = require('morgan');
var cookieParser = require('cookie-parser');
var bodyParser = require('body-parser');

var routes = require('./routes/index');
var users = require('./routes/users');

var app = express();

// view engine setup
app.set('views', path.join(__dirname, 'views'));
app.set('view engine', 'jade');

app.use(favicon());
app.use(logger('dev'));
app.use(bodyParser.json());
app.use(bodyParser.urlencoded());
app.use(cookieParser());
app.use(express.static(path.join(__dirname, 'public')));

app.use('/', routes);
app.use('/users', users);

/// catch 404 and forwarding to error handler
```

```
app.use(function(req, res, next) {
    var err = new Error('Not Found');
    err.status = 404;
    next(err);
});

/// error handlers

// development error handler
// will print stacktrace
if (app.get('env') === 'development') {
    app.use(function(err, req, res, next) {
        res.render('error', {
            message: err.message,
            error: err
        });
    });
}

// production error handler
// no stacktraces leaked to user
app.use(function(err, req, res, next) {
    res.render('error', {
        message: err.message,
        error: {}
    });
});

module.exports = app;
```

The app.js file can be divided into five sections: **dependencies, app configuration, route setting, error handling**, and **export**.

In the top section (dependencies), express, http, path, static-favicon, morgan, cookie-parser, and body-parser modules are required, along with the two routes files, user and index.js. The express module is a function that supplies an app instance when called (this instance is stored in the app variable). The http module is required because to initialize an Express server, the Express app must be attached to an HTTP server. The path module is used twice for its join method—this for cross-operating system compatibility (for instance, in Windows, we would want a backslash, but in Linux and OS X, we would want a forward slash). The four modules required after path are Express middleware modules, which are later passed to app.use in the configuration section. The two routes files export methods that are later used in the routing section of app.js (for example, app.get).

The configuration section consists of the app.set (to configure settings) and app.use (to include middleware) calls.

> **Middleware**
>
> Middleware is a term brought into vogue in the Node community principally by the Connect and Express frameworks. In this context, middleware are simply functions (or in the case of `bodyParser`, submethods) that are called in sequence upon each request and are passed the `request` and `response` objects. Middleware can have various purposes, such as modifying the `request` object for easier access (such as parsing `POST` data into an object), answering certain requests (such as a favicon request), or simply observing incoming requests (such as a logger).

In the configuration section, the default view directory (`views`) and engine (`jade`) are set, and the app is told to use the `static-favicon` (`favicon`), `morgan` (`logger`), `body-parser` (`bodyParser`), `cookie-parser` (`cookieParser`), and `express.static` middleware.

The `static-favicon` middleware simply provides a valid (memory cached) favicon to requests that hit the `/favicon.ico` route. Placing this middleware first in the chain (and caching it in the memory) means that the favicon request is answered as quickly as possible. We can pass in a path to a custom favicon (`favicon('/my/favicon.ico')`) to override the default Express favicon image.

The `morgan` module is Connect's logging middleware. It's set to output development-level logging, even for production. This approach ensures new users know what's available to them, and after gaining experience, they can set the logging levels appropriately.

> Connect was a precursor to Express. The Express framework was originally built on top of Connect; nevertheless, Version 4 is independent of Connect, but still compatible with its middleware (as exemplified by the use of Connect's logger middleware, `morgan`). For more information on Connect, visit `http://www.senchalabs.org/connect`.

The `body-parser` middleware made a brief appearance in *Chapter 2, Exploring the HTTP Object*, in the *There's more...* section of the first recipe, used alongside Connect.

Middleware is generally constructed as is shown in the following code:

```
function (req, res, next) {
  //do stuff
  next();
}
```

The `next` parameter is a sort of a callback mechanism that loads any ensuing middleware. So the positioning of the routes in relation to other middleware is important. For instance, we want to be able to parse cookies before registering routes, but we can only catch `404` errors after it's known that no routes have been matched.

> Alternatively, `next` can be called as a method of `req`: `req.next()`. For more information on middleware, visit `http://www.expressjs.com/guide.html#middleware`.

So underneath the route section is the error-handling section; the first error handler is for `404` errors. As discussed, the positioning of this middleware is important; it will only be reached in two scenarios. The first and target scenario is if none of the routes match the requested. The second scenario is if a matched route doesn't use `res.render` and calls `next`.

The `404` handler generates a `Not Found` error, sets the response status code to `404`, and calls `next`, passing the generated `err` object into it. If the app happens to be in a development environment, the development error handler will render the error to the browser with a stack trace, and no further middleware will be executed because the handler doesn't call `next`.

If we're in a production environment, development logic will be skipped and the production error handler responds accordingly. In the next recipe, we'll be taking a closer look at Express' use of environments. Additionally, any time we call `next` and pass it an error object (that is, one created with the native JavaScript Error constructor), it will be passed through and handled by whichever error handler is relevant (either production or development).

The final section of `app.js` assigns our app to `module.exports`, which allows the `./bin/www` script to load and then initialize our app.

The initialization process

Let's take a look at the `./bin/www` file:

```
#!/usr/bin/env node
var debug = require('debug')('my-application');
var app = require('../app');

app.set('port', process.env.PORT || 3000);

var server = app.listen(app.get('port'), function() {
  debug('Express server listening on port ' + server.address().port);
});
```

The hashbang at the top allows the www file to be executed directly. The best convention, however, would be to use `npm start` to spin up our app.

The `debug` module is used internally across Express and is responsible for the terminal debug output of a running Express app. The `debug` module is a function, calling it with a string as its argument returns a composed function that will return any output passed to it, prefixed by the original string passed to the `debug` module (in this case, `'my-application'`). Our app is required on the line below `debug`. The port is then set on it using either an environmental variable (`PORT`) or defaulting to `3000`.

Accelerating Development with Express

Finally, `listen` is called on the `app`. Once the app has begun listening, the `debug` function is called to output this fact along with the port.

Looking into routes/index.js

In `app.js`, `routes/index.js` is loaded with `require`:

```
var routes = require('./routes/index');
```

Note that the `.js` extension isn't specified, but if a valid module is passed to `require` without its extension, Node will load it just fine. Let's take a look at the following code:

```
var express = require('express');
var router = express.Router();

/* GET home page. */
router.get('/', function(req, res) {
  res.render('index', { title: 'Express' });
});
module.exports = router;
```

The `express.Router()` returns a new router instance (no need to call `new` on this pseudo-constructor). The router instance is essentially a limited version of the object returned from calling `express` (as saved to the app variable in our `app.js` file). It has a subset of router-specific functionality available on app, notably the `use` and verb methods (`get`, `put`, `post`, and `del`). We'll learn more about this in later recipes.

Pushing `router` onto the `exports` object makes any defined route available in `app.js` as `routes`, which is passed to `app.use` as follows:

```
app.use('/', routes);
```

The second argument of `router.get` (the callback function) should look familiar. It follows the pattern of an `http.createServer` callback but is specific to the route. The request (`req`) and response (`res`) parameters are enhanced by Express. We'll look into these in the coming recipes. The function itself simply calls the `res.render` method, which loads a template from `views/index.jade`, passing `title` as a variable, which then outputs the generated content to the client.

See also

- The *Managing server tier environments* recipe
- The *Implementing dynamic routing* recipe
- The *Templating in Express* recipe

Managing server tier environments

An application can go through multiple stages throughout its life cycle—two of the most common stages would be development and production. Specific configurations can be set up to host the app in its various stages. These configured habitats are known as server tiers or environments.

Development and production codes have different requirements. For instance, during development we will most likely want a detailed error output to the client, for debugging purposes. In production, we protect ourselves from opportunistic exploitation by revealing as little internal information as possible.

Express has an env setting that determines its value from an operating system environment variable, NODE_ENV, falling back to the value of 'development' if NODE_ENV isn't set. This allows us to define different settings for different environments within our app.

Getting ready

We'll need our project folder (nca) from the previous recipe.

How to do it...

Let's take a look at the default use of app.get('env') in the generated app.js file:

```
if (app.get('env') === 'development') {
    app.use(function(err, req, res, next) {
        res.render('error', {
            message: err.message,
            error: err
        });
    });
}
```

> The app.get method as used here supplies different functionality compared to router.get. The app.get method in this context is a simple getter; it's the counterpart to app.set. Its functionality is determined by the arguments passed to it. However, if app.get is passed a route and a function, it will behave in the same way as router.get. That is, Express will answer all GET requests to a route with the supplied function.

When the tier is set to development, middleware is inserted into the middleware stack via app.use. Route logic will only get as far as this piece of middleware in the event of an error.

Accelerating Development with Express

In the last recipe, we saw that the generated `app.js` file includes a logger with the logging level set to `'dev'`, which causes the logger to supply colored output to the terminal. In a production environment, it would be better to log to a file.

To achieve this, we'll have to perform some minor refactoring as shown in the following code:

```
//...snip...
var app = express(),
    dev = app.get('env') === 'development';

// view engine setup
app.set('views', path.join(__dirname, 'views'));
app.set('view engine', 'jade');

app.use(favicon());
app.use(logger(dev ? 'dev' : {
  stream: require('fs').createWriteStream('log')
}));

//..snip (rest of the configuration section) ...snip...

/// error handlers

// development error handler
// will print stacktrace
if (dev) {
    app.use(function(err, req, res, next) {
        res.render('error', {
            message: err.message,
            error: err
        });
    });
}
//...snip...
```

To use an environment, we set the special NODE_ENV variable on the command line as we are executing node:

NODE_ENV=production node app.js

On Windows, we use the following command:

set NODE_ENV=production

node app.js

The `development` environment is default, so there's no need to use NODE_ENV to set it.

> Of course, we could set NODE_ENV to anything other than `development` and our alterations would work, since we're only checking if the environment is not `development`.

How it works...

Under the hood, `app.get` will be using `process.env.NODE_ENV` to determine the NODE_ENV variable, checking for a match against any defined environments. If NODE_ENV isn't set, `app.get` falls back to the `development` environment.

When we set up a `dev` variable, we're only interested in checking whether we're dealing with a `development` environment or something else, so it simply resolves to a Boolean based on whether `app.get('env')` returns `'development'`.

So we use our `dev` Boolean to start a ternary expression (shorthand conditional). If `dev` is `true`, we supply the string `'dev'` (the default logging behavior). If `dev` is `false`, we supply an object to `logger`. The object contains a `stream` property that supplies a `writeStream` to a file called `log`. So in any environment other than development, the server will pass all log information to the logfile.

Finally, since we've already determined whether we're in a development environment, there's no need to check `app.get('env')` again. So we replace the conditional check `if ('development' == app.get('env'))` with `if (dev)`.

There's more...

Let's look into some of the ways we can manage our environments.

Setting other environments

We could have other phases in our work flow that would benefit from specific settings. For instance, we may have a staging phase where we emulate as much of the production environment as possible on the development machine for the purpose of testing.

For example, if our production server requires us to run the process on a specific port (say port 80), which we cannot access on our development server (if we do not have root privileges, for instance), we could add a staging environment and set a `port` variable that is only set to 80 in a production environment.

> See *Chapter 11, Taking It Live*, for information on how to safely run Node on port 80.

Accelerating Development with Express

Let's modify the top part of the configuration section as shown in the following code:

```
var app = express(),
    env = app.get('env'),
    dev = env === 'development'
    prd = env === 'production';

process.env.PORT = process.env.PORT || (prd ? 80 : 3000);
```

We defer to the `PORT` operating system environment variable if it is set, enabling this functionality to be overridden if required. If `PORT` isn't set and it's a `production` environment, then we set `process.env.PORT` to `80` or fallback to port `3000`. When starting the app, `./bin/www` uses `process.env.PORT` to determine the port. The `./bin/www` file requires our `app.js` code, thus allowing `app.js` to modify the `PORT` environment variable if required.

So if we set `NODE_ENV` to anything other than `development` or `production` (for example, we could set it to `staging`), the app would be hosting on port `3000` but it would be logging the logfile instead of the console.

We could initialize our staging server with the following code:

NODE_ENV=staging npm start

For Windows, use the following commands:

set NODE_ENV=staging

npm start

This would not be a safe way to run a server, but for testing purposes on Mac OS X or Linux systems, we can try out the `production` environment using the following command:

sudo NODE_ENV=production npm start

On Windows, we simply use the following commands:

set NODE_ENV=production

npm start

> When attempting to run the server with `NODE_ENV` set to `production`, if we see an `EADDRINUSE` or an `EACCESS` error, it's likely that a service is already running on port `80`. We would need to stop this service in to test our code. For instance, if Apache is running on our system, it's probably hosting through port `80`. We can stop Apache with `sudo apachectl -k stop` (or `net stop apache2.2` on Windows).

Changing NODE_ENV permanently

If we are in a staging process, we may not wish to type `NODE_ENV=staging` every time we load our app. The same applies to production. While the server would be started a lot less, we would have to remember to set `NODE_ENV` when restarting.

We can make things easier on Unix-type systems (Linux or Max OS X) with the `export` shell command as follows:

```
export NODE_ENV=staging
```

This command only sets `NODE_ENV` while our terminal is open. To make it permanent, we add this line to our home directory's `rc` file. The `rc` file is named depending upon the shell. For bash, it's located at `~/.bashrc` (where `~` is the home folder). Other shells, such as `sh` and `ksh`, would have `rc` files located at `~/.shrc`, `~/.kshrc` and so on.

To permanently set `NODE_ENV`, we can use the following command:

```
echo -e "export NODE_ENV=staging\n" >> ~/.bashrc
```

Here `staging` is our desired environment and `bash` is our shell.

In Windows, we use `set` and `setx`:

```
set NODE_ENV=staging
```
```
setx NODE_ENV=staging
```

The `set` command takes immediate effect, but is lost once the command prompt is closed. The `setx` command persists the setting, but not until we open a new command prompt, so we use both.

See also

- The *Generating Express scaffolding* recipe
- The *Deploying to a server environment* recipe discussed in Chapter 11, *Taking It Live*
- The *Making an Express web app* recipe
- The *Initializing and using a session* recipe

Implementing dynamic routing

In the very first recipe of this cookbook, *Setting up a router*, we explored various ways to set up routing in Node. Express provides a far superior and very powerful routing interface, which we'll explore in this recipe.

Accelerating Development with Express

Getting ready

In this recipe, we'll work with our `nca` folder.

How to do it...

Let's say we want to add a page for a fictional character named "Mr Page." We'll name the route page, so in the routes section of `app.js`, we add the following code:

```
app.get('/page', function (req, res) {
  res.send('Hello I am Mr Page');
});
```

We can also define flexible routes and grab the requested route using `req.params` as shown in the following code:

```
app.get('/:page', function (req, res) {
  res.send('Welcome to the ' + req.params.page + ' page');
});
```

It's maybe okay to shove our callbacks directly into `app.get` while prototyping ideas, but in the interest of a clutter-free `app.js` let's take our callbacks and load them from `routes/index.js` as follows:

```
var express = require('express');
var router = express.Router();

/* GET home page. */
router.get('/', function(req, res) {
  res.render('index', { title: 'Express' });
});

router.get('/page', function (req, res) {
  res.send('Hello I am Mr Page');
});

router.get('/:page', function (req, res) {
  res.send('Welcome to the ' + req.params.page + ' page');
});

module.exports = router;
```

How it works...

We create the `/page` route using `router.get`. Then we outline how we wish to respond to that route in the callback of `router.get`. In our example, we use `res.send` (an enhanced `res.write`) to output simple text. This is our inflexible dynamic route.

Express also provides flexible route capabilities using placeholders. In the main recipe, we defined a `:page` placeholder. When the placeholder is filled in by a request (for example, `/anyPageYouLike`), the fulfillment of the placeholder is added to `req.params` according to its name. So in this case, `req.params.page` would hold `/anyPageYouLike`.

When a user loads `localhost:3000/page`, they see **Hello I am Mr Page**. When they access `localhost:3000/absolutelyAnythingElse`, they get the **Welcome to the absolutelyAnythingElse** page.

Essentially, the router is a piece of middleware, and every route we add to it decorates the middleware with extra functionality. The entire composed piece of route middleware is then integrated into the app by exporting it from the `routes/index.js` file, loading it into `app.js`, and finally passing it into `app.use`.

There's more...

What other things can we do with Express routes?

Route validation

We can restrict flexible routes to specific character ranges using pieces of Regular Expression syntax shown as follows (in `routes/index.js`):

```
router.get('/:page([a-zA-Z]+)', routes.anypage);
```

We pass a character match, `[a-zA-Z]` along with a plus (+). This will match the characters one or more times. As a result, we limit our `:page` parameter to letters only.

Therefore, `http://localhost:3000/moo` will give the **Welcome to the moo** page, whereas `http://localhost:3000/moo1` will return a `404` error.

Optional routes

We can also define optional routes using the question mark (?), so in `routes/index.js`, we use the following code:

```
router.get('/:page/:admin?', function (req, res) {
  var admin = req.params.admin
  if (admin) {
    if (['add','delete'].indexOf(admin) !== -1) {
      res.send('So you want to ' + req.params.admin + ' ' + req.params.page + '?');
      return;
    }
    res.send(404);
  }
});
```

Accelerating Development with Express

We check for the existence of the `:admin` placeholder. If a route fulfills it, we verify that it is allowed (either `add` or `delete`) and send a tailored response. If the route is not allowed, we send a `404` error.

While the query wildcard (`?`) can be appropriate for lots of similar routes, if we only had our `add` and `delete` routes and there was no possibility of adding more routes later, we could implement this functionality in a much cleaner way.

In `routes/index.js`, we could change the route expression to the following code:

```
router.get('/:page/:admin((add|delete))', function (req, res) {
  res.send('So you want to ' + req.params.admin + ' ' +
    req.params.page + '?');
});
```

So this would do exactly the same thing. A more specific route expression allows for a cleaner (though less powerful) handler function.

Asterisks wildcards

We can use asterisk (`*`) as a wildcard for general matching requirements. For instance, let's add the following route:

```
router.get('/:page/*', function (req, res) {

  var child = req.params[0],
    parent = child ? ' of the ' + req.params.page + ' page' : '';

    res.send('Welcome to the ' +
      (child || req.params.page) + ' page' + parent);

});
```

Now, if we access `localhost:3000/foo/bar`, we get the **Welcome to the bar page of the foo page**, but if we just access `localhost:3000/foo`, we see the **Welcome to the foo page**.

We could also get a little wild and apply this to Mr Page's route as follows (function masked with the snip comment for brevity):

```
router.get('/*page*', /*...snip...*/);
```

Now any route containing the word `page` will get a message from **Mr Page**.

See also

- The *Setting up a router* recipe discussed in *Chapter 1, Making a Web Server*
- The *Making an Express web app* recipe
- The *Templating in Express* recipe

Chapter 7

Templating in Express

A fundamental part of the Express framework is its use of views. A view is simply a file that holds template code. Express helps us to separate our code into operationally distinct concerns. We have server code in `app.js`, route-specific functionality in `routes/index.js`, and then we have our output-generating logic in the `views` folder. A template language provides the basis for defining dynamic logic-driven content, and the template (or view) engine converts our logic into the final HTML, which is served to the user. In this recipe, we'll use Express' default view engine, Jade, to process and present some data.

> In the *There's more...* section, we'll find out how to change the view engine.
>
> A list of supported template engines can be found at `https://www.github.com/visionmedia/express/wiki`. Comparisons of various template engines can be found at `http://paularmstrong.github.com/node-templates/`.

Getting ready

For our data, we'll use the `profiles.js` object created in the first recipe of *Chapter 3, Working with Data Serialization*. We'll need to copy it into the root of our `nca` folder.

How to do it...

Let's keep it simple and strip any routes we've added to `routes/index.js`. We just want our top-level route.

Since Jade is set as the default view engine, we don't need to work with `app.js` in this recipe.

In `routes/index.js`, we'll strip all routes except for index as shown in the following code:

```
router.get('/', function(req, res) {
    res.render('index', { title: 'Express' });
});
```

The `res.render` method loads the Jade template in `views/index.jade`. We're going to use `index.jade` as a view for our `profiles.js` object data, so we need to make it available to our `index` view.

We do this by passing it through the options object of `res.render`:

```
var express = require('express');
var router = express.Router();
var profiles = require('../profiles');

    router.get('/', function(req, res) {
```

```
        res.render('index', { title: 'Profiles',
            profiles: profiles });
});
module.exports = router;
```

Note that we also changed the `title` property to `'Profiles'`.

All we do now is edit `views/index.jade`. The generated `index.jade` file contains the following code:

```
extends layout

block content
  h1= title
  p Welcome to #{title}
```

We're going to add a table to the page that outputs the details of each person in the `profiles.js` object:

```
extends layout

block content

  h1= title
  p Welcome to #{title}

  table#profiles
    tr
      th Name
      th Irc
      th Twitter
      th Github
      th Location
      th Description
    each profile, id in profiles
      tr(id=id)
        each val in profile
          td #{val}
```

> **Off-side coding**
>
> Jade is an off-side (indentation-based) language. Indentation dictates scope, so in all the Jade (and Stylus) recipes ensuring the indentation is correct in our code is of paramount importance.

To test, we start our app using the following command:

`npm start`

Then navigate to `http://localhost:3000` to see something like the following output:

Profiles

Welcome to Profiles

Name	Irc	Twitter	Github	Location	Description
Ryan Dahl	ryah	ryah	ry	San Francisco, USA	Creator of node.js
Isaac Schlueter	isaacs	izs	isaacs	San Francisco, USA	Author of npm, core contributor
Bert Belder	piscisaureus	piscisaureus	piscisaureus	Netherlands	Windows support, overall contributor
TJ Holowaychuk	tjholowaychuk	tjholowaychuk	visionmedia	Victoria, BC, Canada	Author of express, jade and other popular modules
Felix Geisendorfer	felixge	felixge	felixge	Berlin, Germany	Author of formidable, active core developer

How it works...

The `res.render` method pulls the `index.jade` view from the `views` folder, even though the first parameter is simply `index`. Express knows that our intended Jade file is inside the `views` directory because `app.js` contains the following code:

```
app.set('views', __dirname + '/views');
app.set('view engine', 'jade');
```

The second parameter is an object holding two properties: `title` and `profiles`. These object properties become local variables within the Jade view. We output the variables either by `return` value buffering with a preceding equals (=) sign, or by using Jade's interpolation, wrapping it like #{title}.

Jade is a lean-templating language. It uses bracket-stripped markup tags and has an indentation-based syntax with an alternative block expansion option (where we use the colon instead of an indentation to signify nesting). It also has a minimal syntax set to define the `id` and `class` attributes using the hash (#) and dot (.), respectively.

For instance, refer to the following Jade:

```
table#profiles
    th Name
```

The preceding code would create the following HTML:

```
<table id=profiles><th>Name</th></table>
```

Accelerating Development with Express

> To learn more about the Jade language, check out its GitHub page: https://www.github.com/visionmedia/jade.

Jade also processes iteration logic. We used two Jade iterators each to pull the values from our profiles object as follows:

```
each profile, id in profiles
    tr(id=id)
        each val in profile
            td #{val}
```

This code traverses the `profiles` object, loading each ID (`ryan`, `isaac`, `timothy`, and so on) into a new `id` variable and each object containing profile information into a `profile` object variable.

Underneath our first `each` statement, we indent `tr(id=id)`. Unlike JavaScript, indentation in Jade is part of the logic, so getting it right is essential.

This tells Jade that for each profile we want to output a `<tr>` tag with the `id` attribute set to the ID of the `profile`. In this case, we don't use the hash (#) shorthand to set the `id` attribute since we need Jade to evaluate our `id` variable. The `tr#id` syntax would generate `<tr id=id>` for each profile, whereas `tr(id=id)` generates `<tr id=ryan>` or `isaac`, or `timothy`, and so forth.

Underneath `tr` we indent again, indicating that whatever comes next should be nested within the `<tr>` tags. Again, we use `each` to traverse the values of each sub-object, indenting beneath with a `td` that holds each value of the profile.

There's more...

Let's take a look at some of the other templating capabilities and features Express has to offer.

Using other template engines

Express supports various alternative template engines, and unsupported engines can be adapted to Express without excessive hassle.

The `express` executable will only generate Jade or EJS-based project scaffolding. To generate EJS, we simply pass `ejs` to the `-t` flag:

express -t ejs nca

Instead of generating an Express project with EJS as the default view engine, let's convert our existing project (we'll start by copying it to `nca_ejs`).

First, remove `jade` and install `ejs` as shown in the following commands:

npm uninstall jade --save

npm install ejs@~0.8.5 --save

The `--save` flag causes npm to remove the `jade` dependency and add the `ejs` dependency in `package.json` as shown in the following code:

```
{
  "name": "application-name",
  "version": "0.0.1",
  "private": true,
  "scripts": {
    "start": "node ./bin/www"
  },
  "dependencies": {
    "express": "~4.0.0-rc2",
    "static-favicon": "~1.0.0",
    "morgan": "~1.0.0",
    "cookie-parser": "~1.0.1",
    "body-parser": "~1.0.0",
    "debug": "~0.7.4",
    "ejs": "~0.8.5"
  }
}
```

Finally, we change our `view` engine as follows:

```
app.set('views', __dirname + '/views');
app.set('view engine', 'ejs');
```

This technique will work for any Express-supported template engine. There's no need to `require` the EJS module; Express takes care of that behind the scenes.

EJS templates

Since we've set up `nca_ejs`, we may as well go ahead and rewrite our `index` view in embedded JavaScript.

In `nca_ejs/views`, we add a new file, `index.ejs`, and add the following code:

```
<h1> <%= title %></h1>
<p> Welcome to <%= title %></p>

<table>
<tr><th>Name</th><th>Irc</th><th>Twitter</th>
<th>Github</th><th>Location</th><th>Description</th></tr>

<% Object.keys(profiles).forEach(function (id) {%>
```

```
        <tr>
        <% Object.keys(profiles[id]).forEach(function (val) { %>
        <td><%= profiles[id][val]; %></td>
        <% }); %>

        </tr>
    <% }); %>
    </table>
```

The `<%` and `%>` tags denote embedded JavaScript. If JavaScript happens to wrap any HTML code, the HTML is processed as if it's part of the JavaScript. For instance, in our `forEach` callbacks, we have `<tr>` and `<td>`; these are included as output from each loop.

When the opening tag is accompanied by the equals sign (`<%=`), it evaluates any given JavaScript variable and pulls it into the generated output. For example, in our first `<h1>`, we output the `title` variable.

Since the error handlers in `app.js` attempt to render an error template, we'll also need to provide an `error.ejs` view; the following will suffice:

```
<h1><%= message %></h1>
<h2><%= error.status %></h2>
<pre><%= error.stack %></pre>
```

Now if we start our app (`npm start`) and go to `localhost:3000`, we'll see the same profiles table as in our main recipe.

Literal JavaScript in Jade

Jade can also process plain JavaScript. Let's use that to our advantage to output our table headers in a more concise, DRY fashion:

```
    - var headers = ['Name', 'Irc', 'Twitter', 'Github', 'Location',
      'Description'];
    table#profiles
      tr
        each header in headers
          th= header
        each profile, id in profiles
          tr(id=id)
            each val in profile
              td #{val}
```

A dash (–) at the beginning of a line informs Jade that we're using plain JavaScript. Here we simply create a new array called `headers` and then use Jade's `each` iterator to output our headers, using the equals (=) sign to evaluate the `header` variable.

We could alternatively create our array in Jade as follows:

```
headers = ['Name', 'Irc', 'Twitter', 'Github', 'Location',
    'Description'];
```

Jade then compiles this to the embedded JavaScript in the preceding example, including the `var` declarative.

Jade includes

The `include` statement helps us to separate and reuse pieces of template code. Let's put our `profiles` table into its own view. We'll call it `profiles.jade`.

To load `profiles.jade` into the `index.jade` file, we simply edit the `index.jade` file to look as follows:

```
h1= title
p Welcome to #{title}
include profiles
```

Using layout.jade

Also included in a generated project is the `layout.jade` view. This is a special view that is intertwined with Express logic. Any rendered views are packaged into a `body` variable, which is then passed into `layout.jade`. So in our case, we tell `res.render` to assemble `index.jade`. Express converts `index.jade` to HTML, and then internally renders the `layout.jade` view, passing the generated HTML in a `body` variable. The `layout.jade` view allows us to head and foot our views. To disable this feature for the entire app, we use `app.set('view options', {layout:false})`. To prevent it from applying to a particular render, we simply pass `layout:false` to the options object of `res.render`.

See also

- The *CSS preprocessors with Express* recipe
- The *Making an Express web app* recipe
- The *Generating Express scaffolding* recipe

CSS preprocessors with Express

Once we have our HTML, we'll want to style it. We could of course use raw CSS, but Express integrates nicely with some select CSS preprocessors.

Stylus is one such engine. It's written with Express in mind, and its syntax follows many of the design principles found in Jade.

Accelerating Development with Express

In this recipe, we're going to put Stylus in the spotlight, learning how we can use it to apply styles to our `profiles` table from the previous recipe.

Getting ready

We'll need our `nca` folder as it was left in the previous recipe.

How to do it...

First, we need to set up our app to use Stylus.

If we were starting a new project, we could use the `express` executable to generate a Stylus-based Express project as follows:

```
express -c stylus ourNewAppName
```

This would generate a project where `stylus` is a dependency in `package.json`, with an extra line in `app.js` in the configuration section:

```
app.use(require('stylus').middleware(path.join(__dirname,
    'public')));
```

However, since we've already got a project on the hotplate, let's modify our existing app to use Stylus.

In `package.json`, we use the following code:

```
{
  "name": "application-name",
  "version": "0.0.1",
  "private": true,
  "scripts": {
    "start": "node ./bin/www"
  },
  "dependencies": {
    "express": "~4.0.0-rc2",
    "static-favicon": "~1.0.0",
    "morgan": "~1.0.0",
    "cookie-parser": "~1.0.1",
    "body-parser": "~1.0.0",
    "debug": "~0.7.4",
    "jade": "~1.3.0",
    "stylus": "~0.42.3"
  }
}
```

Then on the command line, run the following command:

`npm install`

Finally, in `app.js`, we insert the following code just above the `express.static` middleware:

```
app.use(cookieParser());
app.use(require('stylus').middleware({
  src: __dirname + '/views',
  dest: __dirname + '/public'
}));
app.use(express.static(path.join(__dirname, 'public')));
```

We're going to put our Stylus files in `views/stylesheets`. So let's make that directory and place a new file in it, which we'll call `style.styl`. Express will find this file, placing generated CSS in the corresponding folder (`stylesheets`) of the `public` directory.

To start our Stylus file, we'll copy the current CSS from `/stylesheets/style.css` as follows:

```
body {
  padding: 50px;
  font: 14px "Lucida Grande", Helvetica, Arial, sans-serif;
}
a {
  color: #00b7ff;
}
```

Stylus is fully compatible with plain CSS, but for learning purposes let's convert it into the minimal indentation-based format, shown as follows:

```
body
  padding 50px
  font 14px "Lucida Grande", Helvetica, Arial, sans-serif;
a
  color #00B7FF
```

Now, we'll style our `#profiles` table from the previous recipe.

We can apply consistent padding to our `td` and `th` tags as well as our `#profile` table, utilizing Stylus' `@extend` directive as follows:

```
.pad
  padding 0.5em
#profiles
  @extend .pad
  th
    @extend .pad
  td
    @extend .pad
```

Accelerating Development with Express

As new CSS properties are introduced into browsers, they often come with vendor-specific prefixes until the implementation is considered mature and stable. One such property is `border-radius`; on Mozilla browsers it's `-moz-border-radius`, and on WebKit types it's referenced as `-webkit-border-radius`.

Writing and maintaining this sort of CSS can be quite involved, so let's use a Stylus mixin to make our lives easier:

```
borderIt(rad = 0, size = 1px, type = solid, col = #000)
  border size type col
  if rad
    -webkit-border-radius rad
    -moz-border-radius rad
    border-radius rad
```

Now, we'll apply our mixin to the `#profiles` table and all the `td` elements as shown in the following code:

```
#profiles
  borderIt 20px 2px
  @extend .pad
  th
    @extend .pad
  td
    @extend .pad
    borderIt(col: #000 + 80%)
```

So our `#profiles` table now looks similar to the following screenshot:

Profiles

Welcome to Profiles

Name	Irc	Twitter	Github	Location	Description
Ryan Dahl	ryah	ryah	ry	San Francisco, USA	Creator of node.js
Isaac Schlueter	isaacs	izs	isaacs	San Francisco, USA	Author of npm, core contributor
Bert Belder	piscisaureus	piscisaureus	piscisaureus	Netherlands	Windows support, overall contributor
TJ Holowaychuk	tjholowaychuk	tjholowaychuk	visionmedia	Victoria, BC, Canada	Author of express, jade and other popular modules
Felix Geisendorfer	felixge	felixge	felixge	Berlin, Germany	Author of formidable, active core developer

How it works...

As a module, `stylus` can operate independent of Express. However, it also has a convenient `middleware` method that can be passed into `app.use`.

When the `express` executable generates a Stylus-powered project, only the `src` property is set, which means Stylus pulls files with a `.styl` extension and converts them to `.css` files in the same folder. When we set `dest`, we load our Stylus code from one place and save it in another.

Our `src` is `views` and `dest` is `public`, but even though we put our `styles.styl` in a subdirectory of `views`, Stylus still finds it and places it in the corresponding subdirectory of the `dest` folder.

The `layout.jade` file includes a `link` tag to `/stylesheets/style.css`. So when we created `style.styl` in `views/stylesheets`, the generated CSS was written to `public/stylesheets`. Since our static server directory is set to `public`, requests for `/stylesheets/style.css` are served from `public/stylesheets/style.css`.

We used several Stylus features to create our style sheet.

The `@extend` directive is based on the concept of inheritance. We make a class and then use `@extend` to apply all the qualities of that class to another element. Our use of `@extend` in the recipe creates the following CSS:

```
.pad,
#profiles,
#profiles th,
#profiles td { padding: 0.5em;}
```

The larger our styles base becomes, the more the `@extend` directive tends to ease maintenance and readability.

We make it easier to define a border, with rounded corners if desired, by using a mixin. Stylus mixins allow us to define default values as we set the parameters. If we mixed in `borderIt` with no arguments, it would generate a one pixel-wide, right-angled, solid black border according to its defaults.

We first use `borderIt` on the `#profiles` table, passing in `20px` and `2px`. There's no need to use parentheses—Stylus understands it's a mixin. The first parameter (`20px`) in our mixin is named `rad`. Since `rad` has been specified the `borderIt` mixin goes ahead and outputs the various vendor prefixes along with the desired radius. The second parameter overwrites our `border-width` default.

We do need parentheses when we apply `borderIt` to the `td` elements, because we define our options using `kwarg` (a keyword argument). All we want to do is set the color, so instead of supplying all preceding parameters, we simply reference the desired parameter as a property. The color we pass is `#000 + 80%`. This is not a valid CSS but Stylus understands it.

Accelerating Development with Express

There's more...

Let's explore some more Stylus features and find out how to use the alternative CSS engine, LESS, as Express middleware.

Nested mixins and rest parameters

Let's take a look at reusing mixins in other mixins and Stylus' rest parameter syntax (essentially, it is a single parameter that consumes any parameters that follow and compiles them into an array).

We could soften the edges of our table further by rounding the relevant angles of the corner `<td>` elements, such that they match the rounded nature of the outer border.

We need to be able to set a radius for an individual corner. Vendor implementations differ on their approach to this. In Mozilla-based browsers, the corner is defined after the radius with no dash; for example, refer to the following code:

```
-moz-border-radius-topleft: 9px
```

On the other hand, WebKit conforms to the specification (except the prefix) with the following code:

```
-webkit-border-top-left-radius
```

Let's create another mixin dedicated to create the rounded corners CSS, irrespective of corners being equal.

```
rndCorner(rad, sides...)
  if length(sides) is 2
    -moz-border-radius-{sides[0]}{sides[1]} rad
    -webkit-border-{sides[0]}-{sides[1]}-radius rad
    border-{sides[0]}-{sides[1]}-radius rad
  else
    -webkit-border-radius rad
    -moz-border-radius rad
    border-radius rad
```

The `sides` parameter is a rest parameter. It swallows up all the remaining arguments. We need two sides for a corner, for example, top left. So we use a conditional statement to check if the length of the remaining arguments is 2 (instead of `is`, we could have used `==`).

If we have our sides, we integrate them into the various browser-specific CSS. Note that when including variables in a property, we escape them with curly brackets (`{ }`). If sides aren't specified, we set the radius to all sides, as in this recipe.

Now, we can call this mixin from our `borderIt` mixin as follows:

```
borderIt(rad = 0, size = 1px, type = solid, col = #000)
```

```
  border size type col
  if rad { rndCorner(rad) }
```

We didn't have to wrap the conditional statement with braces. This just allows us to keep our `if` statement and mixin call on the same line. It's the equivalent to the following code:

```
borderIt(rad = 0, size = 1px, type = solid, col = #000)
  border size type col
  if rad
    rndCorner(rad)
```

Finally, we apply our single corners to the relevant `td` elements:

```
tdRad = 9px
#profiles
  borderIt 20px 2px
  @extend .cell
  th
    @extend .cell
  td
    @extend .cell
    borderIt(col: #000 + 80%)
  tr
    &:nth-child(2)
        td:first-child
          rndCorner tdRad top left
        td:last-child
          rndCorner tdRad top right
    &:last-child
        td:first-child
          rndCorner tdRad bottom left
        td:last-child
          rndCorner tdRad bottom right
```

Our first `borderIt` mixin now calls the `rndCorner` mixin inferentially because it sets a radius. The second `borderIt` mixin won't call `rndCorner`, which is great because we want to call it ourselves on specific elements.

We use the special ampersand (`&`) referencer to cite the parent `tr` element. We use CSS `:nth-child(2)` to select the second row of our table. The first row consists of `th` elements. The same applies for `first-child` and `last-child`, which we use to apply the appropriate corners to our `td` elements.

While the `:nth-child` and `:last-child` pseudo selectors won't work in Internet Explorer 8 and below, and neither will `border-radius`. So this is one of the few cases we can use it and still be cross-browser compatible, progressively enhancing it in more modern browsers.

Accelerating Development with Express

Playing with colors

Stylus does some amazing things with color. It has functions that allow us to lighten/darken, (de)saturate, hue adjust, and even mix colors together.

Let's color our table in, writing the adjusting our Stylus code as follows:

```
#profiles
  borderIt 20px, 2px
  @extend .pad
  background: #000;
  color: #fff;
  th
    @extend .pad
  td
    @extend .pad
    background blue + 35%
    borderIt(col: @background)
    color pink - green - brown + gold - green
    color desaturate(@color + 100, 100)
    &:hover
      color @background + 180deg
      background desaturate(@background, 40)
      border-color @background
```

We can reference values of any properties already set for an element. We use the `@background` property lookup variable consistently throughout this piece of code, but in many cases it holds a different value.

To start off, we invert our `#profile` table, setting `color` to `white` and `background` to `black`. We next apply color to our `td` elements, obtaining a lighter shade of blue by adding `35%` to it. We match our `td` borders to their background colors with the `@background` property lookup.

Then we just go wild with color mixing, eventually setting the text color of our `td` to a color not far from the original pink. We then pass `@color` to desaturate while lightening it using the plus (+) symbol. Next, we set the hover text color by adding 180 degrees to our `@background` color, obtaining the complementary hue. We also `desaturate` our background and match `border-color` (`@background` now matches the `desaturated` background, whereas when we set the color on hover, it matched the pre-hover background color).

So now our table looks similar to the following screenshot:

Profiles

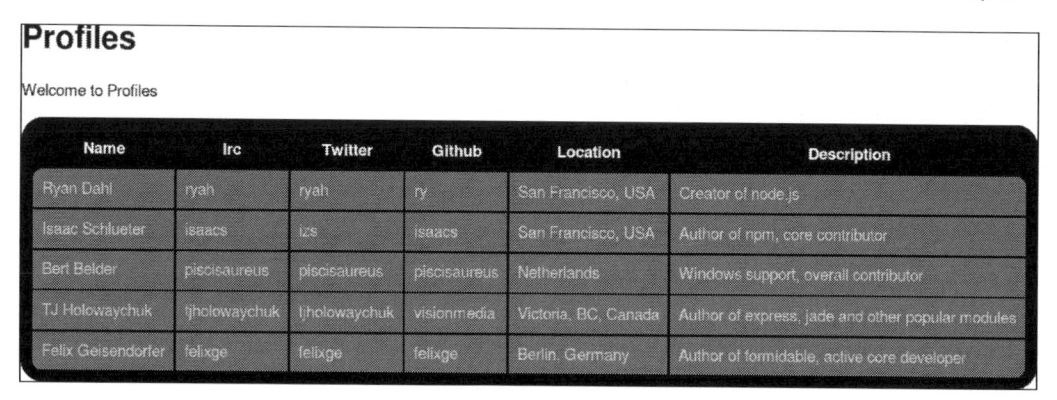

Welcome to Profiles

Name	Irc	Twitter	Github	Location	Description
Ryan Dahl	ryah	ryah	ry	San Francisco, USA	Creator of node.js
Isaac Schlueter	isaacs	izs	isaacs	San Francisco, USA	Author of npm, core contributor
Bert Belder	piscisaureus	piscisaureus	piscisaureus	Netherlands	Windows support, overall contributor
TJ Holowaychuk	tjholowaychuk	tjholowaychuk	visionmedia	Victoria, BC, Canada	Author of express, jade and other popular modules
Felix Geisendorfer	felixge	felixge	felixge	Berlin, Germany	Author of formidable, active core developer

Using LESS

LESS may be suitable as a more familiar and verbose style sheet language compared to Stylus.

> For more information on LESS, visit `http://en.wikipedia.org/wiki/LESS_(stylesheet_language)` and `http://lesscss.org`.

We can use LESS with Express by replacing the following code:

```
app.use(require('stylus').middleware({
    src: __dirname + '/views',
    dest: __dirname + '/public'
}));
```

To use LESS with Express, replace the preceding code with the following code:

```
app.use(require('less-middleware')({
    src: __dirname + '/views',
    dest: __dirname + '/public'
}));
```

To ensure this works, change our `package.json` file as follows:

```
{
  "name": "application-name",
  "version": "0.0.1",
  "private": true,
  "scripts": {
    "start": "node app.js"
  },
  "dependencies": {
    "express": "3.3.4",
    "jade": "*",
```

```
        "less-middleware": "~0.2.0"
    }
}
```

And run the following command:

`npm install`

To test it, we'll rewrite our recipe in LESS.

Some Stylus features have no equivalent in LESS. Instead of using `@extend` to inherit our `pad` class, we'll convert it into a mixin. There are no `if` conditions in LESS either, so we'll declare the `.borderIt` mixin twice, the second time using the `when` statement:

```
body { padding: 50px;
       font: 14px "Lucida Grande", Helvetica, Arial, sans-serif; }

a { color: #00B7FF; }

 .pad() { padding: 0.5em; }

.borderIt (@rad:0, @size:1px, @type: solid, @col: #000) {
  border: @size @type @col;
}

.borderIt (@rad:0) when (@rad > 0) {
  -webkit-border-radius: @rad;
  -moz-border-radius: @rad;
  border-radius: @rad;
}

#profiles {
.borderIt(20px, 2px);
.pad();
th { .pad(); }
td { .pad();
  .borderIt(0,1px,solid,lighten(#000, 80%));
   }
}
```

We save this to `views/styles.less`. Express compiles it to `public/styles.css` and once again our `#profiles` table has rounded corners.

See also

- The *Templating in Express* recipe
- The *Generating Express scaffolding* recipe

Initializing and using a session

If we want to maintain the state between page requests, we use sessions. Express supplies middleware that takes much of the complexity out of managing sessions. In this recipe, we're going to use Express to make a session between a browser and server to facilitate a user login process.

Getting ready

Let's create a fresh project:

`express login`

This will create a new Express skeleton named `login`.

Let's move into the `login` folder and run the following commands:

```
npm install express-session@1.x --save
npm install method-override @1.x --save
```

These are both pieces of Express middleware, which we'll use in our new login app.

How to do it...

We need to add some lines to `app.js`. First, where we require the dependencies, let's require `express-session` and `method-override`:

```
var express = require('express');
var http = require('http');
var path = require('path');
var favicon = require('static-favicon');
var logger = require('morgan');
var cookieParser = require('cookie-parser');
var bodyParser = require('body-parser');
var methodOverride = require('method-override');
var session = require('express-session');
```

Accelerating Development with Express

Then we plug the `method-override` middleware just above `cookieParser`, and the `express-session` middleware just below it, as shown in the following code:

```
app.use(methodOverride());
app.use(cookieParser());
app.use(session({secret:'koobkooC edoN'}));
app.use(express.static(path.join(__dirname, 'public')));
```

Now, let's modify `routes/index.js` as follows:

```
var express = require('express');
var router = express.Router();
var users = {'dave' : 'expressrocks'}; //fake user db

function index(req, res) {
  res.render('index', { title: 'Express',
    user: req.session.user});
}

router.route('/')
  .get(index)
  .post(function login(req, res) {
    var user = req.body.user;
    if (user) {
      Object.keys(users).forEach(function (name) {
        if (user.name === name && user.pwd === users[name]) {
          req.session.user = {
            name: user.name,
            pwd: user.pwd
          };
        }
      });
    }
    index(req, res);
  })
  .delete(function logout(req, res) {
    delete req.session.user;
    index(req, res);
  });

module.exports = router;
```

Finally, let's put a login form together in a file, which we'll call `login.jade`:

```
if user
  form(method='post', action='/')
```

```
      input(name="_method", type="hidden", value="DELETE")
      p Hello #{user.name}!
        a(href='javascript:', onClick='forms[0].submit()') [logout]

  else
    p Please log in
    form(method='post', action='/')
      fieldset
        legend Login
        p
          label(for="user[name]") Username:
          input(name="user[name]")
        p
          label(for="user[pwd]") Password:
          input(type="password", name="user[pwd]")

        input(type="submit")
```

> **_method**
> Note how our logout form uses a hidden input named _method. Setting this value to DELETE overrides the POST method that the form is set to. This is made possible by the method-override middleware inside the configuration section within the app.js file.

We'll include this form within index.jade:

```
h1= title
p Welcome to #{title}

include login.jade
```

Now if we run our app and navigate to http://localhost:3000, we'll see a login form. We enter the username dave and password expressrocks; we will now see a greeting with the option to log out.

How it works...

To use sessions and work with DELETE requests, we have to include some additional middleware. We do this by installing and requiring expression-session and method-override.

We app.use the method-override (methodOveride) middleware just above cookie-parser (cookieParser), and more importantly, underneath the body-parser (bodyParser). The override works via a private hidden form variable (the _method hidden input as defined in our login.jade file). So we need the form data to be parsed with body-parser before method-override can know if such an override is expected.

Accelerating Development with Express

In similar fashion, the `express-session` (`session`) middleware is placed below the `cookie-parser` (`cookieParser`) middleware because a browser session relies on cookie data. When we pass a string to `session`, it becomes the seed for a hash that is used to create signed cookies (which sessions depend on), so it needs to be unique and unknown to outsiders.

The router allows us to attach multiple verbs to a predefined route, using `router.route`. We set up a route to the `/` path and then attach `get`, `post`, and `delete` configurations to it using a chaining API. That is, the call to `router.route` and subsequent verb methods will return an object with those same methods available for us.

We refactor the index `GET` handler from an anonymous function expression to a named function statement (`index`) and then reuse it in our `POST` and `DELETE` routes.

When we set up our routes, we assume that `POST` requests to the `/` path are login attempts, and thus pass them first to the `login` route. We also assume that `DELETE` requests to `/` are to be processed primarily by the `logout` route.

Our `login` route checks the posted login details (using `req.body`, which is supplied to us by the `body-parser` middleware) against our placeholder `users` object. In a real-world scenario, `login` would rather be validating against a database of users.

If everything checks out, we add a `user` object to the session and place the `name` and password (`pwd`) into it.

When pushing user details to the session, we could have taken a shortcut and used the following code:

```
req.session.user = req.body.user;
```

However, doing so could leave us open for an attacker to fill the `req.session.user` object with anything they desire, in potentially large amounts. While any data being entered into a session would be entered by a trusted user (one with login details), and although `body-parser` has built-in safety limits for `POST` data, it is always better to err on the side of conservatism over convenience.

Once the login `POST` handler is done, it calls `index`, passing the `req` and `res` objects along.

Other than being broken out as its own function statement, we make one small addition to the `index` route, by adding a `user` property to the rendering options, and set this new property to `req.session.user`.

Doing so enables `login.jade` to check the `user` variable. If it is set, `login.jade` shows a greeting along with a small form containing a link that sends a `POST` request with a `DELETE` override to the server, thus triggering the `logout` route via `router.delete`.

The `logout` route simply deletes the `user` object from `req.session` and passes control to the `index.route` (by calling the `index` function with `req` and `res`), which pushes a non-existent `req.session.user` back to Jade via `res.render`.

When Jade finds that there is no `user` it displays the login form, which is of course also output to a pre-login request.

There's more...

We can improve the way we interact with sessions.

Custom middleware for site-wide session management

This recipe is fine if we want to pass our login and logout requests to just one route. However, as our routes and views increase, managing the complexities with sessions could become burdensome. We can somewhat mitigate this by creating our own custom middleware for session-handling purposes.

In `routes/index.js`, we can now simply have the following code:

```
var express = require('express');
var router = express.Router();

function index(req, res) {
  res.render('index', { title: 'Express' });
}

router.all('/', index);
router.all('/:page', index);

module.exports = router;
```

We're completely decoupling our session logic from the routes logic, so the login and logout handlers have disappeared. We're sending all requests to the / path to our `index` function. The `all` verb will catch any type of request, whether it's `GET`, `PUT`, `POST`, or `DELETE`, or if it is a more exotic request such as `PATCH` or `SUBSCRIBE`, it will be served by our `index` handler. We also have the `:page` route catching all HTTP methods as well. In a real-life scenario, the `:page` route could be handled separately; however, we'll leave it to be handled by `index` for brevity. Our `index` function has been slightly modified by removing the `user` property from the options argument provided to `res.render`.

Now let's create a file and call it `login.js`, saving it in the root folder of our app (alongside `app.js`). We'll put the following code into the `login.js` file:

```
var users = {'dave' : 'expressrocks'};

module.exports = function (req, res, next) {
```

```
    var method = req.method.toLowerCase(), //cache the method
      user = req.body.user,
      logout = (method === 'delete'),
      login = (user && method === 'post');

    if (logout) { delete req.session.user; }

    if (login) {
      Object.keys(users).forEach(function (name) {
        if (user.name === name && user.pwd === users[name]) {
          req.session.user = {
            name: user.name,
            pwd: user.pwd
          };
        }
      });
    }

    if (!req.session.user) { return next(); }

    res.locals.user = req.session.user;
    next();
};
```

Now we simply include `login.js` as middleware in the configuration section of `app.js`, between the `session` and `express.static` middleware:

```
app.use(session({secret:'koobkooC edoN'}));
app.use(require('./login'));
app.use(express.static(path.join(__dirname, 'public')));
```

Finally, we'll modify both forms that appear in `login.jade`, so we'll replace the following code:

```
form(method='post', action='/')
```

We will replace the preceding code with the following code (in both places where `form` appears):

```
form(method='post')
```

This makes the form POST (or DELETE in the override case) to whatever address it is submitted from. This would be useful in a scenario where we wanted a site global login (and logout) widget rather than a separate login page.

Now all the muscle work is performed by the `login.js` file. The exported function essentially performs the same actions as our recipe but in a route-agnostic manner.

At the top of our function, we determine the HTTP method currently hitting our server and find out if the request body contains any user data (as would be the case in a login attempt). We use the method and the existing user data to determine if a login or logout attempt is being made, holding the Boolean result in the `login` and `logout` variables.

In the event of a `DELETE HTTP` request (a logout attempt as far as our server is concerned), we simply remove the user data from the session.

If we've got a login on our hands (that is, if it's a `POST` request and the `POST` body contains user data), we check our phony database; if there's a match, we load the matched user data into the session.

If the session doesn't contain any logged-in user data, then we exit the function at this point and call `next` to proceed to the following middleware.

Otherwise, the ultimate value of the `user` property is loaded directly into our view as a local variable by setting `res.locals.user` to `req.session.user` at the end of our middleware function. In the same way, we can pass variables to views via the `res.render` options object within a route. So as in the main recipe, `req.session.user` is now available in `login.jade` as user. Finally, we call the `next` function, which passes control to any subsequent middleware. In our case the next piece of middleware is `app.router`.

Flash messages

For this example, we'll work on the previous extension to our recipe (the *Custom middleware for site-wide session management* section).

The `express-flash` module provides a simple interface for `session-based` flash messages. A flash message is held in a session object for one request and then disappears. It's an easy way to generate one-time request associated information, such as an error message.

First, we'll need to install `express-flash` using the following command:

```
npm install express-flash --save #adds the dep to package.json
```

Let's add our new dependency to `app.js`:

```
var express = require('express');
var http = require('http');
var path = require('path');
var favicon = require('static-favicon');
var logger = require('morgan');
var cookieParser = require('cookie-parser');
var bodyParser = require('body-parser');
var methodOverride = require('method-override');
var session = require('express-session');
var flash = require('express-flash');
```

Accelerating Development with Express

In the configuration section, we'll slot `express-flash` into our middleware stack between the `session` middleware and our custom login middleware:

```
app.use(cookieParser());
app.use(session({secret:'koobkooC edoN'}));
app.use(flash());
app.use(require('./login'));
app.use(function (req, res, next) {
  res.locals.flash = req.flash();
  next();
});
app.use(express.static(path.join(__dirname, 'public')));
```

Now, let's modify our `login.js` file from the *Custom middleware for site-wide session management* section. We're going to modify it to flash an error message for invalid login details.

We need to capture our flash message (if any) and pass it as a local variable to our Jade views. The second highlighted piece of code is some custom middleware that does just that.

We could alter the code located at the bottom of our exported function inside the `if (login)` statement block:

```
if (login) {
  var valid = Object.keys(users).some(function (name) {
    return (user.name === name && user.pwd === users[name]);
  });
  if (valid) {
    req.session.user = {
    name: req.body.user.name,
    pwd: req.body.user.pwd
    };
  } else {
    req.flash('error','Login details invalid!');
  }
}
```

This works fine, but we can do better. Let's tidy it up by extracting our validation code into a separate function (placing it at the top of `login.js`):

```
function validate(user, cb) {
  var valid = Object.keys(users).some(function (name) {
    return (user.name === name && user.pwd === users[name]);
  });
  cb((!valid && {msg: 'Login details invalid!'} ));

}
```

Although everything happening in `validate` is synchronous, we've written it in an asynchronous style (that is, passing values through a callback instead of returning values). This is because, in reality, we wouldn't use an object to store user details. We would use a remote database, which would have to be accessed asynchronously. In the next recipe, we'll store our user details in a MongoDB database and asynchronously read it to validate login requests. The `validate` function is structured with this in mind.

Now, we replace the login logic in the `login.js` file's exported function with the following code:

```
if (login) {
  validate(user, function (err) {
    if (err) { req.flash('error', err.msg); return next(); }
      res.locals.user = req.session.user = user;
      next();
  });

  return;
}

if (!req.session.user) { return next(); }
res.locals.user = req.session.user;

next();
}; //closing bracket of module.exports
```

Our `validate` function essentially does the same thing as our first adjustment to the login logic. However, it's tucked out of the way. Also, note the various strategic calls to `next`—when exiting early from an error, adding a user session, or at the very end. Placing these `next` calls within the callback context future-proofs our `validation` function for asynchronous operations, which is important for database interactions.

We use the `callback(err)` style from the `validate` function to let our middleware know whether the login was successful. The `err` object is simply an object containing the error message (`msg`) and it's only passed if `valid` is not true.

If `err` is present, we call `req.flash`, which is a method added to the `req` object by the `express-flash` middleware. It pushes an object called `flash` onto `req.session`. After the request is fulfilled, the object is removed from `req.session`.

We need to make this object available to `login.jade`; this is why we have added some custom middleware after the login middleware to pass `req.flash()` to `req.locals.flash`.

Finally, at the top of `login.jade`, we write the following code:

```
if flash.error
  hr
  b= flash.error
  hr
```

Accelerating Development with Express

If login details are incorrect, the user receives a bold error notification between horizontal lines.

See also

- The *Making an Express web app* recipe
- The *Templating in Express* recipe
- The *Implementing dynamic routing* recipe

Making an Express web app

In this recipe, we're going to combine a lot of previous recipes and throw in a few extra Express features (such as app mounting) to create the foundations of an Express-based web app with integrated administration features.

Getting ready

Let's start fresh. From the command line, we execute the following command:

`express profiler`

The name of our new app will be `Profiler`; it will be the profile manager for members of the Node community.

We need to edit `package.json` using the following code:

```
{
  "name": "Profiler",
  "version": "0.0.1",
  "private": true,
  "scripts": {
    "start": "node ./bin/www"
  },
  "dependencies": {
    "express": "~4.0.0-rc2",
    "static-favicon": "~1.0.0",
    "morgan": "~1.0.0",
    "cookie-parser": "~1.0.1",
    "body-parser": "~1.0.0",
    "debug": "~0.7.4",
    "jade": "~1.3.0",
    "stylus": "~0.42.3",
    "express-flash": "0.0.2",
    "mongodb": "~1.3.23"
  }
}
```

Chapter 7

We've set the name to `Profiler`, adding `stylus`, `mongodb`, and `express-flash` modules.

So we get our dependencies by executing the following command:

npm install

We also need to ensure that MongoDB is installed. See the *Storing and retrieving data with MongoDB* recipe of *Chapter 4, Interfacing with Databases*, for more details.

Mongo needs a folder to store our apps database in our app folder:

mkdir db

Then we can start MongoDB with the following command:

sudo mongod --dbpath db

> At deployment stage, we can start MongoDB as a service using the `--fork` flag.

We'll also push some data into MongoDB to get us started. Let's create a new folder in the `profiler` directory and call it `tools`. Then we pull our `profiles.js` module from *Chapter 1, Making a Web Server*, into it, creating a new file called `prepopulate.js`.

Inside the `prepopulate.js` file, we write the following code:

```
var client = require('mongodb').MongoClient,
  profiles = require('./profiles'),
  users = [{name : 'dave', pwd: 'expressrocks'},
           {name : 'MrPage', pwd: 'hellomynamesmrpage'}
          ],
  tx = 2; //expected amount of transactions

profiles = Object.keys(profiles).map(function (key) {
  return profiles[key];
}); //convert object to array of objects

function e(err) { if (!err) {return;} console.log(err); process.exit(); }

function tidy(db) {tx--; return tx || db.close(); }

client.connect('mongodb://localhost:27017/profiler',
  function (err, db) {
    e(err);

    db.dropDatabase(function (err) {
```

Accelerating Development with Express

```
      e(err);

      db.collection('users').insert(users, function (err) {
        if (err) { return console.log(err); }
        console.log('Added users');
        tidy(db);
      });

      db.collection('profiles').insert(profiles,
        function (err, o) {
          e(err);
          console.log('Added profiles');
          tidy(db);
        });
    });
  });
```

When executed, this gives us a database named `profiler` with a `profiles` and `users` collection.

Finally, we'll use the entire login app of the previous recipe. However, we'll want it with the site-wide session management and flash messages (in the code examples, this folder is called `login_flash_messages`). So let's copy the `login` folder to our new profile directory as `profiler/login`.

How to do it...

There's a lot going on in this recipe, so let's break it down into pieces.

Creating a database bridge

Let's begin with some backend coding. We'll create a new folder called `models` and create a file inside it called `profiles.js`. This is going to be used to manage all of our interactions with the MongoDB profiles collection. In the `models/profiles.js` file, we put the following code:

```
var mongodb = require('mongodb'),
  client = mongodb.MongoClient,
  ObjectID = mongodb.ObjectID,
  profs;

client.connect('mongodb://localhost:27017/profiler', function (err, db) {
  profs = db.collection('profiles');
  [pull, del, add].forEach(function (m) { exports[m.name] = m; })
});

function pull(page, cb) {
```

```
        var p = {},
          //rowsPer = 10, //realistic rowsPer
          rowsPer = 2,
          skip, errs;
        page = page || 1;
        skip = (page - 1) * rowsPer;

        profs.find({}, {limit: rowsPer, skip: skip})
          .each(function (err, doc) {
            if (err) { errs = errs || []; errs.push(err); }
            if (doc) {
              p[doc._id] = doc;
              delete p[doc._id]._id;
              return;
            }
            cb(errs, p);
          });
      }

      function del(profile, cb) {
        profs.remove({_id: ObjectID(profile)}, cb);
      }

      function add(profile, cb) {
        profs.insert(profile.profile, cb);
      }

      exports.pull = exports.add = exports.del = function (_, cb) {
        cb(Error('Profiles Not Ready'))
      }
```

We've defined three functions: `pull`, `del`, and `add`. When a connection to our database has been established, these are loaded onto the `exports` object, replacing the placeholder function (at the bottom) assigned to all the three namespaces. The placeholder simply sends an error through the callback function, indicating that the data isn't ready (this is an unlikely event but should be handled nonetheless). This error is then thrown in our `index` handler in `login/routes/index.js`, and the error-handling logic at the end of `login/app.js` captures the throw, rendering the appropriate output.

Each of our methods operate on the database asynchronously and executes a user callback once data is returned or the operation is complete. We've set a low rows-per-page limit (`rowsPer`) to allow us to test our pagination work (the dividing of content into pages) with the few records we have.

Accelerating Development with Express

We must also modify `login/login.js`, which we created in the previous recipe, to hook up our login app to the MongoDB user collection. The main module can remain untouched. We only have to change the way we validate a user. Everything above `module.exports` changes to the following code:

```
var client = require('mongodb').MongoClient,
  users;

client.connect('mongodb://localhost:27017/profiler',
  function (err, db) {
    users = db.collection('users');
  });

function validate(user, cb) {
  if (!users) {cb({msg: 'User data not ready'});}

  users.findOne({name: user.name, pwd: user.pwd},
    function (err, user) {
      if (err) { throw err; }
      if (!user) {
        cb({msg: 'Invalid login details!'});
        return;
      }
      cb();
    });
}
```

In this case, if our `users` data hasn't been loaded from the database, we return early with a callback, sending an object as the error parameter with the `msg` property explaining that user data isn't ready. This `msg` property would later be passed to the `express-flash` middleware via `req.flash` and be output to the user.

Configuring app.js files

Now let's modify `app.js` (in project root).

The configuration section should look like the following code:

```
app.set('views', path.join(__dirname, 'views'));
app.set('view engine', 'jade');

app.use(favicon());
app.use(logger('dev'));
app.use(bodyParser.json());
app.use(bodyParser.urlencoded());
app.use(cookieParser());
```

```
app.use(require('stylus').middleware({
  src: __dirname + '/views',
  dest: __dirname + '/public'
}));
app.use(express.static(path.join(__dirname, 'public')));

app.use('/', routes);
app.use('/admin', require('./login/app'));
```

We've included the Stylus engine above `express.static` and added an additional `app.use` that actually mounts our login app at the `/admin` route (we copied `login` into our `profiler` directory in the *Getting ready* section of this recipe). We also removed the `/users` route. We can delete the `users.js` file from `routes`; do the same in `login/app.js`, and remove `login/routes/users.js`.

Now we'll set up Stylus in `login/app`:

```
app.use(flash());
app.use(require('stylus').middleware({
  src: __dirname + '/views',
  dest: __dirname + '/public'
}));
app.use(require('./login'));
app.use(express.static(path.join(__dirname, 'public')));
```

The `login` app will pull in our profiles table from the `profiler` app. We've configured it to use Stylus as we'll be applying extra admin-specific Stylus-generated CSS.

The login app is the gatekeeper of our administration section, within which we will be able to add and remove profiles.

Now that our main and mounted apps are suitably prepared, we can move on to editing our views, styles, and routes.

Modifying the profiler app

Let's start with the profiler apps' `index.jade` view:

```
h1= title
p Welcome to #{title}
p: a(href='admin/') [ Admin Login ]
include profiles
```

Since we're including `profiles.jade`, let's script it as follows:

```
- safeMix && safeMix(jade_mixins, 'add', 'del', 'adminScript')

table#profiles
```

```
          tfoot
            - s = (page > 1) ? null : 'display:none'
            td
              a#bck(href="#{(+(page||1)-1)}", style=s) &laquo;
              a#fwd(href="#{(+(page||1)+1)}") &raquo;
          thead
            tr
              th Name
              th Irc
              th Twitter
              th Github
              th Location
              th Description
              if typeof user !== 'undefined'
                th Action
          tbody
            each profile, id in profiles
              tr(id=id)
                each row in profile
                  td= row
                +del(id)
    +add
    +adminScript
```

> Jade mixins are defined and can also be called using the `mixin` keyword. For terseness and better distinction between a definition and invocation, mixins can also be called by prefixing their name with a plus (+) symbol.

The `profiles.jade` file should be saved to the `profiler/views` directory. It is based on our `profiles` table in the previous recipes. However, we've added code to support seamless integration with the login app and some additional HTML structure for pagination.

At the top of `profiles.jade`, we've included a safety net called `safeMix` to ensure our view doesn't choke if our administration-specific mixins aren't present. We'll define `safeMix` shortly in `routes/index.js`. We will pre-check `safeMix` before calling it because we'll reuse `profiles.jade` in the login subapp, where `safeMix` won't be defined by the administration mixins.

We'll define our admin mixins when we come to editing the `login` apps views.

For pagination, we've added a `tfoot` element to hold the back and forward links with a complementary `thead` to hold wrap the `th` elements.

Let's create a new `stylesheets` directory under `views` and place a file in it called `style.styl`.

In `views/stylesheets/style.styl`, we write the following code:

```
body
  padding 50px
  font 14px "Lucida Grande", Helvetica, Arial, sans-serif;
a
  color #00B7FF
rndCorner(rad, sides...)
  if length(sides) is 2
    -moz-border-radius-{sides[0]}{sides[1]} rad
    -webkit-border-{sides[0]}-{sides[1]}-radius rad
    border-{sides[0]}-{sides[1]}-radius rad
  else
    -webkit-border-radius rad
    -moz-border-radius rad
    border-radius rad

borderIt(rad = 0, size = 1px, type = solid, col = #000)
  border size type col
  if rad {rndCorner(rad)}

.pad
  padding 0.5em

tdRad = 9px

#profiles
  width 950px
  borderIt 20px, 2px
  @extend .pad
  background: #000;
  color: #fff;
  th
    @extend .pad
  tbody
    td
      @extend .pad
      background blue + 35%
      borderIt(col: @background)
      color pink - green - brown + gold - green
      color desaturate(@color + 100, 100)
      &:hover
        color @background + 180deg
        background desaturate(@background, 40)
```

```
              border-color @background

      tr
        &:first-child
            td:first-child
              rndCorner tdRad top left
            td:last-child
              rndCorner tdRad top right
        &:last-child
            td:first-child
              rndCorner tdRad bottom left
            td:last-child
              rndCorner tdRad bottom right

  tfoot
    font-size 1.5em
    td
    a
       text-decoration none
       color #fff - 10%
       &:hover
         color #fff
```

This is the same Stylus sheet from the *Playing with color* section under *There's more...* in the *CSS preprocessors with Express* recipe, but with some minor modifications.

Since we've placed our `th` elements under a `thead`, we can simply select our `tbody tr` elements by `:first-child` instead of `:nth-child(2)`. We also add some styling for the new `tfoot` element.

Finally, we'll write the code for the `routes/index.js` file:

```
var express = require('express');
var router = express.Router();
var profiles = require('../models/profiles');

function safeMix(jade_mixins, mixins) {
  mixins = Array.prototype.slice.call(arguments, 1);
  mixins.forEach(function (mixin) {
    jade_mixins[mixin] = jade_mixins[mixin] || safeMix.noop;
  });
}
safeMix.noop = function () {}

router.get('/:pagenum([0-9]+)?', function (req, res) {

  profiles.pull(req.params.pagenum, function (err, profiles) {
```

```
      if (err) { throw err; }

      res.render('index', { title: 'Profiler', profiles: profiles,
         page: req.params.pagenum,    safeMix: safeMix});
   });

});

module.exports = router;
```

Our `index` route makes a call via our `models/profiles.js` module to MongoDB, passing it the desired page number, and retrieves some profiles to display.

It also passes our `safeMix` function (defined prior to our route) through the local object passed to `res.render`. If we don't include dummy mixins in the place of the admin mixins, Node will throw an error. The `safeMix` function takes a `jade_mixins` object (which will be available in the Jade view). Then, in the absence of a pre-existing method, `safeMix` assigns a `no-op` function to properties on the `jade_mixins` object named after each subsequent argument passed.

Internally, Jade mixins are compiled into JavaScript functions before they are executed within our view templates. So we create dummy `no-op` (no operation) functions to prevent a server error. Then when we log in, they are replaced with the administration mixins.

If we navigate to `localhost:3000`, we should now have a functioning `profiler` app.

Modifying the mounted login app

In `login/views`, we currently have `index.jade`, `login.jade`, `error.jade`, and `layout.jade`. In `login.jade`, we want to add two `include` statements as follows:

```
if flash.error
   hr
   b= flash.error
   hr

if user
   form(method='post')
      input(name="_method", type="hidden", value="DELETE")
      p Hello #{user.name}!
         a(href='javascript:', onClick='forms[0].submit()') [logout]

   include admin
   include ../../views/profiles

else
   p Please log in
// rest of the login.jade...
```

Accelerating Development with Express

Rather than repeating code, we reuse our `profiles.jade` view from the main app using a relative path. This means any changes we make to our frontend site are also made to our administration section! The `admin.jade` file is going to contain Jade mixins (which are conceptually similar to Stylus mixins). These mixins are conditionally included in `profiles.jade` (see the previous *Modifying the profiler app* section).

The `admin.jade` file contains the following code:

```
mixin del(id)
  td
    a.del(href='/admin/del?id=#{id}&p=#{page}')
      &#10754;

mixin add
  #ctrl
    a#add(href='#') &oplus;

mixin adminScript
  include adminScript

include addfrm
```

We have two includes in `admin.jade`: one as part of a mixin and the other as a straight include.

The contents of the `addfrm.jade` file should be as follows:

```
- fields = ['Name', 'Irc', 'Twitter', 'Github', 'Location', 'Description'];

form#addfrm(method='post', action='/admin/add')
  fieldset
    legend Add
    each field, i in fields
      div
        label= field
        input(name="profile[#{field.toLowerCase()}]")
    .btns
      button.cancel(type='button') Cancel
      input(type='submit', value='Add')
```

The `adminScript.jade` file should contain the following code:

```
script(src='http://ajax.googleapis.com/ajax/libs/jquery/1.9.2/jquery.min.js')
script.
  document.getElementsByTagName('body')[0].id = 'js';
```

```
$('#add').click(function (e) {
  e.preventDefault();
  $('#profiles, #ctrl').fadeOut(function () {
    $('#addfrm').fadeIn();
  });
});

$('#addfrm .cancel').click(function () {
  $('#addfrm').fadeOut(function () {
    $('#profiles, #ctrl').fadeIn();
  });
});
```

Admin is positioned above profiles in `login.jade`, so `#addfrm` will sit above the `#profiles` table. However, our `adminScript` mixin hides the table, showing it when the **Add** button is clicked on.

We create a `stylesheets` folder under `login/views`, creating the `admin.styl` file in it and write the following code:

```
@import '../../../views/stylesheets/style.styl'

tbody
  td
    .del
      text-decoration none
      color blue + 35% + 180deg
      float right
      &:hover
        color red
#ctrl
  width 950px
  text-align center
  margin-top -2.5em
  a
    color white - 10%
    font-size 1.8em
    text-decoration none
    &:hover
      color @color + 111%

#js
  #addfrm
    display none
#addfrm
```

```
      width 250px
      label
        display block
        float left
        width 100px
        font-weight bold
      .btns
        width @width
        text-align right
```

Now we'll also reuse the Stylus sheet from our main app. The `@import` declarative is handled by Stylus on the server side (unless the extension is `.css`). As a result, our main app's `styles.styl` sheet is combined with `admin.styl` and compiled as one CSS file in `login/public/stylesheets/admin.css`.

To load our `admin.css` file, we must alter the login app's `layout.jade` view as shown in the following code:

```
doctype 5
html
  head
    title= title
    link(rel='stylesheet',href='/admin/stylesheets/admin.css')
    body!= body
```

We've altered the link `href` attribute from `/stylesheet/style.css` to `/admin/stylesheets/admin.css`, ensuring that CSS is loaded from the static server on our subapps route.

Finally, we complete our admin routes in `login/routes/index.js` as follows:

```
var express = require('express');
var router = express.Router();
var profiles = require('../../models/profiles');

router.all('/:pagenum([0-9]+)?', function (req, res) {
  profiles.pull(req.params.pagenum, function (err, profiles) {
    if (err) { console.log(err); }
    res.render('index', { title: 'Profiler Admin', profiles: profiles,
page: req.params.pagenum });
  });
});

router.get('/del', function (req, res) {
  profiles.del(req.query.id, function (err) {
    if (err) { console.log(err); }
```

```
          profiles.pull(req.query.p, function (err, profiles) {
            req.app.locals.profiles = profiles;
            res.redirect(req.header('Referrer') || '/');
          });
        });
      });

      router.post('/add', function (req, res) {
        profiles.add(req.body, function (err) {
          if (err) { console.log(err); }
          res.redirect(req.header('Referrer') || '/');
        });
      });

      module.exports = router;
```

Adding the optional `:pagenum` attribute to the `get` method route enables the navigation of the `profiles` table as in the main app. Adding `:pagenum` to the `post` method route allows users to log in from pages that they may have previously navigated to (for example, this allows a login form to be served from `http://localhost:/admin/2` if a user's session is expired). Likewise, the `del` method route will allow us to log out from any valid page.

We've also added a `/del` and `/add` route to process admin tasks.

We should now be able to log in to `http://localhost:3000/admin` to delete and add profiles as `dave` with the password `expressrocks` or as `Mr.Page` with the password `hellomynamesmrpage`.

> **Login security**
>
> In the next chapter, we will learn how to hash our passwords and log in over SSL.

How it works...

Our app contains a lot of pieces working together. So let's look at it from various angles.

Understanding app mounting

In this recipe, we have two apps working with the same database, sharing views and Stylus sheets. We imported the login app to our new `profiler` folder and mounted it with `app.use` setting `/admin` as its route.

Accelerating Development with Express

This works because Express apps are an assemblage of middleware. So when we mount the login app, it simply integrates with our app as a middleware plugin. Middleware works on the request and response objects. By passing the /admin route into app.use, we limit the login app to work only with requests made under that route.

Data flow

Our app is supported by a MongoDB database that we set up with our prepopulate.js tool. Data flows to and from the database as shown in the following diagram:

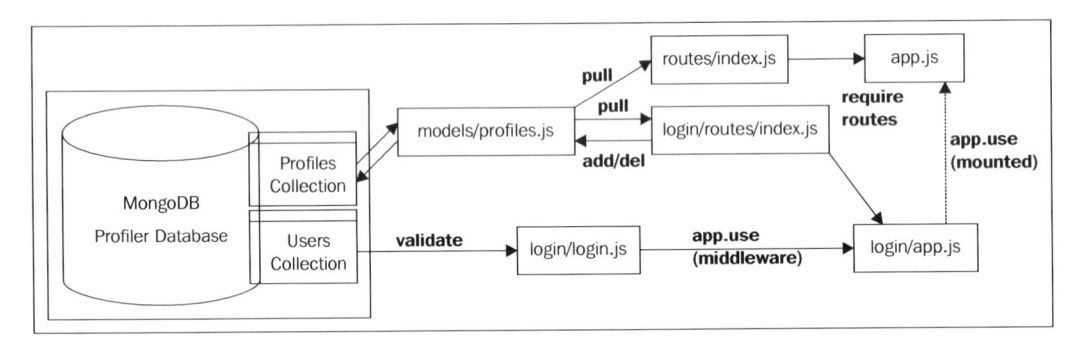

The profiles.js file in the models folder pulls and pushes data to the profiles collection, providing an interface for the routes/index.js files in both master and subapps. Our routes integrate within their respective app.js files and work to interact with models/profiles.js to carry out the desired tasks.

The login.js file simply verifies the user's credentials, performing a search with user-supplied input. The login.js file sits as a piece of middleware within login/app.js, waiting to respond to POST requests that contain a username and password.

Route handling

In both apps, the index route provides a foundation for displaying and navigating the profiles table. In both, we call profiles.pull, passing in req.params.pagenum. The pagenum parameter is loaded onto req.params. It will never be anything but a number—thanks to our restrictions placed on it, though it is optional; so it may not be present.

Our profiles.pull method takes two parameters: the page number and a callback. If the page number isn't present, it sets the page to 1. We determine the rows to be extracted by multiplying our internal rowsPer variable by page - 1 (we want to start at the beginning with page 1; therefore, for the first page, we skip 0 rows). The result is passed through as the skip modifier to MongoDB and rowsPer is passed as the limit property. The skip modifier will pass over a predetermined number of rows before outputting and limit restricts the amount to output; thus we achieve pagination. The profiles.pull callback is initiated either with an error or with an object containing profiles.

In both our `index` routes, we perform minimal error handling. Express tends to capture the errors and output them to the browser for debugging purposes. The `profiles` object is passed to `res.render`, where it is later utilized by the `profiles.jade` view.

In `login/routes/index.js`, two inflexible routes are defined: `/add` and `/del`. The `/del` route is a `GET` route expecting two URL query attributes: `id` and `p`. The `id` parameter is obtained through `req.query.id` and passed to `profiles.del`, which calls the Mongoskin `removeByID` method, effectively deleting a profile from the collection.

As long as no error has occurred, we invoke `profiles.pull` with the `p` URL query attribute (via `req.query.p`), updating the `profiles` object made available in our views by pointing `req.app.locals.profiles` to our new `profiles` object that came through as the second parameter of the `profiles.pull` callback. This ensures that changes to the database are reflected to the user. Finally, we redirect the user back to where they came from.

The `/add` route works much in the same way, except as a `POST` request. If `req.body` is returned as an object, we can simply insert this object straight into MongoDB (since it is JSON-like).

Views

We use a lot of `includes` in our views, and sometimes between apps. The relationships are shown in the following diagram:

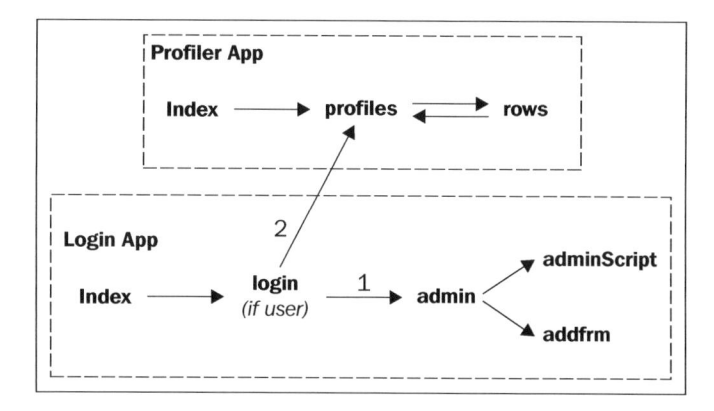

```
┌─────────────────────────────────────────────────────┐
│ Profiler App                                        │
│                                                     │
│    Index  ──────▶  profiles  ◀──────▶  rows         │
│                       ▲                             │
└───────────────────────┼─────────────────────────────┘
                        │
┌───────────────────────┼─────────────────────────────┐
│ Login App            2│                             │
│                       │                             │
│                     login        1      ▸ adminScript│
│    Index  ──────▶  (if user)  ──▶ admin  ◁          │
│                                         ▸ addfrm   │
└─────────────────────────────────────────────────────┘
```

In our main app, the `index` view loads the `profiles` view, and `profiles` utilizes the `rows` view in a partial statement.

In the login app, the `index` view includes the `login` view. The `login` view loads the `profiles` view, and under the right conditions, it also includes the `admin` view (before `profiles`) to provide the administration layer. The `admin` view includes the `addfrm` and `adminScript` views. The mixins defined in `admin` become available to `profiles`.

The `profiles.jade` view is very central to the entire web app: it outputs our data, delivers the optional administration overlay, and provides navigational capabilities. Let's take a look at the navigational portion:

```
table#profiles
  tfoot
    s = (page > 1) ? null : 'display:none'
    td
      a#bck(href="#{(+(page||1)-1)}", style=s) &laquo;
      a#fwd(href="#{(+(page||1)+1)}") &raquo;
```

The `page` variable is passed through from the `index` route and is determined from `req.params.pagenum`. Jade doesn't allow variables to leak into global scope when `var` isn't used, so our `s` variable can be declared without it. If we are on the first page, a link to the previous page is unnecessary, so we add a style attribute containing `display:none` (if we wanted to be neat, we could have a CSS class set `display` and add a class attribute instead). By passing `null`, if the `page` is greater than one, we're telling Jade that we don't want to set the style attribute at all. If `page` is `undefined` or `0`, we bump it to `1`, as a typical user's mind will count starting from `1`, not `0`.

Mixins

The only place we use Jade mixins is in the `login/views/admin.jade` view, but they are essential to the synergy between the admin section and the top-level site. Unless a user is logged in and under the `/admin` route, the mixins are not present in `profiles.jade`. They are only intended for privileged users.

We use mixins to supplement the `profiles` table with an administration layer. The only part of `admin.jade` that isn't a mixin is the final `include` of `addfrm.jade`. As admin is included before `profiles`, `#addfrm` sits above the `profiles` table.

The `adminScript` mixin is, as the name suggests, a `script` block that quickly applies an `id` of `js` to the `body` tag. We use this in `admin.styl` to hide our `#addfrm` (the generated CSS would be `#js #addfrm {display:none}`). This is quicker than directly hiding the element with JavaScript and minimizes the undesirable flash of content effect that can occur when hiding page elements on page load. Therefore, `#addfrm` is not initially visible. In the following screenshot, we can see the visible mixins displayed on the `#profiles` table within the admin section:

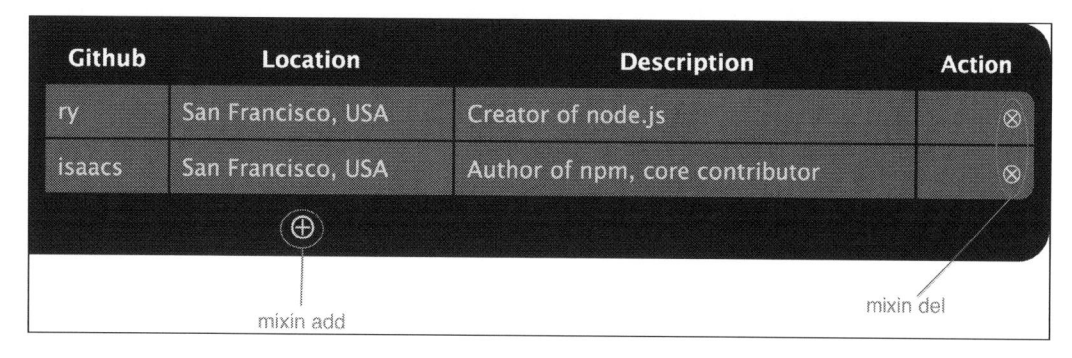

Github	Location	Description	Action
ry	San Francisco, USA	Creator of node.js	⊗
isaacs	San Francisco, USA	Author of npm, core contributor	⊗

mixin add   *mixin del*

Clicking on the **Add** button causes the `#profiles` table to fade out and `#addfrm` to fade in. The `del` mixin takes an `id` argument, which it then uses to generate a link for each profile, such as `/del?id=4f3336f369cca0310e000003&p=1`. The `p` variable is determined from the `page` property passed in at the `res.render` time in the `index` route.

Locals

We use local variables throughout to pull data from our server through our views.

Also, in the `login/app.js` file, we insert some custom middleware that loads the result of `req.flash()` into `res.locals.flash`. The contents of the flash local is dependent on the request/response negotiation, so we use a response-based local.

If `req.flash()` has any content, it will have been set in our `login.js` middleware. This is also where we set our `user` local, passing `req.session.user` to `res.locals.user` on each request to ensure that our view stays up-to-date with user-session data.

Locals are also implicitly set in both the `exports.index` functions of `routes/index.js` and `login/routes/index.js` files by passing an object as the second option of `res.render`. In both cases, we set the `title`, `profiles`, and `page` locals so that our views have the information they need from a functioning app.

Finally, we also utilize the local object to inject the `safeMix` function for use by `profiles.jade` to protect it from throwing when attempting to use undefined mixins.

Styles

Our Stylus files also share a degree of interconnectivity as shown in the following diagram:

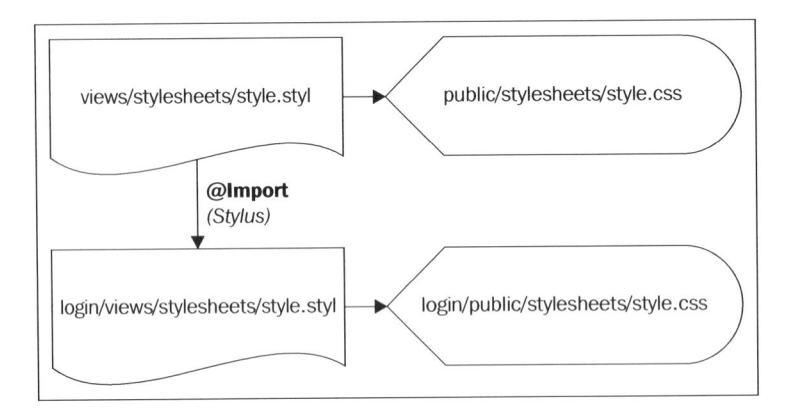

```
┌─────────────────────────────────────────────────────────────┐
│                                                             │
│   views/stylesheets/style.styl  →  public/stylesheets/style.css │
│                │                                            │
│             @Import                                         │
│             (Stylus)                                        │
│                ↓                                            │
│   login/views/stylesheets/style.styl  →  login/public/stylesheets/style.css │
│                                                             │
└─────────────────────────────────────────────────────────────┘
```

User flow

All the aforementioned things work together to provide a website with an admin section.

A user can browse the `profiles` table, using the back and forward links, and they can link to a particular page on the table.

A privileged user can navigate to `/admin`, enter their login details, and proceed to add and delete records. The `/add` and `/delete` routes are protected by the middleware. Unless the user is logged in, the only route that gets delivered to them is the login app's index route asking for login details.

There's more...

Let's look at ways to monitor and analyze our web app.

Benchmarking

Benchmarking a Node website can be very satisfying, but there's always going to be room for improvement.

Apache Bench (`ab`) comes bundled with Apache servers, and while Apache servers have no part in NodeJS, their HTTP benchmarking utility is an excellent tool for stress testing our app's ability to respond to a large amount of simultaneous requests.

We can use it to test the performance benefits or hindrances of any changes to our app. Let's quickly throw 1,000 requests, 50 at a time, at both the site and the admin section as follows:

```
ab -n 1000 -c 50 http://localhost:3000/
ab -n 1000 -c 50 http://localhost:3000/admin
```

Mileage will vary depending on system capabilities. However, since tests are run on the same machine, conclusions can be drawn from differences between tests.

With our test on the two sections, the / route delivers at 120 requests per second, whereas `/admin` serves at just under 160 requests per second. This makes sense because the `/admin` page will only be serving a login form, whereas the / route is pulling data from MongoDB, loading in sub-views via `include` and performing iteration logic on the `profiles` object.

See also

- The *Implementing dynamic routing* recipe
- The *Templating in Express* recipe
- The *CSS preprocessors with Express* recipe
- The *Initializing and using a session* recipe

8
Implementing Security, Encryption, and Authentication

In this chapter, we will cover the following topics:

- Implementing Basic Authentication
- Hashing passwords
- Implementing Digest Authentication
- Setting up an HTTPS web server
- Preventing cross-site request forgery

Introduction

When it comes to production web servers, security is paramount. The importance of security correlates with that of the data or services we provide. But even for the smallest project, we want to ensure our systems aren't vulnerable to attack.

Many web development frameworks provide built-in security, which is a two-sided coin. On one side, we don't have to overly concern ourselves with the details (except for the basics, such as cleaning user input before passing it into a SQL statement), but on the other, we implicitly trust that the vendor has plugged all the holes.

If a largely used server-side scripting platform, such as PHP, is discovered to contain security vulnerability, this can become public knowledge very quickly and every site running the vulnerable version of that framework is open to attack.

Implementing Security, Encryption, and Authentication

With Node, server-side security is almost entirely on our shoulders. Therefore, all we need to do is educate ourselves on the potential vulnerabilities and tighten the security of our systems and alter our code accordingly.

For the most part, Node is minimalistic: if we don't specifically outline something it doesn't happen. This leaves little room for exploitation of unknown parts of our or obscure configuration settings because we coded and configured our system by hand.

Attacks take place from two angles: exploiting technical flaws and taking advantage of user naivete. We can protect our systems by educating ourselves and conscientiously checking and rechecking our code. We can also protect our users by educating them.

In this chapter, we will learn how to implement various types of user-authenticated logins, how to secure these logins, and encrypt any transferred data, along with a technique to prevent the authenticated users from falling victim to exploits of the browser's security model.

Implementing Basic Authentication

The **Basic Authentication** standard has been in place since the 1990s and can be the simplest way to provide a user login. When used over HTTP, it is in no way secure since a plain text password is sent over the connection from the browser to the server.

> For information on Basic Authentication, visit `http://en.wikipedia.org/wiki/Basic_authentication`.

However, when coupled with SSL (HTTPS), Basic Authentication can be a useful method if we're not concerned about a custom-styled login form.

> We will discuss SSL/TLS (HTTPS) in the *Setting up an HTTPS web server* recipe of this chapter. For additional information, visit `http://en.wikipedia.org/wiki/SSL/TLS`.

In this recipe, we'll learn how to initiate and process a Basic Access Authentication request over plain HTTP. In the following recipes, we'll implement an HTTPS server and see an advancement of Basic Authentication (Digest Authentication).

Getting ready

We just need to create a new `server.js` file in a new folder.

How to do it...

Basic Authentication specifies a username, password, and realm, and it works over HTTP. So we'll require the HTTP module and set up some variables as shown in the following code:

```
var http = require('http');

var username = 'dave',
  password = 'ILikeBrie_33',
  realm = 'Node Cookbook';
```

Now we'll set up our HTTP server as shown in the following code:

```
http.createServer(function (req, res) {
  var auth, login;

  if (!req.headers.authorization) {
    authenticate(res);
    return;
  }

  //extract base64 encoded username:password string from client
  auth = req.headers.authorization.replace(/^Basic /, '');
  //decode base64 to utf8
  auth = (new Buffer(auth, 'base64').toString('utf8'));

  login = auth.split(':'); //[0] is username [1] is password

  if (login[0] === username && login[1] === password) {
    res.end('Someone likes soft cheese!');
    return;
  }

  authenticate(res);

}).listen(8080);
```

Note that we make two calls to a function named `authenticate`. We need to create this function, placing it above our `createServer` call:

```
function authenticate(res) {
  res.writeHead(401,
    {'WWW-Authenticate' : 'Basic realm="' + realm + '"'});
  res.end('Authorization required.');
}
```

Implementing Security, Encryption, and Authentication

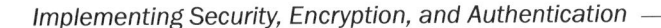

When we navigate to `localhost:8080` in our browser, we are asked to provide a username and password for the `Node Cookbook` realm. If we provide the correct details, our passion for "soft cheese" is revealed.

How it works...

Basic Authentication works via a series of headers sent between the server and browser. When a browser hits the server, the `WWW-Authenticate` header is sent to the browser and the browser responds by opening a dialog for the user to log in.

The browser's login dialog blocks any further content from being loaded in the browser, until the user either cancels or attempts to log in. If the user clicks on the **Cancel** button, they see the **Authorization required** message sent with `res.end` in the `authenticate` function.

However, if the user attempts to log in, the browser sends another request to the server. This time it contains an `Authorization` header in response to the `WWW-Authenticate` header. We check for its existence at the top of the `createServer` callback with `req.headers.authorization`. If the header exists, we skip the call to `authenticate` and go on to verify the user credentials. The `Authorization` header looks like the following syntax:

```
Authorization: Basic ZGF2ZTpJTGlrZUJyaWVfMzM=
```

The text following the `Basic` keyword in the preceding `Authorization` header syntax is a Base64-encoded string that holds the username and password separated by a colon; the decoded Base64 text is as follows:

```
dave:ILikeBrie_33
```

In our `createServer` callback, we decode the Base64 header by first stripping the `Basic` portion from it, load it into a buffer that converts Base64 to binary, and then run `toString` on the result converting it to a UTF-8 string.

> Visit `http://en.wikipedia.org/wiki/Base64` and `http://en.wikipedia.org/wiki/Comparison_of_Unicode_encodings` for information on Base64 and string encodings such as UTF-8.

Finally, we split the login details with a colon, and if the provided username and password match our stored credentials, the user is granted access to the authorized content.

There's more...

Basic Authentication comes bundled with the Express framework as middleware.

Basic Authentication with Express

Connect provides the `basicAuth` middleware, which implements this pattern for us. To implement the same in Express, use the following code:

```
var express = require('express');
var connect = require('connect');

var username = 'dave',
  password = 'ILikeBrie_33',
  realm = 'Node Cookbook';

var app = express();

app.use(connect.basicAuth(function (user, pass) {
  return username === user && password === pass;
}, realm));

app.get('/:route?', function (req, res) {
  res.end('Someone likes soft cheese!');
});

app.listen(8080);
```

If we now head to `http://localhost:8080`, our Express server will behave in the same way as it did in our main recipe.

> See *Chapter 7, Accelerating Development with Express,* for information on using Express to develop web solutions.

See also

- The *Setting up a router* recipe in *Chapter 1, Making a Web Server*
- The *Implementing Digest Authentication* recipe
- The *Setting up an HTTPS web server* recipe

Hashing passwords

Effective encryption is a fundamental part of online security. Node provides the `crypto` module that can be used to generate our own MD5 or SHA1 hashes for user passwords. Cryptographic hashes such as MD5 and SHA1 are known as message digests. Once the input data has been digested (encrypted), it cannot be put back into its original form (of course, if we know the original password, we can regenerate the hash and compare it to our stored hash).

Implementing Security, Encryption, and Authentication

We can use hashes to encrypt a user's password before we store them. If our stored passwords were ever stolen by an attacker, they cannot be used to log in because the attacker will not have the actual plain text passwords. However, since a hash algorithm always produces the same result, it could be possible for an attacker to crack a hash by matching it against hashes generated from the password dictionary (see the *There's more...* section for ways to mitigate this).

> Visit `http://en.wikipedia.org/wiki/Cryptographic_hash_function` for more information on hashes.

In this example, we will create a simple registration form and use the `crypto` module to generate an MD5 hash of a password gained via user input.

As with Basic Authentication, our registration form should be posted over HTTPS; otherwise, the password is sent as plain text.

Getting ready

In a new folder, let's create a new `server.js` file along with an HTML file for our registration form. We'll call it `regform.html`.

We'll use the Express framework to provide the peripheral mechanisms (parsing POST requests, serving `regform.html`, and so on), so Express should be installed. We'll also need the body-parser middleware to process the POST request. Use the following commands to install Express and body-parser middleware:

npm install express

npm install body-parser

We covered more about Express and how to install it in the previous chapter.

How to do it...

First, let's put together our registration form (`regform.html`) as shown in the following code:

```
<form method=post>
  User  <input name=user>
  Pass  <input type=password name=pass>
  <input type=submit>
</form>
```

For the `server.js` file, we'll require `express` and `crypto`. Then create our server as follows:

```
var express = require('express');
var crypto = require('crypto');
```

```
        var bodyParser = require('body-parser');

    var userStore = {},
      app = express();

    app.listen(8080);

    app.use(bodyParser());
```

The `bodyParser` keyword gives us the POST capabilities and our `userStore` object is used to store registered user details. In production, we would use a database.

Now set up a GET route as shown in the following code:

```
app.get('/', function (req, res) {
  res.sendfile('regform.html');
});
```

This uses Express' `sendfile` method to stream our `regform.html` file.

Finally, our POST route will check for the existence of user and pass inputs, returning an error message to the user if either or both are left blank or turning the user's specified password into an MD5 hash. Refer to the following code:

```
app.post('/', function (req, res) {
  if (!req.body.user || !req.body.pass) {
    res.send('Username and password both required');
    return;
  }
  var hash = crypto
      .createHash("md5")
      .update(req.body.pass)
      .digest('hex');

  userStore[req.body.user] = hash;
  res.send('Thanks for registering ' + req.body.user);
  console.log(userStore);

});
```

When we use our form to register, the console will output the `userStore` object, containing all registered usernames and password hashes.

Implementing Security, Encryption, and Authentication

How it works...

The password hashing portion of this recipe is as follows:

```
var hash = crypto
    .createHash("md5")
    .update(req.body.pass)
    .digest('hex');
```

We've used the dot notation to chain some `crypto` methods together.

First, we create a vanilla MD5 hash with the `createHash` method (see the *There's more...* section on how to create unique hashes). We could alternatively create a (stronger) SHA1 hash by passing `sha1` as the argument. The same goes for any other encryption method supported by Node's bundled `openssl` version. We can find out what hashes are supported with the following command:

`node -p "require('crypto').getHashes()"`

> The `-p` flag can be used with the `node` executable to evaluate and print (to screen) whatever string is subsequently passed to it.

Then we call the `update` method to feed our user's password to the initial hash.

> For a comparison of different hash functions, see http://ehash.iaik.tugraz.at/wiki/The_Hash_Function_Zoo.
>
> This site labels certain hash functions as broken, which means a weakness point has been found and published. However, the effort required to exploit such a weakness will often far exceed the value of the data we are protecting.

Finally, we call the `digest` method, which returns a completed password hash. Without any argument, digest returns the hash in the binary format. We pass `hex` (base 16 numerical representation format of binary data; see http://en.wikipedia.org/wiki/Hexadecimal) to make it more readable on the console.

There's more...

The `crypto` module offers some more advanced hashing methods to create even stronger passwords.

Making unique hashes with HMAC

HMAC, Hash-based Message Authentication Code, is a hash with a secret key (authentication code).

To convert our recipe to use HMAC, we change our crypto portion with the following code:

```
var hash = crypto
    .createHmac("md5",'SuperSecretKey')
    .update(req.body.pass)
    .digest('hex');
```

Using HMAC protects us from the use of rainbow tables (precomputed hashes from a large list of probable passwords). The secret key mutates our hash, rendering a rainbow table impotent (unless an attacker discovers our secret key, for instance, by somehow gaining root access to our server's operating system, at which point rainbow tables wouldn't be necessary anyway).

Hardened hashing with PBKDF2

PBKDF2 is the second version of **Password-Based Key Derivation Function**, which is part of the Password-Based Cryptographic standard.

A powerful quality of PBKDF2 is that it generates hashes of hashes, thousands of times over. Iterating over the hash multiple times strengthens the encryption, exponentially increasing the amount of possible outcomes resulting from an initial value to the extent that the hardware required to generate or store all possible hashes becomes infeasible.

The `pbkdf2` method requires four components: the desired password, a salt value, the desired amount of iterations, and a specified length of the resulting hash.

A salt is similar in concept to the secret key in our HMAC in that it mixes in with our hash to create a different hash. However, the purpose of a salt differs. A salt simply adds uniqueness to the hash and it doesn't need to be protected as a secret. A strong approach is to make each salt unique to the hash being generated, storing it alongside the hash. If each hash in a database is generated from a different salt, an attacker is forced to generate a rainbow table for each hash based on its salt rather than the entire database. With PBKDF2, thanks to our salt, we have unique hashes of unique hashes, which further increases the complexity for a potential attacker.

For a strong salt, we'll use the `randomBytes` method of `crypto` to generate 128 bytes of random data, which we will then pass through the `pbkdf2` method with the user-supplied password 7,000 times, finally creating a hash 256 bytes in length.

To achieve this, let's modify our POST route from the recipe as shown in the following code:

```
app.post('/', function (req, res) {
  if (!req.body.user || !req.body.pass) {
    res.send('Username and password both required');
    return;
```

Implementing Security, Encryption, and Authentication

```
    }

    crypto.randomBytes(128, function (err, salt) {
      if (err) { throw err; }
      salt = new Buffer(salt).toString('hex');
      crypto.pbkdf2(req.body.pass, salt, 7000, 256,
        function (err, hash) {
          if (err) { throw err; }
          userStore[req.body.user] = {salt : salt,
            hash : (new Buffer(hash).toString('hex')) };
          res.send('Thanks for registering ' + req.body.user);
          console.log(userStore);
        });
    });
  });
```

Once we have both our hash and salt values, we place them into our `userStore` object. To implement a corresponding login, we would simply compute the hash in the same way using that user's stored salt.

We chose to iterate 7,000 times. When PBKDF2 was standardized, the recommended iteration count was 1,000. However, we need more iteration to account for technology advancements and reductions in the cost of equipment.

See also

- The *Implementing Digest Authentication* recipe
- The *Setting up an HTTPS web server* recipe
- The *Generating Express scaffolding* recipe in *Chapter 7, Accelerating Development with Express*

Implementing Digest Authentication

Digest Authentication combines Basic Authentication with MD5 encryption, thus avoiding the transmission of plain text passwords, making for a more secure login method over plain HTTP.

On its own, Digest Authentication is still insecure without an SSL/TLS-secured HTTPS connection. Anything over plain HTTP is vulnerable to the man-in-the-middle attacks, where an adversary can intercept requests and forge responses. An attacker could masquerade as the server, replacing the expected digest response with a Basic Authentication response, thus gaining the password in plain text.

Chapter 8

Nevertheless, in the absence of SSL/TLS, Digest Authentication at least provides some defense in the area of plain text passwords requiring more advanced circumvention techniques.

So in this recipe, we will create a Digest Authentication server.

Getting ready

To begin with, we simply create a new folder with a new `server.js` file.

How to do it...

As in the *Basic Authentication with Express* recipe, we create an HTTP server. We'll also use the `crypto` module to handle the MD5 hashing:

```
var http = require('http');
var crypto = require('crypto');

var username = 'dave',
  password = 'digestthis!',
  realm = "Node Cookbook",
  opaque;
function md5(msg) {
   return crypto.createHash('md5').update(msg).digest('hex');
}

opaque = md5(realm);
```

We've made an `md5` function as a shorthand interface to the `crypto` hash methods. The `opaque` variable is a necessary part of the `Digest` standard. It's simply an MD5 hash of `realm` (as also used in Basic Authentication). The client returns the opaque value to the server for an extra means of validating responses.

Now, we'll create two extra helper functions, one for authentication and one to parse the `Authorization` header as follows:

```
function authenticate(res) {
  res.writeHead(401, {
    'WWW-Authenticate' : 'Digest realm="' + realm + '"'
    + ',qop="auth",nonce="' + Math.random() + '"'
    + ',opaque="' + opaque + '"'});

  res.end('Authorization required.');
}

function parseAuth(auth) {
```

Implementing Security, Encryption, and Authentication

```
    var authObj = {};
    auth.split(', ').forEach(function (pair) {
      pair = pair.split('=');
      authObj[pair[0]] = pair[1].replace(/"/g, '');
    });
    return authObj;
  }
```

Finally, we implement the server as shown in the following code:

```
  http.createServer(function (req, res) {
    var auth, user, digest = {};

    if (!req.headers.authorization) {
      authenticate(res);
      return;
    }
    auth = req.headers.authorization.replace(/^Digest /, '');
    auth = parseAuth(auth); //object containing digest headers from client
    //don't waste resources generating MD5 if username is wrong
    if (auth.username !== username) { authenticate(res); return; }
    digest.ha1 = md5(auth.username + ':' + realm + ':' + password);
    digest.ha2 = md5(req.method + ':' + auth.uri);
    digest.response = md5([
      digest.ha1,
      auth.nonce, auth.nc, auth.cnonce, auth.qop,
      digest.ha2
    ].join(':'));

    if (auth.response !== digest.response) { authenticate(res); return;
  }
    res.end('You made it!');

  }).listen(8080);
```

Within the browser, this will look exactly the same as Basic Authentication, which is unfortunate because a clear difference between digest and basic dialogs could alert the user about a potential attack.

How it works...

When the server sends the `WWW-Authenticate` header to the browser, several attributes are included, consisting of `realm`, `qop`, `nonce`, and `opaque`.

The `realm` attribute is the same as Basic Authentication, and `opaque` is an MD5 hash of the `realm`.

The `qop` attribute stands for **Quality of Protection** and is set to `auth`. The `qop` attribute can also be set to `auth-int` or simply omitted. By setting it to `auth`, we cause the browser to compute a more secure final MD5 hash. The `auth-int` attribute is still stronger, but browser support for it is minimal.

The `nonce` attribute is a similar concept to a salt; it causes the final MD5 hash to be less predictable from an attacker's perspective.

When the user submits their login details via the browser's authentication dialog, an `Authorization` header is returned containing all of the attributes sent from the server, plus the `username`, `uri`, `nc`, `cnonce`, and `response` attributes.

The `username` attribute is the user's specified alias, `uri` is the path being accessed (we could use this to secure on a route-by-route basis), `nc` is a serial counter that is incremented on each authentication attempt, `cnonce` is the browser's own generated `nonce` value, and `response` is the final computed hash.

In order to confirm an authenticated user, our server must match the value of `response`. To do so, it removes the `Digest` string (including the proceeding space) and then passes what remains out of the `Authorization` header to the `parseAuth` function. The `parseAuth` function converts all the attributes into a handy object and loads it back into our `auth` variable.

The first thing we do with `auth` is check if the username is correct. If we do not have a match, we ask for authentication again. This could save our server from some unnecessary heavy lifting with MD5 hashing.

The final computed MD5 hash is made from the combination of two previously encrypted MD5 hashes along with the server's `nonce` and `qop` values and the client's `cnonce` and `nc` values.

We called the first hash `digest.ha1`. It contains a colon (`:`) delimited string of the `username`, `realm`, and `password` values. The `digest.ha2` hash is the `request` method (`GET`) and the `uri` attribute, again delimited by a colon.

The final `digest.response` property has to match `auth.response`, which is generated by the browser, so the ordering and specific elements must be precise. To create our `digest.response` property we combine `digest.ha1`, `nonce`, `nc`, `cnonce`, `qop`, and `digest.ha2`, each separated by a colon. For easy reading, we put these values into an array running JavaScript's `join` method on them to generate the final string, which is passed to our `md5` function.

If the given username and password are correct, and we've generated `digest.response` correctly, it should match the browser's response header attribute (`auth.response`). If it doesn't, the user will be presented with another authentication dialog. If it does, we reach the final `res.end`. We made it!

Implementing Security, Encryption, and Authentication

There's more...

Let's tackle the logout problem.

Logging out of authenticated areas

There is little to no support in browsers for any official logging out method under Basic or Digest Authentication, except for the closing of the entire browser.

However, we can force the browser to essentially lose its session by changing the `realm` attribute in the `WWW-Authenticate` header.

In a multiuser situation, if we change our global `realm` variable, it will cause all users to log out (if there was more than one). So if a user wishes to log out, we have to assign them a unique realm that will cause only their session to quit.

To simulate multiple users, we'll remove our `username` and `password` variables, replacing them with a users object as shown in the following code:

```
var users = {
            'dave' : {password : 'digestthis!'},
            'bob'  : {password : 'MyNamesBob:-D'},
          },
    realm = "Node Cookbook",
    opaque;
```

Our subobjects (currently containing `password`) will potentially gain three extra properties: uRealm, uOpaque, and forceLogOut.

Next, we'll modify our `authenticate` function as follows:

```
function authenticate(res, username) {
  var uRealm = realm, uOpaque = opaque;
  if (username) {
    uRealm = users[username].uRealm;
    uOpaque = users[username].uOpaque;
  }
  res.writeHead(401, {'WWW-Authenticate' :
     'Digest realm="' + uRealm + '"'
    + ',qop="auth",nonce="' + Math.random() + '"'
    + ',opaque="' + uOpaque + '"'});

  res.end('Authorization required.');
}
```

We've added an optional `username` parameter to the `authenticate` function. If `username` is present, we load the unique `realm` and corresponding `opaque` values for that user, sending them in the header.

Inside our server callback, we replace the following code:

```
//don't waste resources generating MD5 if username is wrong
if (auth.username !== username) { authenticate(res); return; }
```

We replace the preceding code with the following code:

```
//don't waste resources generating MD5 if username is wrong
if (!users[auth.username]) { authenticate(res); return; }

if (req.url === '/logout') {
  users[auth.username].uRealm = realm + ' [' + Math.random() + ']';
  users[auth.username].uOpaque = md5(users[auth.username].uRealm);
  users[auth.username].forceLogOut = true;
  res.writeHead(302, {'Location' : '/'});
  res.end();
  return;
}

if (users[auth.username].forceLogOut) {
  delete users[auth.username].forceLogOut;
  authenticate(res, auth.username);
}
```

We check whether the specified username exists inside our `users` object, saving us from further processing if it doesn't. Provided the user is valid, we check the route (we'll be supplying a logout link to the user). If the `/logout` route has been hit, we set up a `uRealm` property on the logged in user's object and a corresponding `uOpaque` property containing an MD5 hash of `uRealm`. We also add a `forceLogOut` Boolean property, setting it to `true`. Then we redirect the user away from the `/logout` to `/`.

The redirect triggers another request, on which the server detects the presence of our `forceLogOut` property for the currently authenticated user. The `forceLogOut` property is then removed from the `users` subobject to prevent it from getting in the way later. Lastly, we pass control over to the `authenticate` function with the special `username` parameter.

Consequently, `authenticate` includes the user-linked `uRealm` and `uOpaque` values in the `WWW-Authenticate` header, breaking the session. To finish off, we make a few more simple adjustments.

Implementing Security, Encryption, and Authentication

The `digest.ha1` hash requires the `password` and `realm` values, so it's updated as follows:

```
digest.ha1 = md5(auth.username + ':'
    + (users[auth.username].uRealm || realm) + ':'
    + users[auth.username].password);
```

The `password` value is fed in via our new `users` object, and the `realm` value is chosen based on whether our logged-in user has unique realm (a `uRealm` property) set.

We change the last segment of our server's code to the following:

```
if (auth.response !== digest.response) {
    users[auth.username].uRealm = realm + ' [' + Math.random() + ']';
    users[auth.username].uOpaque = md5(users[auth.username].uRealm);
    authenticate(res, (users[auth.username].uRealm && auth.username));
    return;
}
res.writeHead(200, {'Content-type':'text/html'});
res.end('You made it! <br> <a href="logout"> [ logout ] </a>');
```

Note the inclusion of a logout link, the final piece.

New `uRealm` and `uOpaque` attributes are generated if the hashes don't match. This prevents an eternal loop between the browser and server. Without this, when we log in as a valid user and then log out, we'd be presented with another login dialog. If we enter a non-existent user, the new login attempt is rejected by the server as normal. However, the browser attempts to be helpful and falls back to the old authentication details with our first logged-in user and the original realm. But, when the server receives the old login details, it matches the user to their unique realm, demanding authentication for `uRealm`, not `realm`. The browser sees the `uRealm` value and matches our non-existent user back to it, attempting to authenticate that user again, thus repeating the cycle.

By setting a new `uRealm`, we break the cycle because an extra realm is introduced, which the browser has no record of, so it defers to the user by asking for input.

See also

- The *Implementing Basic Authentication* recipe
- The *Cryptographic password hashing* recipe
- The *Setting up an HTTPS web server* recipe

Setting up an HTTPS web server

In large part, SSL is the solution to many of the security vulnerabilities, such as network sniffing and man-in-the-middle attacks, faced over HTTP. Thanks to the core `https` module. It's really simple to set up.

Getting ready

The greater challenge could be in actually obtaining the necessary SSL/TLS certificate. In order to acquire a certificate, we must generate an encrypted private key, and from that we generate **Certificate Signing Request** (**CSR**). This is then passed to **Certificate Authority** (**CA**). CA is a commercial entity specifically trusted by browser vendors—naturally this means we have to pay for it. Alternatively, the CA may generate your private key and CSR on your behalf.

After a verification process, the CA will issue a public certificate enabling us to encrypt our connections.

We can shortcut this process and authorize our own certificate (self-sign), naming ourselves the CA. Unfortunately, if the CA isn't known to a browser, it will warn the user that our site isn't to be trusted and that they may be under attack. This isn't so good for positive brand image. So, while we may self-sign during development, we would most likely need a trusted CA for production.

For development, we can quickly use the `openssl` executable (available by default on Linux and Mac OS X; we can obtain a Windows version from http://www.openssl.org/related/binaries.html) to generate necessary private key and public certificate:

```
openssl req -new -newkey rsa:1024 -nodes -subj '/O=Node Cookbook' -keyout key.pem -out csr.pem
openssl x509 -req -in csr.pem -signkey key.pem -out cert.pem
```

> Windows users would need to run the preceding command slightly different. After installing, we have to right-click on the `openssl.exe` file (typically located at `C:\OpenSSL-Win32\bin`) and select **Run as Administrator**. Then we supply everything after `openssl` in the preceding first command (for example, `req -new...`) into the resultant dialog, repeating the exercise for the second dialog.

This executes `openssl` twice on the command line: once to generate basic private key and CSR and again to self-sign private key, thus generating a certificate (`cert.pem`).

In a real production scenario, our `-subj` flag would hold more details and we would want to acquire our `cert.pem` file from a legitimate CA. But this is fine for private, development, and testing purposes.

Implementing Security, Encryption, and Authentication

Now that we have our key and certificate, we simply need to make our server, so we'll create a new `server.js` file.

How to do it...

Within the `server.js` file we write the following code:

```
var https = require('https');
var fs = require('fs');

var opts = {key: fs.readFileSync('key.pem'),
  cert: fs.readFileSync('cert.pem')};

https.createServer(opts, function (req, res) {
  res.end('secured!');
}).listen(4443); //443 for prod
```

And that's it!

How it works...

The `https` module depends on the `http` and `tls` modules, which in turn rely on the `net` and `crypto` modules. SSL/TLS is transport layer encryption, meaning that it works at a level beneath HTTP, at the TCP level. The `tls` and `net` modules work together to provide an SSL/TLS-encrypted TCP connection, with HTTPS layered on top.

When a client connects via HTTPS (in our case, at the address `https://localhost:4443`), it attempts a TLS/SSL handshake with our server. The `https` module uses the `tls` module to respond to the handshake in a series of fact-finding interchanges between the browser and server. For example, what SSL/TLS version do you support? What encryption method do you want to use? Can I have your public key?

At the end of this initial interchange, the client and server have an agreed shared secret. This secret is used to encrypt and decrypt content sent between the two parties. This is where the `crypto` module kicks in, providing all of the data encryption and decryption functionality.

For us, it's as simple as requiring the `https` module, providing our certificates, then using it just like we would an `http` server.

There's more...

Let's see a few HTTPS use cases.

HTTPS in Express

Enabling HTTPS in Express is just simple as shown in the following code:

```
var express = require('express'),
  fs = require('fs');

var opts = {key: fs.readFileSync('key.pem'),
  cert: fs.readFileSync('cert.pem')};

var app = express(opts),
  https = require('https');

https.createServer(opts, app).listen(4443);

app.get('/', function (req, res) {
  res.send('secured!');
});
```

Securing Basic Authentication with SSL/TLS

We can build anything into our `https` server that we could into an `http` server. To enable HTTPS in our *Basic Authentication with Express* recipe, all we do is alter the following code:

```
https.createServer(function (req, res) {
```

The preceding code is altered to the following code:

```
var opts = {key: fs.readFileSync('key.pem'),
  cert: fs.readFileSync('cert.pem')};

https.createServer(opts, function (req, res) {
```

See also

- The *Cryptographic password hashing* recipe
- The *Implementing Basic Authentication* recipe

Implementing Security, Encryption, and Authentication

Preventing cross-site request forgery

There's a problem with every browser's security model that, as developers, we must be aware of.

When a user has logged in to a site, any requests made via the authenticated browser are treated as legitimate—even if the links for these requests come from an e-mail or are performed in another window. Once the browser has a session, all windows can access that session. This means an attacker can manipulate users' actions on a site they are logged in to with a specifically crafted link or with automatic AJAX calls requiring no user interaction except to be on the page containing the malicious AJAX.

For instance, if a banking web app hasn't been properly CSRF secured, an attacker could convince the user to visit another website while logged in to their online banking. This website could then run a `POST` request to transfer money from the victim's account to the attacker's account without the victim's consent or knowledge.

This is known as a **Cross-Site Request Forgery** (**CSRF**) attack. In this recipe, we'll implement a secure HTML login system with CSRF protection.

Getting ready

We'll be securing our profiler web app from the *Making an Express Web App* recipe in *Chapter 7, Accelerating Development with Express*.

We'll want to get a hold of our `profiler` app, with the `profiler/app.js` and `profiler/login/app.js` files open and ready for editing.

To supply CSRF protection, we'll use the `csrf` middleware. Let's install that and add it to `package.json`:

```
npm install csrf --save
```

Without SSL/TLS encryption, HTML-based logins are subject to at least the same vulnerabilities as Basic Authorization. So for basic security, we'll add HTTPS to our app. So we need our `cert.pem` and `key.pem` files from the previous recipe.

We'll also need to have MongoDB running with our stored user data from recipes in *Chapter 7, Accelerating Development with Express*, since our profiler app relies on it. We can start MongoDB with the following command:

```
sudo mongod --dbpath db
```

If we use Windows, we can instead use the following command:

```
C:\mongodb\bin\mongod.exe   --dbpath db
```

In the preceding command, `c:\mongodb` is where MongoDb has been installed.

Chapter 8

How to do it...

First, let's secure our entire app with SSL, the `profiler/bin/www` file should be altered as follows:

```
#!/usr/bin/env node
var debug = require('debug')('my-application');
var app = require('../app');
var https = require('https');
var fs = require('fs');

app.set('port', process.env.PORT || 3000);

var server = https.createServer({
  key: fs.readFileSync('key.pem'),
  cert: fs.readFileSync('cert.pem')
}, app).listen(app.get('port'), function() {
  debug('Express server listening on port ' + server.address().port);
});
```

We've added the `fs` and `https` modules.

We use `fs.readFileSync` to load the contents of `cert.pem` and `key.pem` to populate the key and cert properties of the `createServer` method's first argument (the options object).

The `app` function (as returned by calling `express`, exported from `app.js`) is fundamentally a callback function that accepts request and response objects. Although, `app` can also take an optional third parameter (`next`), it principally matches the signature of the callback function for the `https` (and `http`) `createServer` method.

The `app.listen` method (as used in the original `./bin/www`) is simply a convenience function that passes `app` into `http.createServer`. In order to provide a secured HTTP, we must use the `https` module and pass `app` in as the second argument of its `createServer` method, first providing the private key and certificate via the first argument (the options object).

The `createServer` method also returns an object with a listen method, so we leave the rest of the listening code as is.

Now, when we run `npm start`, we can (only) access our app at `https://localhost:3000`. Now that we've implemented SSL for our Express app, let's move on to securing against CSRF attacks.

The admin section of profiler is where a CSRF attack could take place, so let's open up `profiler/login/app.js` and add the `csrf` middleware, which we installed in the *Getting ready* section.

Implementing Security, Encryption, and Authentication

First, we add `csrf` to the dependencies in `profiler/login/app.js` as shown in the following code:

```
var express = require('express');
var http = require('http');
var path = require('path');
var favicon = require('static-favicon');
var logger = require('morgan');
var cookieParser = require('cookie-parser');
var bodyParser = require('body-parser');
var methodOverride = require('method-override');
var session = require('express-session');
var flash = require('express-flash');
var csrf = require('csrf');

var routes = require('./routes/index');

var app = express();
```

Then we insert the `express-csrf` middleware by using the following code:

```
//…snip… prior configuration
app.use(cookieParser());
app.use(session({secret:'koobkooC edoN'}));
app.use(csrf());
app.use(flash());
//…snip… rest of configuration section
```

The `csrf` middleware is dependent on the `bodyParser` and `session` middleware, so it must be placed below these.

Now, if we navigate to `https://localhost:3000/admin` and attempt to log in (`dave`, `expressrocks`), we will receive a `403 Forbidden` response, even though we use the correct details.

That's because our login app is now looking for an additional POST parameter called `_csrf` in all of our POST forms, which must match the `_csrf` value stored in the user's `session` object.

Our views need to know the value of `_csrf` so that it can be placed in our forms as a hidden element.

One easy way to supply this is to load it onto the `res.locals` object within the middleware we wrote to supply `req.flash` to our views:

```
app.use(function (req, res, next) {
    res.locals.flash = req.flash();
    res.locals._csrf = req.session._csrf;
```

```
      next();
});
```

Next, we'll create a view called `csrf.jade` in the `login/views` folder as follows:

```
input(type="hidden", name="_csrf", value=_csrf)
```

Now, we include `csrf.jade` in each of our POST forms.

We will include `csrf.jade` in `login.jade` as follows:

```
//prior login jade code above
if user
  form(method='post')
    input(name="_method", type="hidden", value="DELETE")
    include csrf
    p Hello #{user.name}!
      a(href='javascript:', onClick='forms[0].submit()') [logout]

  include admin
  include ../../views/profiles

else
  p Please log in
  form(method="post")
    include csrf
    fieldset
      legend Login
//rest of login.jade
```

We will include `csrf.jade` in `addfrm.jade` as follows:

```
fields = ['Name', 'Irc', 'Twitter', 'Github', 'Location',
'Description'];
form#addfrm(method='post', action='/admin/add')
  include csrf
  fieldset
    legend Add
//rest of addfrm.jade
```

> Updating and maintaining a site with many different POST forms could pose as challenging. We would have to manually alter every single form. See how we can autogenerate CSRF values for all forms in the *There's more...* section.

Implementing Security, Encryption, and Authentication

Now we can log in, add profiles, and log out without a `403 Forbidden` response.

However, our `/del` route is still susceptible to CSRF. The `GET` requests are not typically supposed to trigger any changes on the server. They are intended simply to retrieve information. However, like many other apps in the wild, the developers (that's us) were lazy when they built this particular functionality and decided to coerce a `GET` request to do their bidding.

We could turn this into a `POST` request and then secure it with CSRF, but what about an app that has hundreds of these deviant `GET` methods?

Let's find out how to protect our `/del` route.

In `login/routes/index.js`, add the following code:

```
exports.delprof = function (req, res) {
  if (req.query._csrf !== req.session._csrf) {
    res.send(403);
    return;
  };
    profiles.del(req.query.id, function (err) {
      if (err) { console.log(err); }
        profiles.pull(req.query.p, function (err, profiles) {
          req.app.helpers({profiles: profiles});
          res.redirect(req.header('Referrer') || '/');
        });
      });

}
```

Our changes make it so we can't delete profiles until we include `_csrf` in the query string, and so in `views/admin.jade`:

```
mixin del(id)
  td
    a.del(href='/admin/del?id=#{id}&p=#{page}&_csrf=#{_csrf}')
      &#10754;
//rest of admin.jade
```

How it works...

The `csrf` middleware generates a unique token that is held in the user's session. This token must be included in any action request (logging in, logging out, adding, or deleting) as an attribute named `_csrf`.

If the `_csrf` value in the request body (or query string for `GET`) doesn't match the `_csrf` token stored in the `session` object, the server denies access to that route and therefore, prevents the action from occurring.

How does this prevent a CSRF attack? In a plain CSRF exploit, the attacker has no way of knowing what the `_csrf` value is, so they are unable to forge the necessary POST request.

Our `/del` route protection is less secure. It exposes the `_csrf` value in the address, potentially creating a very small, but nonetheless plausible, window of opportunity for an attacker to grab the `_csrf` value. This is why it's best for us to stick with the POST/DELETE/PUT requests for all action-related endeavors, leaving GET requests for simple retrieval.

> **Cross-site scripting (XSS) circumvention**
>
> This protection is rendered moot in the event of an accompanied XSS exploit, whereby an attacker is able to implant their own JavaScript within the site (for example, through exploiting an input vulnerability). JavaScript can read any elements in the page it resides on and view non-HttpOnly cookies with `document.cookie`.

There's more...

We'll take a look at a way to automatically generate CSRF tokens for login forms, but we should also bear in mind that CSRF protection is only as good as our ability to code tightly.

Auto-securing the POST forms with the CSRF elements

Ensuring that all the POST forms in our app contain a hidden `_csrf` input element could be an arduous task on a site of any significant scale.

We can interact directly with some Jade internals to automatically include these elements.

First, in `login/app.js`, just under where the view engine is set, we add the following line:

```
app.set('view engine', 'jade');
app.locals.compiler = require('./customJadeCompiler');
```

The Jade view engine relies on a special local variable called `compile`. We can overwrite this local variable after setting Jade as our view engine to add some customizations to the way Jade interprets our views.

Let's create `customJadeCompiler.js`, placing it in the `login` directory.

First, we'll require some modules and set up our new compiler class as follows:

```
var jade = require('jade');
var util = require('util');

//inherit from Jade's Compiler
var CompileWithCsrf = function (node, options) {
  jade.Compiler.call(this, node, options);
};
```

Next, we use `util.inherits` to inherit our new compiler's prototype from the Jade's compiler as shown in the following code:

```
//inherit from the prototype
util.inherits(CompileWithCsrf, jade.Compiler);
```

Then we modify Jade's internal `visitTag` method (which we've inherited from `jade.Compiler`) as shown in the following code:

```
CompileWithCsrf.prototype.visitTag = function (tag) {

    if (tag.name === 'form' && tag.getAttribute('method').match(/post/i)) {

        var csrfInput = new jade.nodes.Tag('input')
            .setAttribute('type', '"hidden"')
            .setAttribute('name', '"csrf"')
            .setAttribute('value', '_csrf');

        tag.block.push(csrfInput);

    }
    jade.Compiler.prototype.visitTag.call(this, tag);
};
```

Finally, we load our new compiler into `module.exports`, so it's passed via `require` to the `compiler` option of the `view options` setting in `app.js`:

```
module.exports = CompileWithCsrf;
```

We create a new class-type function, applying the call method to `jade.Compiler`. When we pass the `this` object to the `call` method, we essentially inherit the main functionality of `jade.Compiler` into our own `CompileWithCsrf` class-type function. It's a great way to reuse code.

However, `jade.Compiler` also has a modified prototype, which must be incorporated into our `CompileWithCsrf` function in order to fully mimic `jade.Compiler`.

Using `call` and `util.inherits` allows us to clone the `jade.Compiler` object as `CompileWithCsrf`, which means we can modify it without touching `jade.Compiler` and then allow it to operate in place of `jade.Compiler`.

We modify the `visitTag` method, which processes each tag (for example, `p`, `div`, and so on) in a Jade view. Then we look for the `form` tags with methods set to `post`, using a regular expression since the `method` attribute may be in upper or lowercase, being wrapped in double or single quotes.

If we find `form` with `POST` formatting, we use the `jade.Nodes` constructor to create a new input `node` (a Jade construct, in this case rolling as an HTML element), which we then call `setAttribute` (an internal Jade method) on three times to set the `type`, `name`, and `value` fields. Note `name` is set to `'"_csrf"'` but `value` contains `'_csrf'`. The inner double quotes tell Jade we intend a string. Without them, it treats the second parameter as a variable, which is exactly what we want in the case of `value`. The `value` attribute is, therefore, rendered according to `res.locals._csrf` defined in `app.js` (which is likewise taken from `req.session._csrf` as generated by the `express.csrf` middleware).

Now that our `_csrf` tokens are automatically included in every `POST` form, we can remove the `csrf.jade` includes from the `login.jade` and `addfrm.jade` views.

Eliminating cross-site scripting (XSS) vulnerabilities

Cross-site scripting attacks are generally preventable. All we have to do is ensure any user input is validated and encoded. The tricky part comes where we improperly or insufficiently encode user input.

When we take user input, much of the time we'll be outputting it to the browser at a later stage; this means we must embed it within our HTML.

XSS attacks are all about breaking context. For instance, imagine we had some Jade that links to a user profile by their username:

```
a (href=username)   !{username}
```

This code is exploitable in two ways. First, we used `!{username}` instead of `#{username}` for the text portion of our anchor link element. In Jade, `#{}` interpolation escapes any HTML in the given variable. So if an attacker was able to insert `<script>alert('This is where you get hacked!')</script>` as their username, `#{username}` would render:

```
&lt;script&gt;alert('This is where you get hacked!')&lt;/script&gt;
```

Whereas, `!{username}` would be unescaped (for example, HTML would not be replaced by escape characters such as `&lt;` in place of `<`). The attacking code could be changed from an innocent (though jaunty) `alert` message, to successfully initiated forged requests, and our CSRF protection would be futile since the attack is operating from the same page (JavaScript has access to all data on the page, and the attacker has gained access to our page's JavaScript via XSS).

Jade HTML escapes variables by default, which is a good thing. However, proper escaping must be context aware, and simply converting HTML syntax into its corresponding entity codes is not enough.

Implementing Security, Encryption, and Authentication

The other vulnerable area in our bad Jade code is the `href` attribute. Attributes are a different context to simple nested HTML. Unquoted attributes are particularly susceptible to attack, for instance, consider the following code:

```
<a href=profile>some text</a>
```

If we could set `profile` to `profile onClick=javascript:alert('gotcha')`, our HTML would read as follows:

```
<a href=profile onClick=javascript:alert('gotcha')>some text</a>
```

Again, Jade partially protects us in this sense by automatically quoting variables inserted to attributes. However, our vulnerable attribute is the `href` attribute, which is another sub context of the URL variety. Since it isn't prefixed with anything, an attacker might input their username as `javascript:alert('oh oh!')`, so the output of a `(href=username)` `!{username}` would be as follows:

```
<a href="javascript:alert('oh oh!')">  javascript:alert('oh oh!')
    </a>
```

The `javascript:` protocol allows us to execute JavaScript at the link level, allowing a CSRF attack to be launched when an unsuspecting user clicks on a malicious link.

> These simple examples are elementary. XSS attacks can be much more complex and sophisticated. However, we can follow the Open Web Application Security Projects 8 input sanitizing rules that provide extensive protection against XSS:
>
> https://www.owasp.org/index.php/XSS_(Cross_Site_Scripting)_Prevention_Cheat_Sheet

> **Validator module**
>
> Once we understand how to clean user input, we could use regular expressions to quickly apply specific validation and sanitization methods. However, for a simpler life, we could also use the third-party validator module, which can be installed with npm. Documentation is available on the GitHub page: https://www.github.com/chriso/node-validator.

See also

- The *Setting up an HTTPS web server* recipe
- The *Initializing and using a session* recipe in *Chapter 7, Accelerating Development with Express*
- The *Making an Express web app* recipe in *Chapter 7, Accelerating Development with Express*

9
Integrating Network Paradigms

In this chapter, we will cover the following topics:

- Sending an e-mail
- Sending an SMS
- Communicating with TCP
- Creating an SMTP server
- Implementing a virtual hosting paradigm

Introduction

Node's capabilities extend far beyond simply serving web pages. Node's core focus of supporting various computing tasks and networking objectives with straightforward APIs allows developers like us to unleash our creativity and innovate increasingly interconnected solutions and ideas.

In this chapter, we'll be looking at some fundamental examples of such interconnectivity with the knowledge that we can take these archetypes and grow and combine them into larger applications.

Knowledge of how to implement network paradigms can help us exceed the normal boundaries of a web app, providing advanced functionality to our users and implementing more ways for individuals to connect with our services.

Integrating Network Paradigms

Sending an e-mail

On many platforms, the ability to send e-mail is a standard core feature, but Nodes' minimal approach to core leaves the actual implementation of e-mail protocols up to third-party modules.

Thankfully, there are some excellent module creators in the Node community who have already created modules for sending an e-mail. In this recipe, we'll be using the well-featured third-party `nodemailer` module to send an imaginary newsletter to a list of recipients.

Getting ready

In order to send an e-mail, we'll need a functioning **Simple Mail Transfer Protocol** (**SMTP**) server that we can connect to. In a later recipe, we'll be creating our own SMTP server, but for now, we'll have to acquire some SMTP details to use our client with.

If we have an e-mail address, we will have access to an SMTP server. We can find out the SMTP host address from our provider.

If required, we can obtain access to an SMTP server by signing up for a Gmail account (at `mail.google.com`). Once we have an account, we can use `smtp.gmail.com` as the host, with our Gmail address as the username.

We'll create a new folder with a new file called `mailout.js` to hold our code.

Finally, we'll need the `nodemailer` module on the command line inside our new folder. We can install it with the following command:

```
npm install nodemailer
```

How to do it...

There are three main elements to use `nodemailer`. They are as follows:

- Setting up the SMTP transport
- Putting together the message object (which includes the transport)
- Passing the object to the `sendMail` method

Let's add the `nodemailer` module and create the transport as shown in the following code:

```
var nodemailer = require('nodemailer');

var transport = nodemailer.createTransport('SMTP', {
  host: 'smtp.gmail.com',
  secureConnection: true,
  port: 465,
  auth: {
```

```
      user: "ourGmailAddress@googlemail.com",
      pass: "ourPassword"
    }
  });
```

We will need to fill in our own SMTP settings for the `user` and `pass` values.

We've used the `secureConnection` setting and set the port to `465`, so we can use Gmail's SSL/TLS-secured SMTP server.

Now we incorporate our configured transport into an object that we'll call `msg`, as follows:

```
var msg = {
  transport: transport,
  text:    "Hello! This is your newsletter, :D",
  from:    "Definitely Not Spammers <spamnot@ok.com>",
  subject: "Your Newsletter"
};
```

Notice that we haven't set a `to` property on the object. We're going to mail out to multiple addresses, so `to` will be set dynamically. For testing purposes, we'll create an array of `mailinator` e-mail addresses. Mailinator (http://www.mailinator.com) is a free service that allows us to quickly create temporary e-mail addresses by sending an e-mail to an invented address. We'll create the temporary e-mail addresses with the help of the following code:

```
var maillist = [
  'Mr One <mailtest1@mailinator.com>',
  'Mr Two <mailtest2@mailinator.com>',
  'Mr Three <mailtest3@mailinator.com>',
  'Mr Four <mailtest4@mailinator.com>',
  'Mr Five <mailtest5@mailinator.com>'
];
```

Now, we simply loop through and send our newsletter to each address as follows:

```
maillist.forEach(function (to, i) {
  msg.to = to;
  nodemailer.sendMail(msg, function (err) {
    if (err) {
      console.log('Sending to ' + to + ' failed: ' + err);
      return;
    }

    console.log('Sent to ' + to);

    if (i === maillist.length - 1) { msg.transport.close(); }
  });
});
```

Integrating Network Paradigms

If we point our browser to `http://mailtest1.mailinator.com` (or `mailtest2`, `mailtest3`, and so on), we should see our message in the temporary inbox of `Mailinator`.

How it works...

With Nodemailer's `createTransport` method, we can quickly configure our app with the required SMTP settings, later including these settings in the `msg` object as used by the `sendMail` method.

We don't set an initial `to` property because it's modified through each iteration of `maillist.forEach` before being passed into the `sendMail` method.

The `sendMail` method is asynchronous, as most methods with callbacks are (`forEach` being an exception). After each `sendMail` is called, `forEach` moves on and calls the next `sendMail` method without waiting for the `sendMail` invocation to be completed. This means that the `forEach` loop will finish before all the `sendMail` calls are finished. So, in order to know when all the mails have been sent, we use the index parameter in the `forEach` callback (`i`).

Once `i` is equivalent to the size of our `maillist` array minus one (since array indexes start at 0), all e-mails have been dispatched, so we call `transport.close`.

Nodemailer opens multiple connections (a connection pool) for the SMTP server and reuses those connections for all the e-mails being sent. This ensures fast and efficient e-mailing, and removes the overhead of opening and closing connections for each e-mail sent. The `transport.close` method shuts down the connection pool and thus allows our app to finish execution.

There's more...

Nodemailer is a well-featured, highly-configurable mailing module, as we'll see.

Using sendmail as an alternative transport

Many hosting providers have a `sendmail` service that connects to a default SMTP server, the details of which we need not know. Nodemailer will interface with `sendmail` if we simply alter our `transport` object to the following code:

```
var transport = nodemailer.createTransport("Sendmail");
```

If `sendmail` isn't in our host server's environment PATH variable (to find out, simply type `sendmail` from an SSH prompt), we can instead specify where `sendmail` is by using the following code:

```
var transport = nodemailer.createTransport("Sendmail", "/to/sendmail");
```

> In cases where the system's `sendmail` implementation requires **Line Feed** (**LF**) line endings instead of **Carriage Return Line Feed** (**CRLF**) line endings, the `sendmail` transport will fail.

Creating HTML e-mails

E-mails can contain HTML and gracefully degrade to plain text for basic user agents. To send an HTML e-mail, we simply add the `html` property to our `msg` object, as follows:

```
var msg = {
//prior properties: transport
text:    "Hello! This is your newsletter, :D",
html: "<b>Hello!</b><p>This is your newsletter, :D</p>",
//following properties: from, subject
};
```

The plain text should be included along with the HTML, allowing a fallback for e-mail clients with no HTML support.

If we don't want to write the text portion separately, we can have Nodemailer extract the text from the HTML for us using the `generateTextFromHtml` property, as shown in the following code:

```
var msg = {
  transport: transport,
  html: "<b>Hello!</b><p>This is your newsletter, :D</p>",
  createTextFromHtml: true,
  from:     "Definitely Not Spammers <spamnot@ok.com>",
  subject: "Your Newsletter"
};
```

Sending attachments

What if we wanted to tell a really bad joke using e-mail attachments?

We'll dynamically create a text file and load an image file from disk, both of which we'll attach to an e-mail.

For the image, we'll be using `deer.jpg` (which can be found in the supporting code files). This should go in the same folder as our mail out file (let's call it `mailout_attachments.js`). We'll do this with the help of the following code:

```
var nodemailer = require('nodemailer');
var msg = {
  transport: nodemailer.createTransport('SMTP', {
    host: 'smtp.gmail.com',
    secureConnection: true,
    port: 465,
```

```
      auth: {
        user: "ourGmailAddress@googlemail.com",
        pass: "ourPassword"
      }
    }),
    text:    "Answer in the attachment",
    from:    "The Attacher attached@files.com",
    subject: "What do you call a deer with no eyes?",
    to: "anyemail@anyaddress.com",
    attachments: [
      {fileName: 'deer.txt', contents:'no eye deer.'},
      {fileName: 'deerWithEyes.jpg', filePath: 'deer.jpg'}
    ]
  };

  nodemailer.sendMail(msg, function (err) {
    if (err) {
      console.log('Sending to ' + msg.to + ' failed: ' + err);
    }
    console.log('Sent to ' + msg.to);
    msg.transport.close();
  });
```

Of course, this is a proof of concept for attachments, and isn't the best use of e-mail. Attachments are provided as an array of objects within the `msg` object. Each attachment object must have a `fileName` property, which is the filename given to the attachment in the e-mail. This doesn't have to match the name of the actual file loaded from disk.

The file contents can be written directly via the `contents` property using a string or a `Buffer` object, or we can use `filePath` to stream a file from disk (we can also pass a stream directly to a `sourceStream` property).

See also

- The *Sending an SMS* recipe
- The *Creating an SMTP server* recipe

Sending an SMS

Being able to send SMS text messages to our users is another way for us to connect with them.

It is possible to connect our computer to a GSM modem, interact with specialized libraries (such as **Asterisk**, asterisk.org, combined with **ngSMS**, ozekisms.com), and interface with the libraries and the telephony equipment to send SMS messages.

Chapter 9

There are easier ways though. Services like Twilio provide gateway SMS services, where we contact them via an HTTP REST API and they handle the SMS sending for us.

> For detailed information on REST architecture, see http://en.wikipedia.org/wiki/REST.

In this recipe, we'll convert our newsletter mail out app into a blanket SMS service using the `twilio` module.

Getting ready

This recipe requires a Twilio account (https://www.twilio.com/try-twilio). Once signed up and logged in, we should take note of our Account SID, Auth Token, and Sandbox phone number (we may have to select our country of residence to obtain the appropriate Sandbox number).

We'll need some phone numbers to send texts to for testing purposes. In the Sandbox mode (which is what we'll be using for development), any number we want to text or call must go through a verification process. We do this by selecting the **Numbers** link from the **Account** section and clicking on **Verify a Number**. Twilio will then call that number and expect a PIN provided on screen to be entered for confirmation.

Let's create a new file, `smsout.js`, and install the `twilio` helper module as follows:

```
npm install twilio
```

How to do it...

First we require the `twilio` module and then we configure the settings as follows:

```
var twilio = require('twilio');
var settings = {
  sid : 'Ad054bz5be4se5dd211295c38446da2ffd',
  token: '3e0345293rhebt45r6erta89xc89v103',
  phonenumber: '+14155992671' //sandbox number
}
```

> **Twilio phone number**
> Before we can start interacting with the Twilio service, we have to specify a registered Twilio phone number in order to create our phone. For development purposes, we can simply use the Sandbox number, which can be found from the Twilio dashboard (http://www.twilio.com/user/account). In a production scenario, we would need to upgrade our account and purchase a unique phone number from Twilio.

Integrating Network Paradigms

With our settings present and correct, we're ready to create a Twilio client as follows:

```
var client = require('twilio')(settings.sid, settings.token);
```

Now, we define a list of numbers to text (we'll have to provide our own), much like our `maillist` array in the previous recipe. We will provide these numbers with the help of the following code:

```
var smslist = [
  '+44770xxxxxx1',
  '+44770xxxxxx2',
  '+44770xxxxxx3',
  '+44770xxxxxx4',
  '+44770xxxxxx5'
];
```

> Unless we have upgraded our account, any number on `smslist` must be preverified with Twilio. This can be done through the Twilio numbers account section (https://www.twilio.com/user/account/phone-numbers/).

Then, we simply loop through `smslist` and use `phone` to send an SMS message to each recipient as follows:

```
var msg = 'SMS Ahoy!';
smslist.forEach(function (to) {
  client.sendSms({to: to, body: msg, from: settings.phonenumber},
    function(err, res) { console.log(res.status); });
});
```

This should work fine, except that we won't know for sure whether our message has been sent or not. The initial status of the response data will be queued; we have to check back with Twilio again to confirm that the message was sent. We can pass `res.sid` to `client.sms.messages` to query Twilio for an update on the response data, as follows:

```
client.sendSms({to: to, body: msg, from: settings.phonenumber},
  client.sms.messages(res.sid).get(function (err, res) {
    //process res using it's status property.
  });
});
```

If our SMS hasn't been sent on the first call, we need to wait and check it again. Let's make some final improvements as shown in the following code:

```
var msg = 'SMS Ahoy!';
smslist.forEach(function (to) {
  client.sendSms({to: to,
```

```
      body: msg,
      from: settings.phonenumber}, function (err, res) {
        if (err) { console.log(err); return; }

        (function checkStatus() {
          client.sms.messages(res.sid).get(function (err, res) {
            if (res.status === 'sent') {
              console.log('Sent to ' + res.to);
            } else {
            //if it's not a number (like 404), it's not an error
            //so we wait one second and retry
              if (isNaN(res.status)) {
                setTimeout(checkStatus, 1000, res);
                return;
              }
            //it seems to be a number, let's notify,
            //but carry on with other numbers
              console.log('API error: ', res.body);
            }
          });
        }());
      });
    });
```

Now, the console will output each time a number has been confirmed as sent. When all numbers have been messaged, the process exits.

How it works...

We use the `sendSms` method of the `client` object to make an HTTP request to the Twilio API via the `twilio` module, passing in an object containing the desired recipient, message, and sender followed by a callback function.

Once the request is made, our callback is triggered with two parameters: a potential `err` object and the initial `res` object.

We first check the `err` object. If there has been an error, we log it out and return the function. If not, then our self-calling `checkStatus` function begins to process the `res` object.

The `res.sid` function is passed to `client.sms.messages`, which provides us with an updated instance of our `res` object.

We are looking to see if Twilio has sent our text message yet. If it has, `res.status` will be sent. If it's anything other than this, we want to wait for a short while and then ask Twilio for another update on the status of our queued SMS message. That is, unless the returned status is a `404` error, in which case there has been an issue and we need to notify the user; we continue on to process the next SMS message.

Integrating Network Paradigms

There's more...

The `twilio` module's versatility stretches beyond sending SMS messages. It can also transparently handle Twilio callbacks for us through emitting events.

Making an automated phone call

For this next example to work, we would need to be running our app on a web-exposed server.

> For this code to work, it must be hosted on a live public server. For more information on hosting Node on live servers, see *Chapter 11, Taking It Live*.

To make a call, we start with the usual setup as follows:

```
var twilio = require('twilio');

var settings = {
  sid : 'Ad054bz5be4se5dd211295c38446da2ffd',
  token: '3e0345293rhebt45r6erta89xc89v103',
  url: 'http://nodecookbook.com',
  to: '+447xxxxxxxx1',
  phonenumber: '+14155992671' //sandbox number
};

var client = twilio(settings.sid, settings.token);
```

We've added two properties to our settings: a `to` property, which we'll pass to Twilio as a desired number to call, and a `url` property, which we'll use to tell Twilio to ask for **Twilio Markup Language** (**TwiML**) that will determine the contents of the phone call.

The `twilio` module has a `TwimlResponse` method that returns an object that allows us to dynamically build TwiML using its `say` method, as follows:

```
var response = twilio.TwimlResponse();

//prepare the message
response.say('Meet us in the abandoned factory');
response.say('Come alone', {voice: 'woman'});
```

We also need to provide a server for Twilio to contact, as follows:

```
require('http').createServer(function (req, res) {
  res.writeHead(200, { 'Content-Type':'text/xml' });
  res.end(response+'')
}).listen(80);
```

> For tips on live hosting with Node, see *Chapter 11, Taking It Live*.

Then, we make the following call:

```
client.makeCall({
  to: settings.to,
  url: settings.url,
  from: settings.phonenumber
});
```

> If our account is not upgraded, whatever number we supply to `makeCall` must be verified through the Twilio **Numbers** area in the account section (https://www.twilio.com/user/account/phone-numbers/).

To send a computerized text-to-speech message to the recipient, we instantiate a special `response` object using the `twilio` module's `TwimlResponse` method and pass our desired speech to the response object's `say` method.

The `toString` method is called on `response` (using shorthand string concatenation—`response+''`) as it's passed to `res.end` resulting in an XML document being supplied to Twilio with the following structure:

```
<?xml version="1.0" encoding="UTF-8" ?>
<Response>
  <Say>
    Meet us in the abandoned factory
  </Say>
  <Say voice="woman">
    Come alone
  </Say>
</Response>
```

When Twilio has downloaded this document, it parses it and converts it into computerized speech, which is then played to the recipient of the phone call.

See also

- The *Sending an e-mail* recipe
- The *Communicating with TCP* recipe
- *Chapter 11, Taking It Live*

Integrating Network Paradigms

Communicating with TCP

The **Transmission Control Protocol** (**TCP**) provides the backbone for HTTP communications. With TCP, we can open up interfaces between processes running on separate server hosts and remotely communicate between processes with less overhead and fewer complexities than HTTP.

Node provides us with the `net` module to create TCP interfaces. When it comes to scaling, reliability, load balancing, synchronization, or real-time social communications, TCP is a fundamental element.

In this recipe, we're going to demonstrate the sort of foundation needed to communicate between processes over a network by setting up two TCP servers that can talk to each other as well as a remote TCP client that utilizes two-way communications.

Getting ready

We'll need two new files: `server.js` and `client.js`. Let's place them in a new folder.

How to do it...

First, let's create our first TCP server in `server.js` as follows:

```
var net = require('net');
net.createServer(function(socket) {
  socket.end('Hello, this is TCP\n');
  socket.on('data', function (d) {
    console.log(d+'');
  });
}).listen(8080);
```

We can use the `nc` (netcat) command-line program to test this out in another terminal as follows:

`echo "testing 1 2 3" | nc localhost 8080`

> If we're using Windows, we can download netcat from http://www.joncraton.org/blog/netcat-for-windows.

The response should be **Hello, this is TCP** and the `server.js` console should output `testing 1 2 3`.

Still inside `server.js`, we're going to create another TCP server that opens a second port for `client.js` that can send to and receive messages from our server. Before we do this though, we'll make and use a `PassThrough` stream as a bridge between our two `server.js` TCP servers, as follows:

```
var net = require('net'),
  PassThroughStream = require('stream').PassThrough,
  stream = new PassThroughStream();

net.createServer({allowHalfOpen: true}, function(socket) {
  socket.end('Hello, this is TCP\n');
  socket.pipe(stream, {end: false});
}).listen(8080);

net.createServer(function(socket) {
  stream.on('data', function (d) {
    d+='';
    socket.write(Date() + ' ' + d.toUpperCase());
  });
  socket.pipe(stream);
}).listen(8081);
```

We've replaced `console.log` in the `data` listener of `socket` with an emission from our `events` object. We pick up on this emitted event in the next TCP server (on port 8081) and write the current date and our uppercased data to the client.

All we have to do now is create our client.

Inside `client.js`, we write the following code:

```
var net = require('net');
var client = net.connect(8081, 'localhost', function () {
  process.stdin.resume();
  process.stdin.pipe(client);
}).on('data', function (data) {
  console.log(data + '');
}).on('end', function () {
  console.log('session ended');
});
```

When we run `client.js`, we can interact with it in two ways. First we can send a message to our TCP server on port 8080 using netcat as we did previously. We will send this message with the help of the following command:

```
echo "testing 1 2 3" | nc localhost 8080
```

Integrating Network Paradigms

Our client will output something like the following:

```
Tue Sep 10 2013 21:53:11 GMT+0100 (BST) TESTING 1 2 3
```

We can also type directly into our client and get a similar result.

To run across separate systems, we simply place `server.js` on a remote host and then update the second parameter of `net.connect` from `localhost` to the name of our server, for example:

```
var client = net.connect(8081, 'nodecookbook.com', function () {
```

How it works...

In `server.js`, we create two TCP servers using the `net` module. Our first server on port 8080 confirms that it is indeed a TCP server, and pipes to our `stream` object. This first server is passed an `options` object as the first value with the option `allowHalfOpen` set to `true`. This prevents any FIN packet from closing our server. A FIN packet is a special piece of data sent over TCP to close a connection; it would be sent by netcat in the case of our recipe. We also pass an `options` object as the second argument of pipe, containing an `end` property set to `false` (this option is `true` by default). This stops the same FIN packet that would close our server from forcing our `stream` session to end.

The `stream` object is a `PassThrough` stream, which simply outputs all input. We take advantage of this in both of our TCP servers by using pipe to direct the flow of incoming data, while leaving that data completely unmodified.

> For more on streams, see Chapter 5, *Employing Streams*.

This allows us to listen to `data` events in our port 8081 TCP server. Any data picked up from our event listener is uppercased, prepended with a date, and written to the `socket` object.

Our `client.js` file connects to our port 8081 TCP server and (in the callback function) begins piping from the standard input to the server once a connection is established. This allows us to send messages directly from the standard input to the TCP server (on port 8081), which pipes them to our `PassThrough` stream, which in turn receives the `data` events and sends messages back to our client. Our `client.js` file receives the messages by listening to the `data` event on our client and simply outputs them using `console.log`. It lets us know when the connection has closed by listening to the `end` event.

There's more...

Let's look at some ways we can further harness the power of TCP.

Port forwarding

There can be various reasons to forward a port. As an example, if we wish `SSH` into our server over a mobile connection, we may find that port 22 has been blocked. The same can be applied to corporate firewalls (this could be because a blanket block is applied to all privileged ports except the most common ones such as 80 and 443).

We can use the `net` module to forward TCP traffic from one port to another, essentially circumventing a firewall. So, naturally this should be used only for legitimate cases and with any necessary permission.

First, we'll require `net` and `define` ports to forward from and to, as follows:

```
var net = require('net');
var fromPort = process.argv[2] || 9000;
var toPort = process.argv[3] || 22;
```

So, we can either define ports via a command line or default to forwarding the arbitrary port 9000 to the SSH port.

Now, we create a TCP server that receives connections via `fromPort`, creating a TCP client connection to `toPort`, passing all data between these connections as follows:

```
var fromPort = process.argv[2] || 9000;
var toPort = process.argv[3] || 22;
var net = require('net');

net.createServer(function (socket) {

  var client = net.connect(toPort);

  socket.pipe(client).pipe(socket);

}).listen(fromPort, function () {
  console.log('Forwarding ' + this.address().port + ' to ' +
    toPort);
});
```

We pass the pipe from the socket to the client and from the client to the server to receive and push data between `client` (our bridge connection) and `socket` (the incoming connection). We can chain the two pipes together because the return value of pipe is the writeable stream passed into it. The `client` stream is both readable and writable, so as it's returned from the first pipe, we call the second pipe on it (due to its readable interface) passing in the `socket` stream (which is also both readable and writable).

If we now run our script on the remote server (with no arguments), we can log in to a secure shell from our local computer using port 9000 like the following:

ssh -l username domain -p 9000

Using pcap to watch TCP traffic

With the third-party `pcap` module, we can also observe TCP packets as they travel in and out of our system. This can be useful for analysis and optimization of expected behavior, performance, and integrity.

In order to install the `pcap` module, enter the following command on the command line:

npm install pcap

The following is our code for this section:

```
var pcap = require('pcap');
//may need to put wlan0, eth0, etc. as 1st arg. of createSession
var pcapSession = pcap.createSession("","tcp");
var tcpTracker = new pcap.TCP_tracker();
tcpTracker.on('end', function (session) {
  console.log(session);
});

pcapSession.on('packet', function (packet) {
  tcpTracker.track_packet(pcap.decode.packet(packet));
});
```

> If `pcap` fails to choose the correct device, there will be no output (or maybe unrelated output). In this case, we need to know which device to sniff. If we are connected wirelessly, it may well be `wlan0` or `wlan1`, and if we are wired, it could be `eth0`/`eth1`. We can find out by typing `ifconfig` (Linux, Mac OS X) or `ipconfig` (Windows) on the command line to see which device has an `inet` address matching the network part of our router's IP address (for example, `192.168.1.xxx`).

If we save the preceding code as `tcp_stats.js`, we can run it with the following command:

sudo node tcp_stats.js

The `pcap` module interfaces with privileged ports and therefore must be run as root (for operating systems such as Linux and Mac OS X that enforce privileged ports).

If we navigate to any website and then refresh the page, the `tcpTracker` object's end event triggers our callback listener where we output the `session` object.

To initialize `tcpTracker`, we create a `pcap` session and attach a listener for the `packet` event where we pass each decoded packet into `tcpTracker`.

Upon creating the `pcap` session, we pass an empty string followed by `tcp` to the `createSession` method. The empty string causes `pcap` to automatically choose an interface (if this doesn't work, we can specify the appropriate interface, for example, `eth0`, `wlan1`, or `lo` if we want to analyze `localhost` TCP packets). The second parameter, `tcp`, instructs `pcap` to only listen for TCP packets.

See also

- The *Creating an SMTP server* recipe
- *Chapter 5, Employing Streams*
- The *Implementing a virtual hosting paradigm* recipe

Creating an SMTP server

We don't have to rely on a third-party SMTP server; we can create our own!

In this recipe, we'll create our own internal SMTP server (just like the first SMTP servers) using the third-party `simplesmtp` module, which is an underlying library of the `nodemailer` module from the first recipe of this chapter, *Sending an e-mail*. For information on converting an internal SMTP server to an externally exposed MX record server, see the *There's more...* section at the end of this recipe.

Getting ready

Let's create a file and call it `server.js`, then make a new folder called `mailboxes` containing three subfolders: `bob`, `bib`, and `susie`. We'll also want to have our `mailout.js` file from the first recipe in hand.

We'll also need the `simplesmtp` and `nodemailer` modules. We'll install them with the help of the following command:

`npm install simplesmtp nodemailer`

How to do it...

First, we'll set up some initial variables as follows:

```
var simplesmtp = require('simplesmtp');
var fs = require('fs');
var path = require('path');
var users = [{user: 'node', pass: 'cookbook'}],
  mailboxDir = './mailboxes/',
  catchall = fs.createWriteStream(mailboxDir + 'caught', {flags :
    'a'});
```

Integrating Network Paradigms

Now, we initialize the SMTP server with authentication enabled, as follows:

```
var smtp = simplesmtp
  .createServer({requireAuthentication: true})
  .on('authorizeUser', function (envelope, user, pass, cb) {
    var authed;
    users.forEach(function (userObj) {
      if (userObj.user === user && userObj.pass === pass) {
        authed = true;
      }
    });
    cb(null, authed);
  });
```

Next, we'll react to some `simplesmtp` events in order to process incoming mail. Beginning with the `startData` event, as follows:

```
smtp.on('startData', function (envelope) {
  var rcpt, saveTo;
  envelope.mailboxes = [];
  envelope.to.forEach(function (to) {
    path.exists(mailboxDir + to.split('@')[0], function (exists) {
      rcpt = to.split('@')[0];
        if (exists) {
        envelope.mailboxes.unshift(rcpt);
        saveTo = mailboxDir + rcpt + '/' + envelope.from
          + ' - ' + envelope.date;
        envelope[rcpt] = fs.createWriteStream(saveTo, {flags:
          'a'});
        return;
      }
      console.log(rcpt + ' has no mailbox, sending to caught
        file');
      envelope[rcpt] = catchall;
    });
  });
});
```

Then, the `data` and `dataReady` events will be as follows:

```
smtp.on('data', function (envelope, chunk) {
  envelope.mailboxes.forEach(function (rcpt) {
    envelope[rcpt].write(chunk);
  });
}).on('dataReady', function (envelope, cb) {
  envelope.mailboxes.forEach(function (rcpt) {
```

```
        envelope[rcpt].end();
    });

    cb(null, Date.now());
  });
```

For terser code, we chained these two events together with dot notation. Finally, we tell our SMTP server what port to listen to on the following port:

```
smtp.listen(2525);
```

In production, it would be expedient to specify the port as `25` (or in more advanced cases, `465` or `587`).

Now, let's test our server by converting our `mailout.js` file from the *Sending an e-mail* recipe.

First, we alter our `createTransport` invocation to reflect the values of our custom SMTP server, as follows:

```
var transport = nodemailer.createTransport('SMTP', {
  host: 'localhost',
  secureConnection: false,
  port: 2525,
  auth: {
    user: "node",
    pass: "cookbook"
  }
});
```

Next, we modify the `maillist` array to reflect our mailboxes, as shown in the following code:

```
var maillist = [
  'Bob <bob@nodecookbook.com>, Bib <bib@nodecookbook.com>',
  'Miss Susie <susie@nodecookbook.com>',
  'Mr Nobody <nobody@nodecookbook.com>',
];
```

Bob and Bib are sent together. We also added an address that doesn't have a mailbox (`nobody@nodecookbook.com`) in order to test our catch all functionality.

Now, if we run `server.js` in one terminal and `mailout.js` in another, the output from `mailout.js` should be something like the following:

Sent to Miss Susie <susie@nodecookbook.com>

Sent to Mr Nobody <nobody@nodecookbook.com>

Sent to Bob <bob@nodecookbook.com>, Bib <bib@nodecookbook.com>

Integrating Network Paradigms

If we look in the `mailboxes/bob` directory, we'll see our e-mail from `spamnot@ok.com`, the same for `susie` and `bib`.

The `server.js` file should have the following output:

nobody has no mailbox, sending to caught file

Therefore, upon analyzing the contents of `mailboxes/caught`, we'll see our e-mail in there sent to Mr. Nobody.

How it works...

SMTP is based upon a series of plain text communications between an SMTP client and server over a TCP connection. The `simplesmtp` module carries out these communications for us, yielding a higher-level API for developer interactions.

When we call `simplesmtp.createServer` with `requireAuthorization` set to `true`, our new server (simply called `smtp`) will emit an `authorizeUser` event and will not continue to execute until we have invoked the fourth parameter, `cb` (the callback). The `cb` callback takes two parameters. With the first, we can specify a reason why access is denied via an `Error` object (we simply pass `null`). The second is a Boolean saying whether the user is authorized or not (if not, and the `Error` parameter is `null`, a generic access denied error is sent to the mail client).

We determine the second `cb` parameter by looping through our `users` array, finding out if the username and password are correct (in reality, we may wish to use a database for this part). If there is a match, our `auth` variable is set to `true` and passed to `cb`, otherwise it remains `false` and the client is rejected.

If the client is authorized, `smtp` will emit several events for each envelope (an envelope is an e-mail package containing all the recipients for that e-mail, body text, e-mail headers, attachments, and so on).

In the `startData` event, we are provided with an `envelope` parameter where we use the `envelope.to` property to check whether our recipients have a mailbox. SMTP allows more than one recipient to be specified per e-mail, so `envelope.to` is always an array, even if it contains only one recipient. Therefore, we use `forEach` to loop through `envelope.to` in order to check mailboxes for each recipient stipulated.

We find out the intended recipient mailbox by splitting the address with the @ character, loading it into our `rcpt` variable. We perform no verification on the domain portion of the address, although `simplesmtp` automatically verifies that the domain is genuine before emitting any of the events.

The `rcpt` variable gets added to our `envelope.mailboxes` array, which we added to the envelope before looping through `envelope.to`. We use `envelope.mailboxes` in the later `data` and `dataReady` events.

Still inside the `envelope.to forEach` loop, we add one final property to `envelope` named after the mailbox name (`rcpt`). If the mailbox exists, we create `writeStream` to `saveTo` (a path with a filename determined from combining `envelope.from` with `envelope.date`). We now have an endpoint to each recipient's mailbox ready to receive data. If the mailbox doesn't exist for the recipient, we set `envelope[rcpt]` to `catchall`. The `catchall` variable is the global variable we set at the top of our file. It's a `writeStream` object with the a flag set so that the `caught` file accumulates orphaned e-mails. We create the `catchall` `writeStream` method on initialization and then reuse the same `writeStream` function for all e-mails addressed to non-existent mailboxes. This saves us from creating a `writeStream` function for every badly addressed e-mail received, thus saving resources.

The `data` event is triggered for each chunk of the e-mail body received by the server, giving us `envelope` and `chunk`. We save each `chunk` to its applicable file using `envelope[rcpt].write`, determining the `rcpt` variable by looping through our custom `envelope.mailboxes` array.

The `dataReady` event signifies that all data has been received and the data is ready for processing. Since we've already stored it, we use this event to end the relevant `writeStream` function for each `rcpt` in our mailboxes. The `dataReady` event also requires a callback (`cb`). The first parameter can be an `Error` object, which allows for a final rejection of an e-mail (for instance, if the content of the e-mail was analyzed and found to be spam). The second parameter expects a queue ID to be sent to the mail client; in our case, we simply give `Date.now`.

There's more...

Let's take a look at how to convert our SMTP server into a public mail exchange handler.

Receiving e-mails from external SMTP servers

By removing authorization settings and remotely hosting our SMTP server, listening on port 25, we can allow other mail servers to communicate with our SMTP server so e-mail can be transferred from one network to another (for example, from a Gmail account to our hosted SMTP server).

Let's save our file as `mx_smtp.js` and modify the following accordingly:

```
var simplesmtp = require('simplesmtp');
var fs = require('fs');
var path = require('path');
var  mailboxDir = './mailboxes/',
   catchall = fs.createWriteStream(mailboxDir + 'caught', {flags : 
     'a'});
var smtp = simplesmtp.createServer();
```

Integrating Network Paradigms

We've discarded the `users` variable and changed the `smtp` variable so the object with the `requireAuthentication` property and the accompanying `authorizeUser` event are removed. In order for an external mail program to forward to our SMTP server, it must be able to connect. Since other mail programs don't possess authentication details, we have to open our server to allow them to do so.

The `startData` data and `dataReady` events all remain the same. The final change to the port is as follows:

```
smtp.listen(25);
```

In order for this to work, we must have a live server, which we have root access to (for example, an Amazon EC2 micro instance) and a domain where we can alter the **Mail Exchange** (**MX**) records.

So, for instance, say we're hosting our SMTP server at `mysmtpserver.net` and we want to receive e-mails for `bob@nodecookbook.com`. We point the MX records of `nodecookbook.com` to `mysmtpserver.net` with a priority of 10.

> For an example of how to change DNS records with a registrar, see `http://support.godaddy.com/help/article/680`. For more info on MX records, take a look at `http://en.wikipedia.org/wiki/MX_record`.

Once changes are made, they can take a while to propagate (up to 48 hours, though often faster). We can use `dig mx` (Mac OS X and Linux) or `nslookup set q=MX` (Windows) on the command line to determine if the update to our MX records has occurred.

We must have Node installed on our remote host, ensuring that port 25 is exposed and not in use by any other programs. To check whether other programs are using port 25, log in with SSH and type `netstat -l`. If you see `*:smtp` in the **Active Internet Connections** (only servers) section, a program is already using the port and must be stopped (try `ps -ef` to look for any suspects).

On the live server, we create our `mailboxes` folder containing `bob`, `bib`, and `susie`, copy our `mx_smtp.js` file over, and install `simplesmtp` as follows:

npm install simplesmtp

Now, if everything is properly set up and our MX records are updated, we can execute our `mx_smtp.js` file on the live server. Then, send a test e-mail to `bob@nodecookbook.com` (or at whatever domain we possess, which we have altered the MX records for), wait a few seconds, and then check the `mailboxes/bob` folder. The e-mail should have appeared.

See also

- The *Sending an e-mail* recipe
- The *Deploying to a server environment* recipe discussed in *Chapter 11, Taking It Live*

Implementing a virtual hosting paradigm

If we wish to host multiple sites on one server, we can do so with virtual hosting. Virtual hosting is a way to uniquely handle multiple domain names according to their name. The technique is surprisingly simple—we just look at the incoming `Host` header and respond accordingly. In this task, we're going to implement simple name-based virtual hosting for static sites.

Getting ready

We'll create a folder called `sites`, with `localhost-site` and `nodecookbook` as subdirectories. In `localhost-site/index.html`, we'll write the following:

```
<b> This is localhost </b>
```

And in `nodecookbook/index.html`, we'll add the following code:

```
<h1>Welcome to the Node Cookbook Site!</h1>
```

For local testing, we'll want to configure our system with some extra host names so we can point different domains to our server. To do this, we edit `/etc/hosts` on Linux and Max OS X, or `%SystemRoot%\system32\drivers\etc\hosts` for Windows systems.

At the top of the file, it maps our local loopback IP `127.0.0.1` to `localhost`. Let's change this line to the following:

```
127.0.0.1    localhost      nodecookbook
```

Finally, we want to create two new files: `mappings.js` and `server.js`. The `mappings.js` file will provide static file servers for each domain name, and `server.js` will provide the virtual hosting logic.

We'll be using the `node-static` module to serve our sites; our virtual host will only serve static websites. If we don't already have it, we can install it via `npm` as follows:

npm install node-static

Integrating Network Paradigms

How to do it...

Let's start with `mappings.js`, as follows:

```
var static = require('node-static');

function staticServe (dir) {
  return new (static.Server)('sites/' + dir)
}

exports.sites = {
  'nodecookbook' : staticServe('nodecookbook'),
  'localhost' : staticServe('localhost-site')
};
```

We've used the domains laid out in our system's `hosts` file. In a production scenario, domains would be directed to us by DNS records.

Now, the following is the code for `server.js`:

```
var http = require('http');

var port = 8080,
  mappings = require('./mappings');

var server = http.createServer(function (req, res) {
  var domain = req.headers.host.replace(new RegExp(':' + port + '$'), ''),
    site = mappings.sites[domain] ||
      mappings.sites[mappings.aliases[domain]];

  if (site) { site.serve(req, res); return; }
  res.writeHead(404);
  res.end('Not Found\n');

}).listen(port);
```

Now when we navigate to `http://localhost:8080` or `http://localhost.localdomain:8080`, we get the content in `sites/localhost-site/index.html`, whereas if we go to `http://nodecookbook:8080`, we get the big Node Cookbook welcome message.

How it works...

Any time our server receives a request, we strip the port number (which wouldn't be necessary with port `80` servers) to determine the domain.

We then cross reference the domain with our `mappings.sites` object. If a site is found, we call its `serve` method, which is inherited from the `node-static` library. In `mappings.js`, each `exports.sites` property contains a `node-static Server` instance pointed at the relevant site directory. We've used our custom `staticServer` function as a wrapper to keep the code a little tidier.

To use the static `Server` instance, we call its `serve` method, passing through the `req` and `res` objects, as in `server.js`, thusly:

```
if (site) { site.serve(req, res); return; }
```

The `site` variable is an instance of `static.Server` pointing to the appropriate site folder for the given domain name.

If `server.js` fails to find a site in `mapping.js` for the requested domain, we simply pass a `404` error back to the client.

There's more...

What about going beyond static hosting into dynamic hosting, or what if we want to use an SSL/TLS certificate with our sites? You could achieve this with the help of this section.

Virtual hosting Express apps

Express/Connect comes with the `vhost` middleware, which allows us to implement dynamic Express-based virtual hosting with ease.

Let's create a new folder (we could call it `express_virtual_hosting`) in which we'll install Express with the following commands:

mkdir express_virtual_hosting

cd express_virtual_hosting && npm install express

We'll create a `sites` folder in our new directory so we can create two new Express apps inside, like so:

```
mkdir sites && cd sites
express nodecookbook && express localhost-site
cd nodecookbook && npm install && cd ..
cd localhost-site && npm install && cd ..
```

We'd also need to modify two parts of each site's `app.js` file; first we slip `module.exports` into the app variable instantiation as follows:

```
var app = module.exports = express();
```

This allows us to `require` our app later.

Integrating Network Paradigms

Then, we add an `if module.parent` conditional statement just before the call to `listen`, using the following code:

```
if (module.parent) {return;}
http.createServer(app).listen(app.get('port'), function(){
   console.log('Express server listening on port ' + app.get('port'));
});
```

This stops apps that we have required (instead of run directly) from creating HTTP servers and thus allows us to handle the front-facing server logic.

In our `nodecookbook` app, let's add the following to `views/index.jade`:

```
h1 Welcome to the Node Cookbook site!
```

And in the `localhost-site` app, we add the following code to `views/index.jade`:

```
b this is localhost
```

With our sites set up, we can modify `mappings.js` as follows:

```
function appServe (dir) {
   return require('./sites/' + dir + '/app.js')
}

exports.sites = {
   'nodecookbook' : appServe('nodecookbook'),
   'localhost' : appServe('localhost-site')
};
```

We've removed the `node-static` module since we're using Express instead. Our `staticServe` convenience function has been modified as `appServe`, which simply loads each Express app using `require` according to its mapping in `exports.servers`.

And we'll update `server.js` with the following:

```
var express = require('express'),
  mappings = require('./mappings'),
  app = express.createServer();

Object.keys(mappings.sites).forEach(function (domain) {
   app.use(express.vhost(domain, mappings.sites[domain]));
});

app.listen(8080);
```

We create a master app and then loop through `mappings.sites`, passing each subapp into `app.use` with `express.vhost`. The `vhost` middleware takes two arguments. The first is the `domain`. We get each `domain` from the `mappings.sites` keys. The second is an Express app. We retrieve each Express app from the values in `mappings.sites`.

We simply request the `domain` and the `vhost` middleware lines up the relevant domain with the relevant app to deliver the correct site.

Server Name Indication (SNI)

Prior to **Server Name Indication** (**SNI**), name-based virtual hosting for sites served over SSL/TLS was a complex administration issue (requiring every hostname to be stored in a multidomain certificate).

This is because an encrypted connection is established based upon a certificate that specifies a domain name before any HTTP headers are received by the server. Therefore, the server cannot provide a certificate that is specific to one domain. As a result, the browser would vividly warn the user that the connection may be unsafe since the domain name listed on the certificate didn't match the domain being accessed. In order to avoid this scenario, a virtual host would have to buy a certificate containing every domain hosted, and then reapply for a new certificate every time a new domain was added or removed.

SNI forwards the requested domain to the server at the beginning of the SSL/TLS handshake, allowing our server to choose the appropriate certificate for a domain and preventing the browser from telling our users that they may be under attack.

The `https.Server` function (inheriting from `tls.Server`) has the `addContext` method, which allows us to specify hostname and certificate credentials for multiple individual domains.

Let's enable TLS-compatible virtual hosting by making a few changes. First, in `mappings.js`, we'll add another convenience function called `secureShare`, as follows:

```
function secureShare(domain) {
  var site = {
    content: staticServe(domain),
    cert: fs.readFileSync('sites/' + domain + '/certs/cert.pem'),
    key: fs.readFileSync('sites/' + domain + '/certs/key.pem')
  };
  return site;
} ;
```

Next, we'll alter the way we load the sites, calling `secureShare` instead of `staticServe`, with the following code:

```
exports.sites = {
  'nodecookbook.com' : secureShare('nodecookbook.com'),
  'davidmarkclements.com' : secureShare('davidmarkclements.com')
};
```

Integrating Network Paradigms

For this example to work in a production scenario, we'll have to replace the sample domains with the ones that we control and obtain genuine certificates signed by a trusted Certificate Authority.

> We can test locally by following the instructions in the supporting code files for this chapter (under `secure_virtual_hosting/howto`).

Let's change our `sites` folder structure to conform to alterations made in `mappings.js` by renaming `nodecookbook` to `nodecookbook.com` and `localhost-site` to `davidmarkclements.com`, changing the latter's `index.html` file to the following:

```
<b>This is DavidMarkClements.com virtually AND secure</b>
```

Each `site` folder also needs a `certs` folder containing our `cert.pem` and `key.pem` files. These files must be certificates purchased specifically for the domain.

In `server.js`, we change the top of our script to the following:

```
var https = require('https');
var fs = require('fs');
```

Underneath our `mappings` variable, we create another variable called `defaultContext`:

```
mappings = require('./mappings'),
  defaultContext = {key: mappings.sites['nodecookbook.com'].key,
    cert: mappings.sites['nodecookbook.com'].cert}
```

The filesystem (`fs`) module is required to load our credentials. As we've replaced `http` with `https`, we will alter our `createServer` call as follows:

```
var server = https.createServer(defaultContext, function (req,
  res) {
```

Simply adding `s` to `http` does the trick. Even though we'll be defining contexts on a per domain basis, the `https` module requires a key and certificate (or alternatively a **pfx** file) for it's `createServer` method—so we simply choose a certificate and key combination and supply this method as the `options` object to `https.createServer`.

In `mappings.js`, our `secureShare` function returns an object containing three properties: `content`, `key`, and `cert`, where `content` holds the static server. So, in `server.js`, we update the following line:

```
if (site) { site.serve(req, res); return; }
```

We will then change the preceding line to the following line:

```
if (site) { site.content.serve(req, res); return; }
```

As we're hosting on a live server, we expose it to the incoming web connections by binding to `0.0.0.0`, thusly:

```
}).listen(port, '0.0.0.0');
```

We could also change the port variable to `443` to serve directly over the HTTPS port (we must run the server as root to do this, which has security implications in a live environment; see *Chapter 11, Taking It Live*, for how to do this safely).

And finally, we add the following to the bottom of `server.js`:

```
Object.keys(mappings.sites).forEach(function (hostname) {
  server.addContext(hostname, {key: mappings.sites[hostname].key,
    cert: mappings.sites[hostname].cert});
});
```

This loads the `key` and `cert` properties for each domain based on the settings laid out in `mappings.js`.

Provided we have trusted CA-certified credentials for each specified domain and we're using a modern browser, we can navigate to each site using HTTPS without a receiving a warning.

> **The caveat**
>
> There is a catch—SNI only works in modern browsers, although modern browsers in this context exclude Internet Explorer 7/8 and Safari when run on Windows XP, as well as Android Gingerbread (versions 2.x) and Blackberry browsers. If we provide a default certificate via the `options` object of `https.createServer`, the user will still be able to view the site on older browsers, but they will receive the same warnings as if we weren't using SNI (the older browsers don't indicate the hostname in SSL/TLS negotiations, so our SNI handling never occurs). Depending on the intended market, we may have to use alternative methods until these older browsers are used in sufficiently low numbers in relation to our purposes.

See also

- The *Serving static files* recipe discussed in *Chapter 1, Making a Web Server*
- The *Dynamic routing* recipe discussed in *Chapter 7, Accelerating Development with Express*
- The *Setting up an HTTPS web server* recipe discussed in *Chapter 8, Implementing Security, Encryption, and Authentication*
- The *Deploying to a server environment* recipe discussed in *Chapter 11, Taking It Live*

10
Writing Your Own Node Modules

In this chapter, we will cover the following topics:

- Creating a test-driven module specification
- Writing a functional module mock-up
- Refactoring with prototypical inheritance
- Extending a module's API
- Deploying a module to npm

Introduction

A thriving module ecosystem has been one of the core goals of Node since its inception. The framework leans heavily toward modularization. Even the core functionality (such as HTTP) is made available through the module system.

It's almost as easy to create our own modules as it is to use core and third-party modules. All we need to know are a few best practices and how the module system works.

A great module is the one that performs a specific function to a high standard, and great code is the result of multiple development cycles. In this chapter, we're going to develop a module from scratch, beginning with defining its **Application Programming Interface** (**API**) to creating our module over a series of development cycle iterations. We'll finally deploy it to **npm** for everyone's benefit.

Writing Your Own Node Modules

Creating a test-driven module specification

We're going to create our module by loosely following the **test-driven development** (**TDD**) model (refer to http://en.wikipedia.org/wiki/Test-driven_development for more information). JavaScript is asynchronous, so the code can be executed in multiple time streams at once. This can sometimes make for a challenging mental puzzle.

A test suite is a particularly powerful tool when it comes to JavaScript development. It provides a quality assurance process and inspires confidence in a module's user base when tests are passing.

What's more, we can define our tests upfront as a way to map out the intended API before we even begin development.

In this recipe, we'll be doing just that by creating a test suite for a module that extracts the statistical information from MP3 files.

Getting ready

Let's create a new folder named `mp3dat`, with a file inside named `index.js`. Then, we will create two subfolders: `lib` and `test`, both containing `index.js`.

We'll also need some MP3 files to test. For simplicity, our module will only support MPEG-1 layer 3 files with error protection turned off. Other types of MP3 files include MPEG-2 and MPEG-2.5. MPEG-1 (no error protection) will be the most common type, but our module can easily be extended later. We can retrieve an MPEG-1 layer 3 file from http://www.paul.sladen.org/pronunciation/torvalds-says-linux.mp3. Let's place this file in our new `mp3dat/test` folder and name it `test.mp3`.

> The focus of this chapter is to create a fully functioning module; however, prior knowledge of MP3 file structures is not required.

The details regarding MP3 files in this chapter can safely be scanned over, while the information pertaining to module creation is of key importance. However, we can learn more about MP3 files and their structure from http://en.wikipedia.org/wiki/MP3.

How to do it...

Let's open `test/index.js` and set up some variables as shown in the following code:

```
var assert = require('assert');
var mp3dat = require('../index.js');
var testFile = 'test/test.mp3';
```

The `assert` module is a core Node module used specifically for building test suites. The general idea is we assert that something should be true (or false), and if the assertion is correct, the test passes. The `mp3dat` variable requires our primary (currently blank) `index.js` file that will in turn load the `lib/index.js` file, which holds the actual module code.

The `testFile` variable points to our `test.mp3` file from the perspective of the root of our module (the `mp3dat` folder). This is because we run our tests from the root of the module directory.

Now, we'll decide our API and write the corresponding tests. Let's model our module after the `fs.stat` method. We'll retrieve data about the MP3 file using an `mp3dat.stat` method, which will take two arguments: a file path and a callback function to be invoked once the stats have been gathered.

The `mp3dat.stat` callback will take two arguments. The first argument will be the error object, which should be set to `null` if there is no error, and the second one will contain our `stats` object.

The `stats` object will contain the `duration`, `bitrate`, `filesize`, `timestamp`, and `timesig` properties. The `duration` property will, in turn, contain an object that holds the `hours`, `minutes`, `seconds`, and `milliseconds` keys.

For example, our `test.mp3` file should return something like the following code:

```
{ duration: { hours: 0, minutes: 0, seconds: 5, milliseconds: 186 },
  bitrate: 128000,
  filesize: 82969,
  timestamp: 5186,
  timesig: '00:00:05' }
```

Now that we've conceptualized our API, we can map it out to assertion tests as a means of enforcing this API throughout the module's development.

Let's start with `mp3dat` and `mp3dat.stat`, as shown in the following code:

```
assert(mp3dat, 'mp3dat failed to load');
assert(mp3dat.stat, 'there should be a stat method');
assert(mp3dat.stat instanceof Function, 'stat should be a
Function');
```

To test the `mp3dat.stat` function, we actually have to call it and then perform further tests within its callback, as shown in the following code:

```
mp3dat.stat(testFile, function (err, stats) {

  assert.ifError(err);

  //expected properties
```

Writing Your Own Node Modules

```
assert(stats.duration, 'should be a truthy duration property');
assert(stats.bitrate, 'should be a truthy bitrate property');
assert(stats.filesize, 'should be a truthy filesize property');
assert(stats.timestamp, 'should be a truthy timestamp
  property');
assert(stats.timesig, 'should be a truthy timesig property');
```

Now that we've established the expected `stats` properties, we can go further and specify what these properties should look like; still within the callback we write the following code:

```
//expected types
assert.equal(typeof stats.duration, 'object', 'duration should
  be an object type');
assert(stats.duration instanceof Object, 'durations should be an
  instance of Object');
assert(!isNaN(stats.bitrate), 'bitrate should be a number');
assert(!isNaN(stats.filesize), 'filesize should be a number');
assert(!isNaN(stats.timestamp), 'timestamp should be a number');

assert(stats.timesig.match(/^\d+:\d+:\d+$/), 'timesig should be
  in HH:MM:SS format');

//expected duration properties
assert.notStrictEqual(stats.duration.hours, undefined, 'should
  be a duration.hours property');
assert.notStrictEqual(stats.duration.minutes, undefined, 'should
  be a duration.minutes property');
assert.notStrictEqual(stats.duration.seconds, undefined, 'should
  be a duration.seconds property');
assert.notStrictEqual(stats.duration.milliseconds, undefined,
  'should be a duration.milliseconds property');

//expected duration types
assert(!isNaN(stats.duration.hours), 'duration.hours should be a
  number');
assert(!isNaN(stats.duration.minutes), 'duration.minutes should
  be a number');
assert(!isNaN(stats.duration.seconds), 'duration.seconds should
  be a number');
assert(!isNaN(stats.duration.milliseconds),
  'duration.milliseconds should be a number');

//expected duration properties constraints
assert(stats.duration.minutes < 60, 'duration.minutes should be
  no greater than 59');
assert(stats.duration.seconds < 60, 'duration.seconds should be
  no greater than 59');
```

```
    assert(stats.duration.milliseconds < 1000, 'duration.seconds
      should be no greater than 999');

    console.log('All tests passed');  //if we've gotten this far we
      are done.
});
```

Now, let's run our test. From the `mp3dat` folder, we will use the following command:

`node test`

The preceding command should return the following text:

`AssertionError: there should be a stat method`

This result is exactly right as we haven't written the `stat` method yet.

> **Test frameworks**
>
> We're using a vanilla Node environment to create some very straightforward tests. As implementations become more complex, it would be worthwhile to consider using a test framework. Test frameworks provide an enhanced execution environment for tests by supplying extra functions in the global namespace that help us describe our tests. Along with these functions, test frameworks can produce more helpful and well-formatted result output.
>
> Mocha (`http://visionmedia.github.io/mocha`) is an excellent choice because it supports a variety of styles and offers a myriad of reporting formats (from the cross-language **Test Anything Protocol** (**TAP**) to a Nyan Cat command-line progress bar).

How it works...

When the tests are run, the `assert` module will throw `AssertionError` to let the developer know that their code is not currently lining up with their predefined assertions regarding the desired API.

In our unit test file (`test/index.js`), we mainly used the simple `assert` function (an alias for `assert.ok`). The `assert` function requires that the first argument passed to it be truthy. Otherwise, it throws `AssertionError` where the second argument is provided for the error message (the opposite of `assert.ok` is `assert.fail`, which expects a falsey value).

Our test fails at the following line:

```
    assert(mp3dat.stat, 'there should be a stat method');
```

This is because `mp3dat.stat` is `undefined` (a falsey value).

Writing Your Own Node Modules

The first argument of `assert` can be an expression. For instance, we use `stats.duration.minutes < 60` to set a constraint for the `duration.minutes` property, and use the `match` method on `timesig` to verify a correct time pattern of HH:MM:SS.

We also use `assert.equal` and `assert.notStrictEqual`. The `assert.equal` function is a test that applies equality with type coercion (for example, equivalent to ==) and `assert.strictEqual` requires that the values and types match—`assert.notEqual` and `assert.notStrictEqual` are the corresponding antipathies.

We use `assert.notStrictEqual` to ensure the existence of the `duration` object's subproperties (`hours`, `minutes`, and so on).

There's more...

There are many testing frameworks that provide extra descriptive syntax, enhanced functionality, asynchronous testing capabilities, and more. Let's sample one.

Unit tests with should.js

The third-party `should` module sits nicely on top of the core `assert` module, thus adding some syntactic sugar to both in order to simplify and increase the descriptive powers of our tests.

Let's install it using the following command:

npm install should

Now, we can rewrite our tests with `should` as shown in the following code:

```
var should = require('should');
var mp3dat = require('../index.js');
var testFile = 'test/test.mp3';

should.exist(mp3dat);
mp3dat.should.have.property('stat');
mp3dat.stat.should.be.a.Function;

mp3dat.stat(testFile, function (err, stats) {
  should.ifError(err);

  //expected properties
  stats.should.have.property('duration');
  stats.should.have.property('bitrate');
  stats.should.have.property('filesize');
  stats.should.have.property('timestamp');
  stats.should.have.property('timesig');
```

```
    //expected types
    stats.duration.should.be.an.Object;
    stats.bitrate.should.be.a.Number;
    stats.filesize.should.be.a.Number;
    stats.timestamp.should.be.a.Number;

    stats.timesig.should.match(/^\d+:\d+:\d+$/);

    //expected duration properties
    stats.duration.should.have.keys('hours', 'minutes', 'seconds',
'milliseconds');

    //expected duration types and constraints
    stats.duration.hours.should.be.a.Number;
    stats.duration.minutes.should.be.below(60).and.be.a.Number;
    stats.duration.seconds.should.be.below(60).and.be.a.Number;
    stats.duration.milliseconds.should.be.below(1000).and.be.a.Number;

    console.log('All tests passed');

});
```

The `should` module allows us to write more concise and descriptive tests. Its syntax is natural and self-explanatory. We can read up on various `should` methods at `https://www.github.com/visionmedia/should.js`, which is its GitHub page.

> **Chai.js**
> Similar to the way Mocha supports various test framework approaches, Chai provides multiple assertion styles, including the `should` syntax among others. Refer to `http://chaijs.com/` to learn more.

See also

- The *Writing a functional module mock-up* recipe
- The *Extending the module's API* recipe
- The *Deploying a module to npm* recipe

Writing a functional module mock-up

Now that we have our tests written (see the previous recipe), we are ready to create our module (incidentally, from here on, we'll be using the `should` version of our unit tests as opposed to `assert`).

Writing Your Own Node Modules

In this recipe, we'll write our module in a simple functional style to demonstrate a proof of the concept. In the next recipe, we'll refactor our code into a more common modular format, which will be centered on reusability and extendibility.

Getting ready

Let's open our main `index.js` file and link it to the `lib` directory via `module.exports`:

```
module.exports = require('./lib');
```

This allows us to place the meat of our module code neatly inside the `lib` directory.

How to do it...

We'll open up `lib/index.js` and begin by requiring the `fs` module, which will be used to read an MP3 file, and setting up a `bitrates` map that cross-references hex-represented values to bitrate values as defined by the MPEG-1 specification:

```
var fs = require('fs');

//half-byte (4bit) hex values to interpreted bitrates (bps)
//only MPEG-1 bitrates supported
var bitrates = { 1:32000, 2:40000, 3:48000, 4:56000, 5:64000,
    6:80000, 7:96000, 8:112000, 9:128000, A:160000, B:192000,
    C:224000, D:256000, E:320000 };
```

Now, we'll define two functions: `findBitRate` to locate and translate the bitrate half-byte and `buildStats` to crunch all the gathered information into our previously determined final `stats` object, as shown in the following code:

```
function buildStats(bitrate, size, cb) {
  var magnitudes = [ 'hours', 'minutes', 'seconds',
      'milliseconds'],
    duration = {}, stats,
    hours = (size / (bitrate / 8) / 3600);

  (function timeProcessor(time, counter) {
    var timeArray = [], factor = (counter < 3) ? 60 : 1000 ;
    if (counter) {
      timeArray = (factor * +('0.' +
        time)).toString().split('.');
    }

    if (counter < magnitudes.length - 1) {
      duration[magnitudes[counter]] = timeArray[0] ||
        Math.floor(time);
```

```
          duration[magnitudes[counter]] =
            +duration[magnitudes[counter]];
          counter += 1;
          timeProcessor(timeArray[1] ||
            time.toString().split('.')[1], counter);
          return;
        }
          //round off the final magnitude
          duration[magnitudes[counter]] =
            Math.round(timeArray.join('.'));
    }(hours, 0));

    stats = {
      duration: duration,
      bitrate: bitrate,
      filesize: size,
      timestamp: Math.round(hours * 3600000),
      timesig: ''
    };

    function pad(n){return n < 10 ? '0'+n : n}
    magnitudes.forEach(function (mag, i) {
     if (i < 3) {
     stats.timesig += pad(duration[mag]) + ((i < 2) ? ':' : '');
     }
    });

    cb(null, stats);
 }
```

The `buildStats` function takes `bitrate`, `size`, and `cb` as arguments. It uses `bitrate` and `size` to calculate the number of seconds in the track and then uses this information to generate the `stats` object, which it passes through the `cb` function.

To get `bitrate` into `buildStats`, let's write the `findBitRate` function, as shown in the following code:

```
    function findBitRate(f, cb) {
       fs.createReadStream(f)
         .on('data', function (data) {
           var i;
           for (i = 0; i < data.length; i += 2) {
             if (data.readUInt16LE(i) === 64511) {
               this.pause();
               cb(null, bitrates[data.toString('hex', i + 2, i +
                 3)[0]]);
               break;
             };
```

Writing Your Own Node Modules

```
    }
  }).on('end', function () {
    cb(new Error('could not find bitrate, is this definitely an
      MPEG-1 MP3?'));
  });
}
```

Finally, we expose a `stat` method that utilizes our functions to produce the `stats` object:

```
exports.stat = function (f, cb) {
  fs.stat(f, function (err, fstats) {
    findBitRate(f, function (err, bitrate) {
      if (err) { cb(err); return; }
      buildStats(bitrate, fstats.size, cb);
    });
  });
}
```

Now, let's run our `should` tests from the previous recipe, *Creating a test-driven module specification*:

node test

It will generate the following output:

All tests passed

How it works...

The `exports` object is a central part of the Node platform. It's the other half of `require`. When we require a module, any properties added to `exports` are exposed through `require`. So, let us see what happens when we use the following line:

```
var mp3dat = require('mp3dat');
```

We can now access `exports.stat` through `mp3dat.stat` or even through `require('mp3dat').stat` (assuming we have `mp3dat` installed as a module; refer to the *Deploying a module to npm* recipe later in this chapter).

If we want to expose one function for the entire module, we use `module.exports`, as we did in the `index.js` file that we set up in the *Getting ready* section of this recipe.

Our `stat` method first calls `fs.stat` with the user-supplied filename (`f`). We use the supplied `fstats` object to retrieve the size of our file, which we pass to `buildStats`. This is after we have called `findBitRate` to retrieve the MP3's `bitrate` value, which we also pass to `buildStats`.

The `buildStats` callback is passed straight up and through to our `stat` method's callback; the execution of the user callback originates within `buildStats`.

The `findBitRate` function creates a `readStream` of the user-supplied file (`f`) and loops through each emitted `data` chunk two bytes at a time, thus reducing the search time by half. We can do this because we're looking for a two-byte sync word, which will always be at a position divisible by two. In hex, the sync word is `FFFB`. As a 16-byte little-endian unsigned integer, it's equivalent to `64511` (this is true only for MPEG-1 MP3 files without error protection).

The next four bits (half byte) that follow the MP3 sync word contain the bitrate value. So, we pass this through the `Buffer.toString` method, requiring the hex output that we match against our `bitrates` object map. In the case of our `test.mp3` file, the half-byte hex value is `9` and represents a bitrate of `128000` bits per second.

Once we find our bitrate, we execute the callback and invoke `this.pause`, which pauses the stream and prevents the `end` event from being triggered. The `end` event will only occur when a bitrate has not been discovered, in which case we send an error back through the callback.

The `buildStats` function receives `bitrate` and divides it by `8`, thus giving us the bytes per second (8 bits to a byte). Dividing the total number of bytes of the MP3 file by the bytes per second renders the number of seconds. We then further divide it by 3,600 to get the `hours` variable, which is then passed onto the embedded `timeProcessor` function. The `timeProcessor` function simply loops through the `magnitudes` array (`hours`, `minutes`, `seconds`, and `milliseconds`) until `seconds` has been accurately converted and apportioned to each magnitude, which gives us our `duration` object. Again, we use the calculated duration (in whichever form) to construct our `timestamp` and `timesig` properties.

> **Streams**
> Refer to *Chapter 5, Employing Streams*, for more in-depth recipes that use streams.

There's more...

Examples of how to use a module can be a great resource for end users. Let's write an example for our new module.

Writing a module use case example

We'll create an `examples` folder within the `mp3dat` folder and a file named `basic.js` (for an example depicting basic usage), within which we will write the following code:

```
var mp3dat = require('../index.js');

mp3dat.stat('../test/test.mp3', function (err, stats) {
  console.log(stats);
});
```

Writing Your Own Node Modules

This should cause the console to output the following code:

```
{ duration: { hours: 0, minutes: 0, seconds: 5, milliseconds: 186
  },
  bitrate: 128000,
  filesize: 82969,
  timestamp: 5186,
  timesig: '00:00:05' }
```

See also

- The *Creating a test-driven module specification* recipe
- The *Refactoring with prototypical inheritance* recipe
- The *Deploying a module to npm* recipe
- *Chapter 5, Employing Streams*

Refactoring with prototypical inheritance

The functional mock-up created in the previous recipe, *Writing a functional module mock-up*, can be useful for getting familiar with a concept and may be perfectly adequate for small, simple modules with narrow scope.

However, the prototype pattern (among others), often used in Node's core modules, is commonly used by module creators and is fundamental to native JavaScript methods and objects.

Prototypical inheritance is more memory efficient. Methods sitting on a prototype are not instantiated until called; instead of being recreated on each invocation, they're reused.

On the other hand, it can be slightly slower than our previous recipe's procedural style because the JavaScript engine has the added overhead of traversing prototype chains. Nevertheless, it's (arguably) more appropriate to think of and implement modules as entities in their own right, which a user can create instances of (for example, a prototype-oriented approach). This makes the modules easier to programmatically extend through cloning and prototype overrides. This leads to great flexibility being afforded to the end user while the core integrity of the module's code stays intact.

In this recipe, we'll rewrite our code from the previous task according to the prototype pattern.

Getting ready

Let's start editing `index.js` in `mp3dat/lib`.

How to do it...

To begin, we'll need to create a constructor function (a function called using `new`), which we'll name `Mp3dat`:

```
var fs = require('fs');

function Mp3dat(f, size) {
  if (!(this instanceof Mp3dat)) {
    return new Mp3dat(f, size);
  }
  this.stats = {duration:{}};
}
```

We've also required the `fs` module as we did in the previous task.

Let's add some objects and methods to our constructor's prototype:

```
Mp3dat.prototype._bitrates = { 1 : 32000, 2 : 40000, 3 : 48000, 4 :
56000, 5 : 64000, 6 : 80000, 7 : 96000, 8 : 112000, 9 : 128000, A :
160000, B : 192000, C : 224000, D : 256000, E : 320000 };

Mp3dat.prototype._magnitudes = [ 'hours', 'minutes', 'seconds',
'milliseconds'];
Mp3dat.prototype._pad = function (n) { return n < 10 ? '0' + n : n; }

Mp3dat.prototype._timesig = function () {
  var ts = '', self = this;;
  self._magnitudes.forEach(function (mag, i) {
    if (i < 3) {
      ts += self._pad(self.stats.duration[mag]) + ((i < 2) ? ':' : '');
    }
  });
  return ts;
}
```

Three of our new `Mp3dat` properties (`_magnitudes`, `_pad`, and `_timesig`) were contained in the `buildStats` function in some form. We've prefixed their names with the underscore symbol (_) to signify that they are private. This is merely a convention; JavaScript doesn't actually privatize them.

Now, we'll reincarnate the previous recipe's `findBitRate` function as shown in the following code:

```
Mp3dat.prototype._findBitRate = function(cb) {
  var self = this;
    fs.createReadStream(self.f)
```

```
      .on('data', function (data) {
        var i = 0;
          for (i; i < data.length; i += 2) {
            if (data.readUInt16LE(i) === 64511) {
              self.bitrate = self._bitrates[data.toString('hex', i +
                2,
                i + 3)[0]];
              this.pause();
              cb(null);
              break;
            };
          }
      }).on('end', function () {
        cb(new Error('could not find bitrate, is this definitely an
          MPEG-1 MP3?'));
      });
    }
```

The only differences here are that we load the filename from the object (`self.f`) instead of loading it via the first parameter, and we load `bitrate` onto the object instead of sending it through the second parameter of `cb`.

Now to convert `buildStats` into the prototype pattern, we will write the following code:

```
    Mp3dat.prototype._buildStats = function (cb) {
      var self = this,
      hours = (self.size / (self.bitrate / 8) / 3600);

      self._timeProcessor(hours, function (duration) {
        self.stats = {
          duration: duration,
          bitrate: self.bitrate,
          filesize: self.size,
          timestamp: Math.round(hours * 3600000),
          timesig: self._timesig(duration, self.magnitudes)
        };
        cb(null, self.stats);

      });
    }
```

Our `_buildStats` prototype method is significantly smaller than its `buildStats` cousin from the previous task. Not only have we pulled its internal `magnitudes` array, `pad` utility function, and time signature functionality (wrapping it into its own `_timesig` method), we've also outsourced the internal recursive `timeProcessor` function to a prototype method equivalent. This is shown in the following code:

```
Mp3dat.prototype._timeProcessor = function (time, counter, cb) {
  var self = this, timeArray = [], factor = (counter < 3) ? 60 :
    1000,
    magnitudes = self._magnitudes, duration = self.stats.duration;

  if (counter instanceof Function) {
    cb = counter;
    counter = 0;
  }

  if (counter) {
    timeArray = (factor * +('0.' + time)).toString().split('.');
  }
  if (counter < magnitudes.length - 1) {
    duration[magnitudes[counter]] = timeArray[0] ||
      Math.floor(time);
    duration[magnitudes[counter]] =
      +duration[magnitudes[counter]];
    counter += 1;
    self._timeProcessor.call(self, timeArray[1] ||
      time.toString().
      split('.')[1], counter, cb);
    return;
  }
    //round off the final magnitude (milliseconds)
    duration[magnitudes[counter]] =
      Math.round(timeArray.join('.'));
    cb(duration);
}
```

Finally, we will write the `stat` method (with no underscore prefix since it's intended for public use) and export the `Mp3dat` object:

```
Mp3dat.prototype.stat = function (f, cb) {
  var self = this;
  fs.stat(f, function (err, fstats) {
    self.size = fstats.size;
    self.f = f;
    self._findBitRate(function (err, bitrate) {
      if (err) { cb(err); return; }
      self._buildStats(cb);
    });
  });
}

module.exports = Mp3dat();
```

Writing Your Own Node Modules

We can ensure all is present and correct by running the tests we built in the first recipe. On the command line from the `mp3dat` folder, we use the following command:

node test

The preceding command should generate the following output:

All tests passed

How it works...

In the previous recipe, we had an `exports.stat` function that called the `findBitRate` and `buildStats` functions to get the `stats` object. In our refactored module, we add the `stat` method onto the prototype and export the entire `Mp3dat` constructor function via `module.exports`.

We don't have to pass `Mp3dat` to `module.exports` using `new`. Our function generates the new instance, when invoked directly, with the following code:

```
if (!(this instanceof Mp3dat)) {
  return new Mp3dat();
}
```

This is really a fail-safe strategy. It's more efficient (though marginally) to initialize the constructor using `new`.

The `stat` method in our refactored code differs from the `exports.stat` function in the previous task. Instead of passing the filename and size of the specified MP3 as parameters to `findBitRate` and `buildStats` respectively, it assigns them to the parent object via `this` (which is assigned to `self` so that we can retain a reference to the outer function's context within the callback passed to `findBitRate`).

It then invokes the `_findBitRate` and `_buildStats` methods to ultimately generate the `stats` object and pass it back to the user's callback.

After running `mp3dat.stats` on our `test.mp3` file, our refactored `mp3dat` module object will contain the following code:

```
{ stats:
   { duration: { hours: 0, minutes: 0, seconds: 5, milliseconds:
     186 },
     bitrate: 128000,
     filesize: 82969,
     timestamp: 5186,
     timesig: '00:00:05' },
  size: 82969,
  f: 'test/test.mp3',
  bitrate: 128000 }
```

In the former recipe, however, the returned object would simply be as follows:

```
{ stat: [Function] }
```

The functional style reveals the API. Our refactored code allows the user to interact with the information in multiple ways (through the `stats` and `mp3dat` objects). We can also extend our module and populate `mp3dat` with other properties later on, outside of the `stats` object.

There's more...

We can structure our module to make it even easier to use.

Adding the stat function to the initialized mp3dat object

If we want to expose our `stat` function directly to the `mp3dat` object, thus allowing us to view the API directly (for example, with `console.log`), we can add it by removing `Mp3dat.prototype.stat` and altering `Mp3dat` as follows:

```
function Mp3dat() {
  var self = this;
  if (!(this instanceof Mp3dat)) {
    return new Mp3dat();
  }
  self.stat = function (f, cb) {
    fs.stat(f, function (err, fstats) {
      self.size = fstats.size;
      self.f = f;
      self._findBitRate(function (err, bitrate) {
        if (err) { cb(err); return; }
        self._buildStats(cb);
      });
    });
  }
  self.stats = {duration:{}};
}
```

Then, our final object contains the following code:

```
{ stat: [Function],
  stats:
   { duration: { hours: 0, minutes: 0, seconds: 5, milliseconds: 186 },
     bitrate: 128000,
     filesize: 82969,
     timestamp: 5186,
     timesig: '00:00:05' },
```

Writing Your Own Node Modules

```
      size: 82969,
      f: 'test/test.mp3',
      bitrate: 128000 }
```

Alternatively, if we're not concerned about pushing the `stats` object and other `Mp3dat` properties to the module user, we can leave everything as it is, except we need to change the following line:

```
module.exports = Mp3dat()
```

The preceding line needs to be changed to the following:

```
exports.stat = function (f, cb) {
   var m = Mp3dat();
   return Mp3dat.prototype.stat.call(m, f, cb);
}
```

This code uses the `call` method to apply the `Mp3dat` scope to the `stat` method, which allows us to piggyback off of the `stat` method, and will return an object with the following:

```
{ stat: [Function] }
```

This is just as in the case of the first write of our module, except we still have the prototype pattern in place. This second approach is ever so slightly more efficient.

Allowing multiple instances

Our module is a singleton as it returns the already initialized `Mp3dat` object. This means that no matter how many times we require and assign it to variables, a module user will always refer to the same object, even if `Mp3dat` is required in different submodules loaded by a parent script.

This means that bad things will happen if we try to run two `mp3dat.stat` methods at the same time. In a situation where our module is required multiple times, two variables containing the same object could end up overwriting each other's properties, which results in unpredictable (and frustrating) code. The most likely upshot is that `readStreams` will clash.

One way to overcome this is to alter the following line:

```
module.exports = Mp3dat()
```

The preceding line needs to be altered to the following:

```
module.exports = Mp3dat
```

Then, we will load two instances with the following code:

```
var Mp3dat = require('../index.js'),
    mp3dat = Mp3dat(),
       mp3dat2 = Mp3dat();
```

If we want to provide both singleton and multiple instances, we have to add the following `spawnInstance` method to our constructor's prototype:

```
Mp3dat.prototype.spawnInstance = function () {
  return Mp3dat();
}

module.exports = Mp3dat();
```

The preceding block then allows us to create multiple instances of `Mp3dat` with the following code:

```
var mp3dat = require('../index.js'),
    mp3dat2 = mp3dat.spawnInstance();
```

Both `mp3dat` and `mp3dat2` would be separate `Mp3dat` instances in this case, as shown in the following code:

```
var mp3dat = require('../index.js'),
    mp3dat2 = require('../index.js');
```

In the preceding case, both `mp3dat` and `mp3dat2` would be the same instance.

See also

- The *Writing a functional module mock-up* recipe
- The *Extending the module's API* recipe
- The *Deploying a module to npm* recipe

Extending a module's API

There are many ways by which we can extend our module. For example, we could make it support more MP3 formats, but this is merely leg work. All it takes is finding out the different sync words and bitrates for different types of MP3 and then adding these at the relevant places.

For a more interesting venture, we could extend the API, creating more options for our module users.

Since we use a stream to read our MP3 file, we can allow the user to pass in either a filename or a stream of MP3 data, which offers both ease (with a simple filename) and flexibility (with streams). This way, we could start a download stream, STDIN stream, or in fact, any stream of MP3 data.

Writing Your Own Node Modules

Getting ready

We'll pick up our module from where we left it at the end of the *Allowing for multiple instances* subsection in the *There's more...* section of the previous recipe.

How to do it...

First, we'll add some more tests for our new API. In `tests/index.js`, we'll pull out the callback function from the `mp3dat.stat` call into the outer scope, and we'll name it `cb`:

```
function cb (err, stats) {
  should.ifError(err);

  //expected properties
  stats.should.have.property('duration');

  //...all the other unit tests here

  console.log('passed');

};
```

Now, we'll call `stat` along with a method that we're going to write and name it `statStream`:

```
mp3dat.statStream({stream: fs.createReadStream(testFile),
   size: fs.statSync(testFile).size}, cb);

mp3dat2.stat(testFile, cb);
```

Note that we're using two `Mp3dat` instances (`mp3dat` and `mp3dat2`). So, we can run the `stat` and `statStream` tests side by side. Since we're creating `readStream`, we require `fs` at the top of our [tests/index.js] file as follows:

```
var should = require('should');
var fs = require('fs');
var mp3dat = require('../index.js'),
    mp3dat2 = mp3dat.spawnInstance();
```

We'll also place a few top-level `should` tests for the `statStream` method as follows:

```
should.exist(mp3dat);
mp3dat.should.have.property('stat');
mp3dat.stat.should.be.a.Function;
mp3dat.should.have.property('statStream');
mp3dat.statStream.should.be.a.Function;
```

Now, to live up to our tests' expectations!

Chapter 10

Within `lib/index.js`, we add a new method to the prototype of `Mp3dat`. Instead of taking a filename for the first parameter, it will accept an object (which we'll name `opts`) that must contain the `stream` and `size` properties:

```
Mp3dat.prototype.statStream = function (opts, cb) {
  var self = this,
    errTxt = 'First arg must be options object with stream and size',
    validOpts = ({}).toString.call(opts) === '[object Object]'
      && opts.stream
      && opts.size
      && 'pause' in opts.stream
      && !isNaN(+opts.size);
  lib
  if (!validOpts) {
    cb(new Error(errTxt));
    return;
  }

  self.size = opts.size;
  self.f = opts.stream.path;

  self.stream = opts.stream;

  self._findBitRate(function (err, bitrate) {
    if (err) { cb(err); return; }
    self._buildStats(cb);
  });

}
```

Finally, just a few modifications to `_findBitRate` and we're done:

```
Mp3dat.prototype._findBitRate = function(cb) {
  var self = this,
    stream = self.stream || fs.createReadStream(self.f);
    stream.on('data', function (data) {
      var i = 0;
        for (i; i < data.length; i += 2) {
          if (data.readUInt16LE(i) === 64511) {
            self.bitrate = self._bitrates[data.toString('hex', i +
              2, i + 3)[0]];
            this.pause();
            cb(null);
            break;
          };
  //rest of the _findBitRate function...
```

Writing Your Own Node Modules

We conditionally hook onto either a passed-in stream, or we create a stream from a given filename.

Let's run our tests using the following command (from the `mp3dat` folder):

node tests

The following result should be obtained:

passed

passed

One output is for `stat` and the other is for `statStream`.

How it works...

We were already using a stream to retrieve our data. We simply expose this interface to the user by modifying `_findBitRate` so that it either generates its own stream from a filename, or if a stream is present in the parent constructor's properties (`self.stream`), it simply plugs that stream into the process that was already in place.

We then make this functionality available to the module user by defining a new API method: `statStream`. We conceptualize this first by making tests for it, and then defining it through `Mp3dat.prototype`.

The `statStream` method is similar to the `stat` method (in fact, we can merge the two; refer to the *There's more...* section for more details). Apart from checking the validity of the input, it simply adds one more property to an `Mp3dat` instance: the `stream` property, which is taken from `opts.stream`. For convenience, we cross-reference `opts.stream.path` with `self.f` (this may or may not be available depending on the type of stream). This technique is essentially redundant but may be useful for debugging purposes on the user's part.

At the top of `statStream`, we have the `validOpts` variable, which has a series of expressions connected by the `&&` conditionals. This is shorthand for a bunch of `if` statements. If any of these expression tests fail, the `opts` object is not valid. One expression of interest is `'pause' in opts.stream`, which tests whether `opts.stream` is definitely a stream or inherited from a stream (all streams have a `pause` method, and `in` checks for the property throughout the entire prototype chain). Another noteworthy expression among the `validOpts` tests is `!isNaN(+opts.size)`, which checks whether `opts.size` is a valid number. The `+` operator that precedes it converts the number to a `Number` type and `!isNaN` checks whether it is a number using "not a number" (there is no `isNumber` in JavaScript, so we use `!isNaN`).

There's more...

Now, we have this new method. Let's write some more examples. We'll also see how we can merge `statStream` and `stat` together and further enhance our module by causing it to emit events.

Chapter 10

Creating the STDIN stream example

To demonstrate usage with other streams, we will write an example using the `process.stdin` stream as follows:

```
//to use try :
// cat ../test/test.mp3 | node stdin_stream.js 82969
// the argument (82969) is the size in bytes of the mp3

if (!process.argv[2]) {
  process.stderr.write('\nNeed mp3 size in bytes\n\n');
  process.exit();
}

var mp3dat = require('../');
process.stdin.resume();
mp3dat.statStream({stream : process.stdin, size: process.argv[2]},
function (err, stats) {
  if (err) { console.log(err); }
  console.log(stats);
});
```

We've included comments in the preceding example to ensure our users understand how to use it. All that we do here is receive the `process.stdin` stream and the file size and then pass them to our `statStream` method.

Creating the PUT upload stream example

In the *There's more...* section of the *Handling file uploads* recipe of *Chapter 2, Exploring the HTTP Object*, we created a PUT upload implementation.

We'll take the `put_upload_form.html` file from that recipe and create a new file named `HTTP_PUT_stream.js` in our `mp3dat/examples` folder:

```
var mp3dat = require('../../mp3dat');
var http = require('http');
var fs = require('fs');
var form = fs.readFileSync('put_upload_form.html');
http.createServer(function (req, res) {
  if (req.method === "PUT") {
    mp3dat.statStream({stream: req, size:req.headers['content-length']}, function (err, stats) {
      if (err) { console.log(err); return; }
      console.log(stats);
    });

  }
```

321

Writing Your Own Node Modules

```
    if (req.method === "GET") {
      res.writeHead(200, {'Content-Type': 'text/html'});
      res.end(form);
    }
  }).listen(8080);
```

Here, we create a server that serves the `put_upload_form.html` file. The HTML file allows us to specify a file to upload (which must be a valid MP3 file) and then sends it to the server.

In our server, we pass `req` (which is a stream) to the `stream` property and `req.headers['content-length']`, which gives us the size of MP3 in bytes, as specified by the browser via the `Content-Length` header.

We then finish by logging `stats` to the console (we can also extend this example by sending `stats` back to the browser in the JSON form).

Merging stat and statStream

There's a lot of similar code between `stat` and `statStream`. With a bit of restructuring, we can merge them into one method, which allows the user to pass either a string containing a filename or an object containing the `stream` and `size` properties straight into the `stat` method.

First, we'd need to update our tests and examples. In `test/index.js`, we should remove the following code:

```
mp3dat.should.have.property('statStream');
mp3dat.statStream.should.be.an.instanceof(Function);
```

Since we're merging `statStream` into `stat`, our two calls to `stat` and `statStream` should now look like the following:

```
mp3dat.stat({stream: fs.createReadStream(testFile),
    size: fs.statSync(testFile).size}, cb);
mp3dat2.stat(testFile, cb);
```

The `statStream` line in `examples/stdin_stream.js` should become:

```
mp3dat.stat({stream : process.stdin, size: process.argv[2]}
```

In `HTTP_PUT_stream.js`, this line should be as follows:

```
mp3dat.stat({stream: req, size: req.headers['content-length']}
```

In `lib/index.js`, we trash the `streamStat` method by inserting a `_compile` method:

```
Mp3dat.prototype._compile =  function (err, fstatsOpts, cb) {
  var self = this;
  self.size = fstatsOpts.size;
  self.stream = fstatsOpts.stream;
```

322

```
      self._findBitRate(function (err, bitrate) {
        if (err) { cb(err); return; }
        self._buildStats(cb);
      });
    }
```

Finally, we modify our `Mp3dat.prototype.stat` method as follows:

```
    Mp3dat.prototype.stat = function (f, cb) {
      var self = this, isOptsObj = ({}).toString.call(f) === '[object Object]';

      if (isOptsObj) {
        var opts = f, validOpts = opts.stream && opts.size
            && 'pause' in opts.stream && !isNaN(+opts.size);
        errTxt = 'First arg must be options object with stream and size'

        if (!validOpts) { cb(new Error(errTxt)); return; }

        self.f = opts.stream.path;
        self._compile(null, opts, cb);
        return;
      }

      self.f = f;
      fs.stat(f, function (err, fstats) {
        self._compile.call(self, err, fstats, cb);
      });
    }
```

The code that actually generates the `stats` object has been placed into the `_compile` method. If the first argument is an object, we assume it is a stream and `stats` takes on the role of the former `statStream` method, calling `_compile` and returning from the function early. If not, we assume a filename and invoke `_compile` within the `fs.stat` callback with JavaScript's `call` method, ensuring our `this/self` variable carries through the `_compile` method.

Integrating the EventEmitter

Throughout this book, we have generally received data from modules via callback parameters or through listening to events. We can extend our `modules` interface further, which allows users to listen to events by causing Node's `EventEmitter` to adopt our `Mp3dat` constructor.

We need to require the `events` and `util` modules, then hook up `Mp3dat` with `EventEmitter` by assigning the `this` object of `Mp3dat` to it, and then give it the super powers of `EventEmitter` using `util.inherits`:

```
    var fs = require('fs'),
      EventEmitter = require('events').EventEmitter,
```

Writing Your Own Node Modules

```
util = require('util');

function Mp3dat() {
  if (!(this instanceof Mp3dat)) {
    return new Mp3dat();
  }
  EventEmitter.call(this);
  this.stats = {duration:{}};
}

util.inherits(Mp3dat, EventEmitter);
```

All we do now is go through the existing methods of `Mp3dat` and insert the `emit` events at relevant places. We can emit `bitrate` (using `emit`) once it's found, as shown in the following code:

```
Mp3dat.prototype._findBitRate = function(cb) {
//beginning of _findBitRate method
    for (i; i < data.length; i += 2) {
      if (data.readUInt16LE(i) === 64511) {
        self.bitrate = self._bitrates[data.toString('hex', i +
          2,
          i + 3)[0]];
        this.pause();
        self.emit('bitrate', self.bitrate);
        cb(null);
        break;
      };
  //rest of _findBitRate method
```

In the preceding code, we would invoke our callback with an error. We can also emit that error, as shown in the following code:

```
//last part of _findBitRate method
  }).on('end', function () {
    var err = new Error('could not find bitrate, is this
      definetely an MPEG-1 MP3?');
    self.emit('error', err);
    cb(err);
  });
```

Then, there's the time signature, which is defined as follows:

```
Mp3dat.prototype._timesig = function () {
  //_timesig function code....
    self.emit('timesig', ts);
    return ts;
}
```

And of course, the `stats` object is defined as follows:

```
Mp3dat.prototype._buildStats = function (cb) {
//_buildStats code
  self._timeProcessor(hours, function (duration) {
    //_timeProcessor code
      self.emit('stats', self.stats);
      if (cb) { cb(null, self.stats); }
  });
}
```

We've also added `if (cb)` to `_buildStats` since a callback may no longer be necessary if the user opts to listen to events instead.

If a module user is dynamically generating the `Mp3dat` instances, they may wish to have a way to hook into a spawned instance event:

```
Mp3dat.prototype.spawnInstance = function () {
  var m = Mp3dat();
  this.emit('spawn', m);
  return m;
}
```

Finally, to allow chaining, we can also return the `Mp3dat` instance from the `stat` function from two places. First, from within the `isOptsObj` block as follows:

```
Mp3dat.prototype.stat = function (f, cb) {
//stat code
  if (isOptsObj) {
    //other code here
      self._compile(null, opts, cb);
      return self;
  }
```

Then, right at the end of the function, as shown in the following code:

```
  //prior stat code
  self.f = f;
  fs.stat(f, function (err, fstats) {
    self._compile.call(self, err, fstats, cb);
  });
  return self;
}
```

This is because we return early from the function depending on the detected input (filename or stream), so we have to return `self` from two places.

Writing Your Own Node Modules

Now, we can write an example for our new user interface. Let's make a new file in `mp3dat/examples` named `event_emissions.js`; look at the following code:

```
var mp3dat = require('../index');

mp3dat
  .stat('../test/test.mp3')
  .on('bitrate', function (bitrate) {
    console.log('Got bitrate:', bitrate);
  })
  .on('timesig', function (timesig) {
    console.log('Got timesig:', timesig);
  })
  .on('stats', function (stats) {
    console.log('Got stats:', stats);
    mp3dat.spawnInstance();
  })
  .on('error', function (err) {
    console.log('Error:', err);
  })
  .on('spawn', function (mp3dat2) {
    console.log('Second mp3dat', mp3dat2);
  });
```

See also

- The *Creating a test-driven module specification* recipe
- The *Handling file uploads* recipe in *Chapter 2, Exploring the HTTP Object*
- The *Deploying a module to npm* recipe
- *Chapter 5, Employing Streams*

Deploying a module to npm

npm is the official package manager for Node. When we deploy a module to npm, we are uploading it to the official npm repository (which happens to be a CouchDB database).

Now that we've created a module, we can share it with the rest of the world using the same integrated tool that we retrieve modules with; that is, `npm`.

Getting ready

Building on the final state of `mp3dat` from the previous recipe, *Extending a module's API* (including all the changes we made in the *There's More...* section so that we can accept streams or filenames via the same `stat` method and our module also emits events), we'll make sure this canonical `mp3dat` is in a directory called `mp3dat`.

Before we can deploy to npm, we need to make a package.json file; so, let's do that for our module. In mp3dat, we'll create package.json and add some information (of course, we can always customize to whatever details work for us):

```
{
  "author": "David Mark Clements <contact@davidmarkclements.com>
    (http://davidmarkclements.com)",
  "name": "mp3dat",
  "description": "A simple MP3 parser that returns stat infos in a
    similar style to fs.stat for MP3 files or streams. (MPEG-1
    compatible only)",
  "version": "0.0.2",
  "homepage": "http://nodecookbook.com/mp3dat",
  "repository": {
    "type": "git",
    "url": "git://github.com/davidmarkclements/mp3dat.git"
  },
  "license": "MIT",
  "main": "./lib/index.js",
  "scripts": {
    "test": "node test"
  },
  "engines": {
    "node": "~0.10..20"
  },
  "dependencies": {},
  "devDependencies": {}
}
```

We can, of course, insert our own name and the name of the package. Another method to create a package.json file is use the npm init command, which asks a series of questions via the command line and then generates the package.json file.

We can specify a repository in package.json. It's a good idea to use an online repository such as GitHub to manage version control, share code, and allow others to work on your code. Refer to http://help.github.com to get started.

The main property is important. It defines the entry point to our module, which in our case is ./lib/index.js (although we could have specified ./index.js, which loads ./lib/index.js). By defining scripts.test as node test, we can now run npm test (or npm mp3dat test once mp3dat is installed via npm) to execute our unit tests.

We'll be deploying our module to npm the way we left it in the previous recipe, where stat and statStream were both merged into stat, and we have integrated our module with the EventEmitter.

Writing Your Own Node Modules

> Note that we've set the version as 0.0.2—the first version was deployed in the first edition of *Node Cookbook*.

How to do it...

In order to deploy to npm, we must have a developer account. We will do this by executing the following command:

`npm adduser`

Then, we fill in our desired username, password, and contact e-mail. That's it; we are now registered!

Before we go ahead and publish our module, we need to test whether npm will install it on our system without a hitch. Inside mp3dat, we use the following command:

`sudo npm install -g`

On Windows and Mac OS X, this command can (and should) be called with sudo.

Then, if we run node from the command line, we should be able to require mp3dat:

`require('mp3dat')`

This command executes without getting an error message. If it worked, we can go ahead and publish our module! Within mp3dat, we use the following command:

`npm publish`

Now, if we go to a completely different folder (say our home folder) and type in the following, npm should install our package from its repository:

`npm uninstall mp3dat`

`npm install mp3dat`

We can double-check whether the package is present with the following command:

`npm search mp3dat`

If this is taking too long, we can go to http://www.npmjs.org/ in our browser. Our module will probably be on the home page (which contains the most recently published modules). Otherwise, we can hit http://www.npmjs.org/search?q=mp3dat to head to our module's npm registry page directly.

Chapter 10

How it works...

`npm` is a command-line script written in Node that provides some excellent tools for developing and publishing modules. The tools really do what they say on the tin: `adduser` adds a user, `install` installs, and `publish` publishes. It's really very elegant.

On the server side, the `npm` registry is backed by a CouchDB database that holds all the JSON-like data for each package. There's even a CouchDB `_changes` field that we can hook into. On the command line, we can use the following command:

```
curl
http://isaacs.couchone.com/registry/_changes?feed=continuous&include_
docs=true
```

Then, we can watch modules as they are added and modified in real time. If nothing happens, we can always open another terminal and type in the following commands in it:

```
npm unpublish --force
npm publish
```

This will cause the CouchDB changes feed to update.

There's more...

npm has some really nice features; let's take a look at some of them.

npm link

The `npm link` command can be useful for module authors.

Throughout development, if we want to require `mp3dat` as a global module each time we make changes, for example, as `require('mp3dat')`, we can update the global package by running the following command:

```
sudo npm install . -g
```

However, `npm link` provides an easier solution when we run the following command:

```
sudo npm link
```

Within our `mp3dat` folder, a symlink is created from our global `node_modules` folder to our working directory. This causes Node to treat `mp3dat` as an installed global module; however, any changes that we make to our development copy will be reflected globally. When we are done developing the module and want to freeze it on our system, we will simply unlink as follows:

```
sudo npm unlink -g mp3dat
```

.npmignore and npm versions

Our `example` files may be handy on GitHub, but we may decide whether there is any benefit in publishing them to the npm repository. We can use an `.npmignore` file to keep certain files out of published `npm` packages. Let's create `.npmignore` in the `mp3dat` folder and put the following line in it:

```
examples/
```

Now, when we republish to the `npm` registry, our new package will be without the `examples` folder. Before we can publish though, we either have to unpublish or change the version of our package (or we could use the `--force` argument). Let's change the version and then publish again:

```
npm version 0.0.3 --message "added .npmignore"
npm publish
```

Changing the version will also alter our `package.json` file to the new version number.

See also

- The *Writing a functional module mock-up* recipe
- The *Refactoring with prototypical inheritance* recipe
- The *Extending the module's API* recipe
- The *Accessing CouchDB changes stream with Cradle* recipe in *Chapter 4, Interfacing with Databases*

11
Taking It Live

In this chapter, we will cover the following topics:

- Deploying an app to a server environment
- Automatic crash recovery
- Continuous deployment
- Hosting with a Platform as a Service provider

Introduction

Node is an excellent platform of choice to construct and provide online services. Whether it's a simple, lean website, a highly versatile web app, or services that transcend beyond HTTP, at some point we must deploy our creations.

This chapter focuses on what it takes to bring our Node apps live.

Deploying an app to a server environment

Virtual Private Servers (**VPS**), Dedicated Servers, or **Infrastructure as a Service** (**IaaS**), for example, the likes of Amazon EC2 or Rackspace and owning our own server machines all have one thing in common: they have total control over the server environment.

However, with great power comes great responsibility, and there are a few challenges we need to be aware of. This recipe will demonstrate how to overcome these challenges as we safely initialize a Node web app on port `80`.

Getting ready

We will, of course, need a remote server environment (or our own setup). It's important to research the best package for our needs.

Dedicated Servers can be expensive. The hardware to software ratio is 1:1; we're literally renting a machine.

VPS can be cheaper since they share the resources of a single machine (or cluster), so we're only renting out the resources it takes to host an instance of an operating system. However, if we begin to use resources beyond those assigned, we could hit penalties (downtime, excessive charges) since excessive usage can affect other VPS users.

IaaS can be relatively cheap, particularly when upscaling is involved (when we need more resources), though IaaS tends to contain a pay-as-you-go element to its pricing, which means the costs aren't fixed and could require extra monitoring.

Our recipe assumes the usage of a Unix/Linux server with the `sshd` (SSH Service) running.

> SSH stands for **Secure Shell**. Find out more about the SSH protocol at `http://en.wikipedia.org/wiki/Secure_Shell`.

Furthermore, we should have a domain pointed at our server. In this recipe, we'll assume the domain name as `nodecookbook.com`. Finally, we must have Node installed on our remote server. If difficulties arise, we can use the instructions available at `https://www.github.com/joyent/node/wiki/Installation`, or to install via a package manager, we can use the instructions at `https://www.github.com/joyent/node/wiki/Installing-Node.js-via-package-manager`.

We'll be deploying the `login` app from the second-to-last recipe of *Chapter 7, Accelerating Development with Express*, so we need this to hand.

How to do it...

To ready our app for transfer to the remote server, we'll remove the `node_modules` folder (we can rebuild it on the server), as follows:

```
rm -fr login/node_modules
```

Then we compress the `login` directory by executing the following command:

```
npm pack login
```

This will generate a compressed archive named after the app's name and version as given in the `package.json` file, which will generate the filename `application-name-0.0.1.tgz` for an untouched Express generated `package.json` file.

On the command line in the same directory that we ran `npm` pack, let's rename the packed file to `login.tgz`, as follows:

mv application-name-0.0.1.tgz login.tgz #Linux/Mac OS X

rename application-name-0.0.1.tgz login.tgz ::Windows.

Next, we upload `login.tgz` to our server. For example, we could use SFTP as follows:

sftp root@nodecookbook.com

Once logged in to the server via SFTP, we can issue the following commands:

cd /var/www

put login.tgz

It's not necessary to upload to the `/var/www` directory; it's just a natural place to put a website.

This assumes that we have logged in to our server via SFTP from the directory holding `login.tgz`.

Next, we use the SSH service on the server as follows:

ssh -l root nodecookbook.com

> If we're using a Windows desktop, we could use the SFTP and SSH services into our server using putty. For more information about putty, see `http://www.chiark.greenend.org.uk/~sgtatham/putty/`.

Once logged in to the remote server, we navigate to `/var/www` and decompress `login.tar.gz` as follows:

tar -xvf login.tar.gz

As `login.tar.gz` decompresses, it recreates our `login` folder on the server.

To rebuild the `node_modules` folder, we enter the `login` folder and use `npm` to regenerate the dependencies as follows:

cd login

npm -d install

Most servers have a shell-based editor, such as `nano`, `vim`, or `emacs`. We can use one of these editors to change one line in `app.js` (or otherwise us the SFTP service over a modified `app.js`), as follows:

```
app.listen(80, function () { process.setuid('www-data'); });
```

Taking It Live

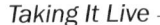

We're now listening to the standard HTTP port, meaning we can access our app without suffixing a port number to its web address. However, since we'll be starting the app as `root` (necessary in order to bind to port 80), we will also pass a callback to the `listen` method, which changes access privileges of the app from `root` to `www-data`.

In some cases, dependent upon file permissions, reading or writing to files from our app may no longer work. We can fix this by changing ownership as follows:

```
chown -R www-data login
```

Finally, we can start our app with the help of the following command:

```
cd login
nohup node app.js &
```

We can ensure that our app is running as `www-data` with the help of the following command:

```
ps -ef | grep node
```

How it works...

We modified `app.listen` to bind to port 80 and added a callback function that resets the user ID from `root` to `www-data`.

Adding a callback to `listen` isn't limited to Express; it works the same way with a plain `httpServer` instance.

Running a web server as `root` is bad practice. If our app was compromised by an attacker, they would have `root` access to our system via our app's privileged status.

To demote our app, we call `process.setuid` and pass in `www-data.process.setuid`. This takes either the name of the user, or the user's UID. By passing in a name, we cause `process.setuid` to block the event loop (essentially freezing operations) while it cross-references the user string to its UID. This eliminates the potential sliver of time where the app is bound to port 80 and also running as `root`. In essence, passing a string to `process.setuid` instead of the underlying UID means nothing can happen until the app is no longer working as `root`.

We call our process with `nohup` and follow up with an ampersand (`&`). This means we freely end our SSH session without causing our app to terminate along with the session.

The ampersand turns our process into a background task, so we can do other things (like exit) while it runs. `nohup` means ignore the **Hang-Up Signal** (**HUP**). HUP is sent to any running processes initiated via SSH whenever the SSH session is terminated. Essentially, using `nohup` allows our web app to outlive the SSH session.

There's more...

There are other ways to start our app independent from our session, and to bind to port `80` without running the app as `root`. Plus, we can also run multiple apps and proxy them to port `80` with `http-proxy`.

Using screen instead of nohup

An alternative to using `nohup` to achieve independence from our SSH session is `screen`. We would use it as follows:

```
screen -S myAppName
```

This will give us a virtual terminal, from which we can run the following commands:

```
cd login
node app.js
```

After this, we can leave the virtual terminal by pressing *Ctrl + A* followed by *D*. We would then return to our initial terminal. The virtual terminal will continue to run after we have logged out of SSH. We can also log back in to SSH at any time and run the following command:

```
screen -r myAppName
```

Here, we will be able to see any console output and stop (*Ctrl + C*) and start the app.

Using authbind for privileged ports

For this example, we should the SSH service on our server as a non-root user by running the following command:

```
ssh -l dave nodecookbook.com
```

An alternative way to bind to port `80` is with `authbind`, which can be installed via our server's package manager. For instance, if our package manager is `apt-get`, we could run the following command:

```
sudo apt-get install authbind
```

The `authbind` utility works by preempting the operating system policies on port binding and exploiting an environment variable called `LD_PRELOAD` upon execution. Therefore, it never needs to be run with `root` privileges.

> For more details on `authbind`, see http://en.wikipedia.org/wiki/Authbind.

Taking It Live

To get it working for us, we have to perform some simple configuration work as follows:

sudo touch /etc/authbind/byport 80

sudo chown dave /etc/authbind/byport 80

sudo chmod 500 /etc/authbind/byport 80

This tells `authbind` to allow the user, `dave`, to bind processes to port `80`.

We no longer need to change the process UID, so we edit the penultimate line of `app.js` to the following:

```
app.listen(80);
```

We should also change ownership of the `login` folder as follows:

chown -R dave login

Now, we can start our server without touching the `root` access at all, as follows:

nohup authbind node app.js &

The `authbind` utility can cause our app to work out of the box, with no modifications necessary. However, it currently lacks IPv6 support so it's not yet future-proof.

Hosting multiple processes from port 80

What about serving multiple processes with the default HTTP port?

We can achieve this with the third-party `http-proxy` module. To install this module, we need to run the following command:

npm install http-proxy

Let's say we have two apps: one (our `login` app) to be hosted at `login.nodecookbook.com` and the other (the `server.js` file from the very first recipe of this book) at `nodecookbook.com`. Both domains point to the same IP.

The `server.js` file will be listening to port `8080` and we'll modify `login/app.js` to listen again to port `3000` as shown in the following code:

```
app.listen(3000, '127.0.0.1');
```

We also added a second argument defining what address to bind to (rather than any address). This prevents our server from being accessed by the port.

Let's create a file in a new folder, call it `proxy.js`, and write the following:

```
require('http-proxy')
  .createServer({router : {
    'login.nodecookbook.com': 'localhost:3000',
```

```
      'nodecookbook.com': 'localhost:8080'
}}).listen(80, function () {
   process.setuid('www-data');
});
```

The object passed to `createServer` contains a router property, which in turn is an object instructing `http-proxy` to route incoming traffic on a particular domain to the correct locally-hosted process according to its port.

We finish off by binding to port `80` and degrading from `root` to `www-data`.

To initialize our app, we must run the following commands:

nohup node login/bin/www &

nohup node server.js &

nohup node proxy.js &

Since we're binding our proxy server to port `80`, these commands must be run as `root`. If we're operating SSH with a non-root account, we simply prefix these three commands with `sudo`.

See also

- The *Automatic crash recovery* recipe
- The *Continuous deployment* recipe
- The *Hosting with a Platform as a Service provider* recipe

Automatic crash recovery

When we create a site, the server and site logic is all tied up in one process, whereas with other platforms, the server code is already in place. If our site code has bugs, the server is very unlikely to crash, and thus, in many cases the site can stay active even if one part of it is broken.

With a Node-based website, a small bug can crash the entire process, and this bug may only be triggered once in a blue moon.

As a hypothetical example, the bug could be related to character encoding on POST requests. When someone like Felix Geisendörfer completes and submits a form, suddenly our entire server crashes because it can't handle umlauts.

In this recipe, we'll look at using Upstart, an event-driven `init` service available for Linux servers, which isn't based upon Node, but is nevertheless a very handy accomplice.

Taking It Live

Getting ready

We will need Upstart installed on our server. http://upstart.ubuntu.com contains instructions on how to download and install it. If we're already using an Ubuntu or Fedora remote server, then Upstart will already be integrated.

How to do it...

Let's make a new server that purposefully crashes when we access it via HTTP, as follows:

```
var http = require('http');
http.createServer(function (req, res) {
  res.end("Oh oh! Looks like I'm going to crash...");
  throw 'crash ahoy!';
}).listen(8080);
```

After the first page loads, the server will crash and the site goes offline.

Let's call this code `server.js` placing it on our remote server under `/var/www/crashingserver`.

Now, we create our Upstart configuration file, saving it as `/etc/init/crashingserver.conf` on our server, as follows:

```
start on started network-services

respawn
respawn limit 100 5

setuid www-data

exec /usr/bin/node /var/www/crashingserver/server.js >> \
  /var/log/crashingserver.log 2>&1

post-start exec echo "Server was (re)started on $(date)" | mail -s 
  "Crashing Server (re)starting" dave@nodecookbook.com
```

Finally, we initialize our server as follows:

start crashingserver

When we access http://nodecookbook.com:8080 and refresh the page, our site is still accessible. A quick look at `/var/log/crashingserver.log` reveals that the server did indeed crash. We could also check our inbox to find the server restart notification.

How it works...

The name of the Upstart service is taken from the particular Upstart configuration filename. We initiate the `/etc/init/crashingserver.conf` Upstart service with start `crashingserver`.

The first line of the configuration ensures our web server automatically recovers even when the operating system on our remote server is restarted (for example, due to a power failure, required reboot, and so on).

The `respawn` variable is declared twice; once to turn on respawning and then to set `respawn limit`—a maximum of 100 restarts every 5 seconds. The limit must be set according to our own scenario. If the website has low traffic, this number might be adjusted to, say, 10 restarts in 8 seconds.

We want to stay alive if at all possible, but if an issue is persistent, we can take that as a red flag that a bug is having a detrimental effect on user experience or system resources.

The next line initializes our server as the `www-data` user, and sends the output to `/var/log/crashingserver.log`.

The final line sends out an e-mail just after our server has been started, or restarted. This is so we can be notified that there are probably issues to address with our server.

There's more...

Let's implement another Upstart script that notifies us if the server crashes beyond its `respawn limit`. We'll also look at another way to keep our server alive.

Detecting a respawn limit violation

If our server exceeds the `respawn limit`, it's likely there is a serious issue that should be solved as soon as possible. We need to know about it immediately. To achieve this in Upstart, we can create another Upstart configuration file that monitors the `crashingserver` daemon, sending an e-mail if the `respawn limit` is transgressed. We will do this with the help of the following code:

```
task

start on stopped crashingserver PROCESS=respawn

script
  if [ "$JOB" != '' ]
    then echo "Server "$JOB" has crashed on $(date)" | mail -s \
    $JOB" site down!!" dave@nodecookbook.com
  fi
end script
```

Taking It Live

Let's save this under `/etc/init/sitedownmon.conf`.

Then we run the following commands:

`start crashingserver`

`start sitedownmon`

We define this Upstart process as a task (it only has one thing to do, after which it exits). We don't want it to stay alive after our server has crashed.

The task is performed when the `crashingserver` daemon has stopped during a respawn (for example, when the `respawn limit` has been broken).

Our script stanza (directive) contains a small bash script that checks for the existence of the `JOB` environment variable (in our case, it would be set to `crashingserver`) and then sends an e-mail accordingly. If we don't check its existence, a `sitedownmon` variable seems to trigger false positives when it is first started and sends an e-mail with an empty `JOB` variable.

We could later extend this script to include more web servers, simply by adding one line to `sitedownmon.conf` per server, as follows:

`start on stopped anotherserver PROCESS=respawn`

Staying up with forever

There is a simpler Node-based alternative to Upstart called `forever`. We need to run the following command to install `forever`:

`sudo npm -g install forever`

First we simply initiate our server with `forever` as follows:

`forever server.js`

We then access our site. Some of the terminal output will contain the following, but we'll still be able to access our site (although it will have been crashed and restarted):

`warn: Forever detected script exited with code: 8`

`warn: Forever restarting script for 1 time`

To deploy our site on a remote server, we log in to our server via SSH, install `forever`, and run the following command:

`forever start server.js`

While this technique is certainly less complex, it's also less robust. Upstart provides core kernel functionality and is therefore system critical. If Upstart fails, the kernel panics and the whole operating system will restart.

Nevertheless, `forever` is used widely in production on Nodejitsu's PaaS stack, and its attractive simplicity may be viable for less mission-critical production environments.

See also

- The *Deploying an app to a server environment* recipe
- The *Hosting with a Platform as a Service provider* recipe
- The *Continuous deployment* recipe

Continuous deployment

The more streamlined our processes, the more productive we can be. Continuous deployment is about committing small ongoing improvements to a production server in a time saving, efficient way.

Continuous deployment is especially relevant to team collaboration projects. Instead of working on separate forks of the code and spending extra time, money, and effort on integration, everyone works on the same code base so integration is seamless.

In this recipe, we'll create a deployment flow using Git as a version control tool. While this may not be enough supportive to Node, it can certainly boost productivity for coding, deploying, and managing Node projects.

> If we're a little unfamiliar with Git, we can gain insight from GitHub's help documentation available at `http://help.github.com`.

Getting ready

We'll need Git installed on both our server and desktop systems. Instructions for different systems can be found at `http://book.git-scm.com/2_installing_git.html`.

If we're using Linux with the `apt-get` package manager, we can run the following command to install Git:

```
sudo apt-get install git git-core
```

If we are installing Git for the first time, we'll have to set the personal information configuration settings as follows:

```
git config --global user.name "Dave Clements"
git config --global user.email "dave@nodecookbook.com"
```

Taking It Live

We'll be using our `login` app, which we deployed to our server in the first recipe. So let's use the SSH service on our server and enter the `/var/www/login` directory as follows:

```
ssh -l root nodecookbook.com -t "cd /var/www/login; bash"
```

Since we'll not be running our app as `root`, we'll keep things simple and change the listening port in `login/app.js` to `8000` as follows:

```
app.listen(8000);
```

How to do it...

Once we've logged in to our server and installed Git (see the *Getting ready* section) in the `login` folder, we run the following:

```
git init
git add *
git commit -m "initial commit"
```

Next, we create a bare repository (it has a record of all the changes but no actual working files), which we'll be pushing changes to. This helps to keep things consistent.

We'll call the bare repository `repo`, because this is the repository we'll be pushing our changes to and we'll create it within the `login` folder, as follows:

```
mkdir repo
echo repo > .gitignore
cd repo
git --bare init
```

Next, we hook up our bare repository `repo` to the `login` app repository, and push all the commits to `repo`, as follows:

```
cd ..
git remote add repo ./repo
git push repo master
```

Now, we'll write a Git hook that instructs the `login` repository to pull any changes from the bare `repo` repository, and then restarts our `login` app whenever `repo` is updated via a remote Git push, as follows:

```
cd repo/hooks
touch post-update
chmod +x post-update
nano post-update
```

With the file open in `nano`, we write the following code:

```
#!/bin/sh

cd /root/login
env -i git pull repo master

exec forever restart /root/login/app.js
```

Then we can save our hook by pressing *Ctrl + O* and afterwards exit using *Ctrl + X*.

If we ever make Git commits to the `login` repository, the two repositories could go out of sync. To fix this, we create another hook for the `login` repository as follows:

```
#!/bin/sh
git push repo
```

We store this in `login/.git/hooks/post-commit`, ensuring it has been made executable using `chmod +x post-commit`.

We'll be making commits to the `repo` repository remotely via the SSH protocol. Ideally, we want to create a system user just for Git interactions. We will do this with the help of the following code:

useradd git

passwd git   #set a password

mkdir /home/git

chown git /home/git

We've also created home directories for the `git` user to make it easy for `forever` to store logs and PID files. We'll need to make `git` the owner of the `login` app, allowing us to manage it using Git through SSH, as follows:

cd /var/www

chown -R git login

Finally (for the server-side setup), we log in as the `git` user and start our app using `forever`, as follows:

su git

forever start /var/www/login/app.js

Assuming our server is hosted at `nodecookbook.com`, we could now access the `login` app at `http://nodecookbook.com:8000`.

Taking It Live

Back on our desktop, we clone the `repo` repository as follows:

```
git clone ssh://git@nodecookbook.com/var/www/login/repo
```

> While the Git command-line app is available for Windows, those who use Git with bash or those who prefer a GUI could benefit from Msysgit. Check out `http://msysgit.github.io` for more information.

This will give us a `repo` directory containing all the generated files perfectly matching our original `login` folder. We can then enter the `repo` folder and make a change to our code (say, altering the port in `app.js`), as follows:

```
app.listen(9000);
```

Then, we commit the change and push to our server as follows:

```
git commit -a -m "changed port"
git push
```

On the server side, our app should have automatically restarted, resulting in our app now being hosted from `http://nodecookbook.com:9000` instead of `http://nodecookbook.com:8000`.

How it works...

We created two Git repositories. The first is the `login` app itself. When we ran `git init`, a `.git` directory was added to the `login` folder. The `git add *` command adds all of the files in the folder and `commit -m "initial commit"` plants our additions into Git's version control system. So, now our entire code base is recognized by Git.

The second is `repo`, which is created with the `--bare` flag. This is a sort of skeleton repository providing all of the expected Git functionality, but lacking the actual files (it has no working tree).

While it may seem overly complex to use two repositories, it actually simplifies things greatly. Since Git does not allow pushes to a branch that is currently checked in, we will have to create a separate dummy branch so we can check out of the master and into the dummy branch. This creates problems with the Git hooks and restarting our app. The hooks try to start the app for the wrong branch. The branches can also quickly become out of sync, and the hooks only add fuel to the fire.

As `repo` is within the `login` directory, we create a `.gitignore` file telling Git to disregard this subdirectory. Even though `login` and `repo` are on the same server, we add `repo` as a remote repository. This puts some necessary distance between the repositories and allows us to later use our first Git hook to cause `login` to pull changes from `repo`. A Git push from `repo` to `login` wouldn't cause `login` to update its working directory, whereas pulling from `repo` into `login` does initiate a merge.

After our `remote add` command, we perform an initial push from the master branch (`login`) to `repo`; now they're singing off the same hymn sheet.

Then we create our hooks.

Git hooks are executable files, which reside in the repository's `hook` folder. There are a variety of available hooks (already in the folder, but suffixed with `.sample`). We used two hooks—`post-update` and `post-commit`. One executes after an update (for example, once changes have been pulled and integrated into `repo`), and one after a commit.

The first hook, `login/repo/hooks/post-update`, essentially provides our continuous deployment functionality. It changes its working directory from `repo` to `login` using `cd`, and commands a `git pull` command. The `git pull` command is prefixed with `env -i`. This prevents problems with certain Git functionality that would otherwise execute the Git commands on behalf of `repo` no matter what directory we sent our hook script to. Git utilizes a `$GIT_DIR` environment variable to lock us in to the repository that the hook is called from. The `env -i` prefix deals with this by telling `git pull` to ignore (`-i`) all environment variables.

Having updated the working directory, our hook then goes on to call `forever restart`, causing our app to reinitialize with the committed changes in place.

Our second hook is little more than a polyfill to ensure code base consistency in the event that commits are made directly to the `login` repository. Making commits directly to the `login` directory won't update the working tree, nor will it cause our app to restart, but the code between `login` and `repo` will at least maintain synchronicity.

For the sake of damage limitation (if we were ever compromised), we create a specific account for handling Git updates over SSH, giving it a home directory, taking ownership of the `login` app, and executing the primary initialization of our app.

Once the server is configured, it's plain sailing. After cloning the `repo` repository to our local development environment, we simply make a change, add and commit that change, and then push to the server.

The server receives our push request, updates repo, initiates the `post-update` hook, which makes `login` pull the changes from `repo`, after which the `post-update` hook uses `forever` to restart `app.js`, and thus we have a continuous deployment workflow.

We can potentially have as many clones from as many locations as we like, so this method lends itself well to geographically-independent team collaboration projects, both large and small.

Taking It Live

> One project that could be really worth our attention is JS-Git (https://github.com/creationix/js-git). The goal of this project is to implement Git using pure JavaScript that's compatible both, with Node and modern browsers. Once a certain level of maturity is reached and JS-Git starts seeing action in the wild, implementing the guts of this recipe could become as easy as installing and configuring a Node module or two.

There's more...

We could avoid uploading modules by using `npm install` in the `post-update` hook. Also, Git hooks don't have to be written in shell script, we can write them in Node!

Building module dependencies on update

Some Node modules are written in pure JavaScript; others have C or C++ bindings. Those with C or C++ bindings have to be built from source—a task which is system specific. Unless our live server environment is identical to our development environment, we shouldn't simply push code build for one system onto another.

Furthermore, to save on transfer bandwidth and have faster synchronizations, we could have our Git hooks install all modules (native bindings and JavaScript) and have Git ignore the `node_modules` folder entirely.

So in our local repository, let's do the following:

```
echo node_modules >> .gitignore
```

Then, we'll change the `post-update` hook in our bare remote repository (`login/repo/hooks`) to the following:

```
#!/bin/sh
cd /root/login
env -i git pull repo master && npm rebuild && npm install
exec forever restart /root/login/app.js
```

We've added `&& npm rebuild && npm install` to the `git pull` line (using `&&` to ensure they benefit from the `env -i` command).

Now if we added a module to `package.json`, and did a `git commit -a` followed by `git push`, our local `repo` would push `package.json` to the remote `repo`. This would trigger the `post-update` hook to pull changes into the main `login` repository, and follow this up with an `npm rebuild` command (to rebuild any C/C++ dependencies) and an `npm install` command (to install any new modules).

Writing a Node Git hook for integrated testing

Continuous deployment is an extension of continuous integration, which generally carries the expectation that a thorough test suite is run against any code changes for quality assurance.

Our `login` app (being a basic demonstration site) doesn't have a test suite (for info on test suites, see *Chapter 10, Writing Your Own Node Modules*), but we can still write a hook that executes any tests that could be added to login in the future.

What's more, we can write it in Node, which has the added bonus of functioning cross platform (on Windows, for example, although we'd have to change the hashbang) as follows:

```
#!/usr/bin/env node
var npm = require("npm");

npm.load(function (err) {
    if (err) { throw err; }

    npm.commands.test(function (err) {
        if (err) { process.exit(1); }
    });

});
```

We would place this code on the server under `login/repo/hooks/pre-commit` and make it executable (`chmod +x pre-commit`).

The first line sets `node` as the script's interpreter directive (much like how `#!/bin/sh` sets the `sh` shell for shell scripts). Now we're in Node country.

We use npm programmability to load the `package.json` file for our app, and then run the test script (if any is specified).

We then add the following to our `package.json` file:

```
{
    "name": "application-name"
,   "version": "0.0.1"
,   "private": true
,   "dependencies": {
       "express": "2.5.5"
    ,  "jade": ">= 0.0.1"
    },
    "scripts": {
      "test": "node test"
    },
    "devDependencies": {"npm": "1.1.18"}
}
```

Taking It Live

Then run the following command:

`npm -d install`

Now, whenever we push to `repo`, any changes will only be committed if they pass the tests. As long as we have a well-written test suite, this is a great way to maintain good code.

> For our `scripts.test` property, we used `node test` (as in *Chapter 10, Writing Your Own Node Modules*). However, there are more advanced test frameworks available to us, such as Mocha (`http://visionmedia.github.com/mocha/`).

> This Node Git hook is adapted (with permission) from a gist by Domenic Denicola, which can be found at `https://gist.github.com/2238951`.

See also

- The *Deploying an app to a server environment* recipe
- The *Automatic crash recovery* recipe
- The *Creating a test-driven module API* recipe discussed in *Chapter 10, Writing Your Own Node Modules*
- The *Hosting with a Platform as a Service provider* recipe

Hosting with a Platform as a Service provider

A **Platform as a Service** (**PaaS**) for Node incorporates all of the concepts discussed in the previous three chapters and boils deployment down to a very basic, yet powerful, set of commands. When it comes to deployment, PaaS can make our lives very easy. With one simple command, our app is deployed, and with another we can seamlessly update and reinitialize.

In this example, we'll learn how to deploy to Nodejitsu, one of the leading Node-hosting platform providers.

Getting ready

First, we'll install `jitsu`, Nodejitsu's deployment and app management command-line app, as follows:

```
sudo npm -g install jitsu
```

Before we proceed, we must sign up for an account as follows:

```
jitsu signup
```

The app will take us through the trivial signup process and create an account for us, which we must confirm by e-mail.

> Nodejitsu will provide a free 30 day trial, after which we have to sign up for a plan (https://www.nodejitsu.com/pricing/), unless we have an open source project, in which case we can apply for free hosting (http://opensource.nodejitsu.com).

Once we've received our e-mail, we use the provided voucher, for instance:

```
jitsu users confirm dave 0b4c2692-395a-4a54-af55-7c6392e796a6
```

As in the first recipe, we'll use the `login` app from the *Initializing and using a session* recipe of *Chapter 7, Accelerating Development with Express*.

How to do it...

First of all, we enter the `login` folder and make some modifications to `package.json`, as follows:

```
{
  "name": "application-name",
  "version": "0.0.1",
  "private": true,
  "scripts": {
    "start": "node ./bin/www"
  },
  "engines": {
    "node": "0.10.x"
  },
  "subdomain": "login",
  "dependencies": {
    "express": "~4.0.0-rc2",
    "static-favicon": "~1.0.0",
    "morgan": "~1.0.0",
    "cookie-parser": "~1.0.1",
    "body-parser": "~1.0.0",
    "debug": "~0.7.4",
    "jade": "~1.3.0",
    "express-session": "~1.0.2",
```

Taking It Live

```
    "method-override": "~1.0.0"
  }
}
```

And now we deploy `jitsu` by running the following command:

`Jitsu deploy`

If we navigate to our specified subdomain at http://login.nodejitsu.com, or alternatively http://login.jit.su, we will see our `login` app (if a subdomain isn't available, `jitsu` will suggest alternatives).

How it works...

We made some modifications to `package.json`. The name of our app is the only alteration that is necessarily made by directly editing `package.json`. The other additions could have been made on our behalf by the `jitsu` executable. It is important to set the name of the app because in `jitsu`, apps are managed by their name.

If we had not appended the `subdomain` and `engines` properties to `package.json`, `jitsu` would have asked for the particulars. When we run `jitsu`, it gets deployed and regenerates `package.json` on our behalf.

The `subdomain` property specifies the label prefix to `nodejitsu.com`, from where we host our app (for example, `login.nodejitsu.com`). The engines property defines which versions of Node our app is designed for. The `start` subproperty in `scripts` is also essential as it informs Nodejitsu of the ignition script—the file that starts the app.

There's more...

Let's find out how to access our Nodejitsu app via a custom domain, and how to provision a database backend through the `jitsu` executable.

Assigning custom domains to Nodejitsu apps

To prepare our app to serve through a custom domain, we make an amendment to `package.json` as shown in the following code:

```
//bottom of package.json file..
  "subdomain": "login",
    "domains": ["login.nodecookbook.com"],
}
```

Then, we push our changes with `jitsu` as follows:

`jitsu apps update ncb-login`

The app is now ready to receive traffic via `http://login.nodecookbook.com`, but before traffic can reach it, we must match our domain's A records with those of Nodejitsu.

We can get the current list of Nodejitsu A records with `dig` (or a similar command-line app), as follows:

`dig nodejitsu.com`

The process for changing A records depends upon our domain providers. We can generally find it in the DNS area of our provider's control panel/administration area.

Provisioning a database with jitsu

In the last recipe of *Chapter 7, Accelerating Development with Express*, we built a MongoDB backed Express app. Now we're going to take the `profiler` app live with Nodejitsu, making use of the database provisioning capabilities of `jitsu`.

So, let's provision a Mongo database for the profiler database as follows:

`jitsu databases create mongo profiler`

`jitsu` will provision our database through a third-party database PaaS provider (in Mongo's case, the PaaS provider is MongoHQ). The output provides us with the MongoDB URL for our new database, which will look something like the following code:

```
data:    Connection url:
  mongodb://nodejitsu_dave:6easrcf3vi0c4gkq48h3udo3@
  ds045998.mongolab.com:45998/nodejitsu_dave_nodejitsudb5369862890
```

So, we update the connection URL in `profiler/tools/prepopulate.js` as follows:

```
client.connect('mongodb://nodejitsu_dave:6easrcf3vi0c4gkq48h3udo3@
  ds045998.mongolab.com:45998/nodejitsu_dave_
  nodejitsudb5369862890',
  function (err, db) { // rest of our populating
```

We'll also need to remove or comment out the code related to `dropDatabase` in `prepopulate.js`—this clears user settings on the remotely provisioned databases, which we don't want to do, as follows:

```
//previous code
   //db.dropDatabase(function (err) {
      // e(err);

         db.collection('users').insert(users, function (err) {
           if (err) { return console.log(err); }
           console.log('Added users')
           tidy(db);
         });
```

```
            db.collection('profiles').insert(profiles, function (err, o) {
              e(err);
              console.log('Added profiles')
              tidy(db);
            });

      //});
    //rest of the code
```

Then, we run it from the `profiler/tools` folder as follows:

`node prepopulate.js   #might have to npm install first...`

This fills our remote database with profiles and login data.

We update our database URI in two other places, `profiler/models/profiles.js` and `profiler/login/login.js`. In both places, the third line is altered to run the following:

```
client.connect('mongodb://nodejitsu_dave:6easrcf3vi0c4gkq48h3udo3@
  ds045998.mongolab.com:45998/
  odejitsu_dave_nodejitsudb5369862890',
  function (err, db) { // rest of the code....
```

If we are using Nodejitsu's trial offering, we may only be able to run one app at a time. In this case, we will need to run the following:

`jitsu stop ncb-login`

Then, finally, we can type the following:

`jitsu deploy`

`jitsu` will ask us for certain settings (`subdomain`, `scripts.start`, and `engines`). We can just press *Enter* and stick to the defaults (unless of course `profiler.nodejitsu.com` is already taken, in which case we should choose a different URL). `jitsu` will then deploy our app; we should be able to access it at `profiler.nodejitsu.com`.

See also

- The *Deploying an app to a server environment* recipe
- The *Automatic crash recovery* recipe
- The *Continuous deployment* recipe

Index

Symbols

$.get method 74
@background property 208
_compile method 322
--max-old-space-size method 26
.npmignore 330
_read method 139, 140
--save flag 199
_transform method 144, 147
<tr> tag 198
_write function 139
_write method 138, 144

A

Add button 231, 237
admin_lock variable 115
admin user
 creating 112, 113
 modifying operations, locking 113-115
aggregation 102, 103
AJAX
 browser-server transmission via 70-79
API
 about 79
 extending 317-325
app
 deploying, to server environment 331-337
app.get method 187
app.js file
 configuring 224, 225
 picking apart 182-185
app.listen method 261
apply function 69
app mounting 233

Asterisk
 URL 274
asterisks wildcards
 defining 194
Atomicity Consistency Isolation Durability (ACID) 107
attachments
 sending 273, 274
authbind
 URL 335
 used, for privileged ports 335, 336
authenticated areas
 logging out 254-256
authenticate function 254
auth-int attribute 253
automated phone call
 making 278, 279
automatic crash recovery 337-340

B

Base64 encoding
 URL 167, 244
basename property 29
basename variable 9
Basic Authentication
 implementing 242-245
 securing, with SSL/TLS 259
 URL 242
 with Express 245
Benchmarking 238, 239
BigCouch
 CouchDB, scaling with 109
 URL 109
Binary JSON (BSON) 104
body-parser
 about 39

POST data, accessing with 39, 40
bodyParser method 40
boundary parameter 50
broken downloads
  resumes, enabling from 57
Browserify
  about 158
  installing 158
  URL 158
browser-server transmission
  via AJAX 70-79
Buffer.concat method 174
Buffer.copy method 25
bufferOffset property 54
bufferOffset variable 25
bufferSize property 25
Buffer.slice variable 56
buffertools.concat function 149
Buffer.toString method 309
Buffer variable 25
buildStats function 307-311
bytesOut variable 56
bytesSent parameter 56

C

CA 257
cacheAndDeliver function 20, 22
cache.clean method 27, 28
cache[f].content property 24, 25
cache.store[f] method 27
cache.store function 27
callback function 140
callback parameter 139
call method 93, 316
Cancel button 244
Can I use
  URL 44
Carriage Return Line Feed (CRLF) 273
cb function 63, 133
cb parameter 55, 288
Certificate Authority. *See* **CA**
Certificate Signing Request (CSR) 257
Chai
  URL 305
changeUser method 95
checkAndSave function 108

checkStatus function 277
chmod 17
chunk parameter 140
chunks property 54
chunk variable 131, 132
clean method 27
client
  multipart data, uploading as 49-52
clientScript variable 174
colorMatches function 149
colors
  playing with 208
Comma Separated Values. *See* **CSV**
connect
  about 39, 184
  POST data, accessing with 39, 40
  URL 184
connection.query method 96
content caching
  in memory, for immediate delivery 18-21
content changes
  reflecting 20, 21
contents property 274
Continuous deployment 341-347
CORS
  URL 64
CouchDB
  data retrieval, with Cradle from 109-115
  data, storing with Cradle 107-109
  scaling, with BigCouch 109
  URL 107
CouchDB changes stream
  accessing, with Cradle 115-117
CouchDB HTTP interface
  exposing, to remote connections 115
Cradle
  used, for retrieving data 109-115
  used, for storing data to CouchDB 107-109
Create a new application button 80
createConnection method 96
createHash method 248
createQuotesView function 110
createServer method 39, 174, 261
createTransport method 272
Cross-browser real-time logic
  used, with Socket.IO 162-166
Cross-Origin Resource Sharing. *See* **CORS**

cross-site request forgery
  preventing 260-268
Cross-Site Request Forgery (CSRF) 260
cross-site scripting attacks
  eliminating 267
Cryptographic password hashing
  about 246-250
  URL 246
CSRF elements
  POST forms, auto-securing with 265-267
CSS preprocessors
  used, with Express 201-210
CSV 90
CSV file
  writing to 90-93
ctime property 21
curl
  URL 29
custom domains
  assigning, to Nodejitsu apps 350
custom events 165, 166
custom middleware
  for site-wide session management 215-217

D

data
  retrieving from CouchDB, with Cradle 109-115
  retrieving, with MongoDB 99-106
  retrieving, with Redis 118-121
  storing to CouchDB, with Cradle 107-109
  storing, with MongoDB 99-106
  storing, with Redis 118-121
database
  provisioning, with jitsu 351, 352
database bridge
  creating 222-224
data event
  consuming via 132-134
Data flows 234
db.create method 108
debug function 186
decide function 129-135
development tool
  WebSockets, using as 176, 177

Digest Authentication
  implementing 251-256
digest method 248
digest.response property 253
DNS records, changing
  with registrar, URL 290
Document Object Model (DOM)
  URL 66
download throttling
  implementing 52-57
duplex stream 127
duration object 309
duration property 301
dynamic routing
  implementing 191-194

E

EJS templates 199, 200
e-mail
  receiving, from external SMTP server 289, 290
  sending 270-274
emit method 165
encoding parameter 139
enctype attribute 41
engine.io
  about 163
  URL 163
envelope parameter 288
envelope.to property 288
err object 185
EventEmitter
  integrating 323-325
exist parameter 16
exports object 308
exports.stat function 314
Express
  Basic Authentication, using with 245
  CSS preprocessors, using with 201-210
  HTTPS, enabling in 259
Express framework
  templating in 195-201
Express scaffolding
  generating 180-186
  initialization process 185

Express web app
  making 220-238
external connections
  Redis, securing from 125
external SMTP server
  e-mail, receiving from 289, 290

F

favicon gotcha 17
feed variable 128
field parameter 43
file limits, Unix systems
  URL 56
fileName property 274
filenames
  preserving, with formidable 44
file parameter 43
files
  uploading, via PUT 44-46
files parameter 51
file uploads
  handling 40-46
findBitRate function 307-311
find method 102
flash messages 217-220
forceLogOut property 255
forEach method 49
forever
  staying up with 340
formidable
  filenames, preserving with 44
  used, to accept POST data 43
from.array method 91
from parameter 166
fs.exists method 16
fs.readFile method 15, 31
fs.stat function 21
fs.stat method 21, 25, 301
fstats object 308
fs.watch method
  about 176
  URL 176
fullname property 61-66
functional module mock-up
  writing 305-309

G

generateTextFromHtml property 273
GitHub
  URL 341
git pull command 345
Google Hot Trends
  cross referencing, with Twitter tweets 85-87
greater complexity
  preparing for 136, 137

H

handleAbort variable 56
handler parameter 87
Hang-Up Signal (HUP) 334
hardened hashing
  with PBKDF2 249, 250
Hash-based Message Authentication Code.
  See **HMAC**
hash functions
  URL 248
HMAC
  unique hashes, making with 249
hotTrends.xmlHandler method 86
hours variable 309
href attribute 232, 268
HTML e-mails
  creating 273
HTTP client
  Node, using as 47-52
http.createServer method 8
http.get method 47
http.request method 47, 49
HTTPS
  enabling, in Express 259
https.Server function 295
HTTPS web server
  setting up 257, 258

I

id attribute 45
include statement 201
INCR command 176
indexing 102, 103
inherit method 143
initialization process 185

init method 171
insert method 102
inspect method 37
INSTALL button 7
integrated testing
  Node Git hook, writing for 347
isUpdated variable 21
ix variable 149

J

Jade
  about 196
  include statement 201
  literal JavaScript, using 200
JavaScript Object Notation. *See* JSON
jitsu
  database, provisioning with 351, 352
JS-Git
  URL 346
JSON
  object, converting to 59-62
jsonHander method 87
jsonHandler method 82, 84
JSONP
  about 62, 63
  URL 62
JSONP responses
  constructing 62, 63
JSONStream
  URL 161
JSONStream.parse function 136
JSON with Padding. *See* JSONP

L

large file generation
  URL 52
lastChanged variable 21
layout.jade
  using 201
length property 140
LESS
  URL 209
  using 209, 210
limit
  updating 103-105
Line Feed (LF) 273

Linux Apache MySQL PHP (LAMP) 94
listen method 165
literal JavaScript
  used, in Jade 200
load function 78
locals 237
log function 130
loop function 55, 56

M

Mail Exchange. *See* MX records
Mailinator
  URL 271
main property 327
makeCall function 82
mappings.sites object 293
md5 function 251
message event 165
middleware
  URL 185
middleware method 205
mixin keyword 226
mixins 236, 237
Mocha
  URL 303, 348
modifiers
  updating 103-105
modifying operations
  locking, to admin user 113-115
module
  deploying, to npm 326-329
module dependencies
  building, on update 346
module's request
  URL 48
module's wiki page
  URL 32
MongoDB
  data, retrieving with 99-106
  data, storing with 99-106
  without MongoDB 105, 106
MongoDB server
  URL 99
mounted login app
  modifying 229-233

mp3dat object
  stat function, adding to 315, 316
Mp3dat object 313
mp3dat.stat method 301
mp3dat variable 301
MP3 files
  URL 300
MPEG-1 layer 3 file retrieval
  URL 300
msg parameter 165
msg property 224
Msysgit
  URL 344
multilevel routing 10, 11
multi method 120
multipartAssembler function 51, 52
multipart data
  uploading, as client 49-52
multiple instances
  allowing 316
multiple processes
  hosting, from port 80 336, 337
MX records
  URL 290
MySQL server
  results, receiving from 98
  SQL, connecting to 94-98
  SQL, sending to 94-98

N

NeDB to MongoDB
  URL 106
nested mixins parameter 206
nested mixins rest parameter 206, 207
netcat
  URL 280
network latency
  overcoming 120, 121
next parameter 184
ngSMS
  URL 274
Node
  used, as HTTP client 47-52
Node-based WebSocket client
  creating 157, 158

NODE_ENV
  changing 191
Node Git hook
  writing, for integrated testing 347
Node installation
  URL 332
  via package manager, URL 332
Nodejitsu
  URL 349
Nodejitsu apps
  custom domains, assigning to 350
nodemailer
  using 270
Node processes
  streaming 144-150
Node Redis module
  speeding up 120
Node Static 32
NodeZoo
  URL 12
nonce attribute 253
no-op function 229
npm
  module, deploying to 326-329
npm init command 327
npm install command 181
npm link command 329
npm rebuild command 346
npm version 330

O

object
  converting, to JSON 59-62
  converting, to XML 64-70
Object.create method 85
Object Out of Bounds (OOB) 56
once method 23
on method 23
optimist module
  URL 97
optional routes
  defining 193, 194
options method 92
other environments
  setting 189, 190

other template engines
  using 198, 199
output parameter 79

P

PaaS
  hosting with 348-352
pagenum parameter 234
page variable 236
parseAuth function 253
parse method 37
parseString function 70
parseString method 66
parseString variable 69
partial application 69, 70
path.basename method 31
pathname property 29
PBKDF2
  hardened hashing, using with 249, 250
pcap
  used, to watch TCP traffic 284, 285
performance
  optimizing, with streaming 22-28
pipe method 134, 135
pipes
  playing with 134-137
Platform as a Service. *See* **PaaS**
pop method 140
port
  forwarding 283
port 80
  multiple processes, hosting from 336, 337
port property 157
POST data
  accepting, formidable used 43
  accessing, with body-parser 39, 40
  accessing, with connect 39, 40
  processing 35-40
postData variable 37
POST forms
  auto-securing, with CSRF elements 265-267
POST method 213
POST requests
  sending 48, 49
POST server
  protecting 37

privileged ports
  authbind, used for 335, 336
process.argv property 48
process memory overruns
  protecting against 26-28
profile object 198
profiler app
  modifying 225-229
profiles.pull method 234
profiles variable 66
prototypical inheritance
  about 310
  refactoring with 310-317
PUBLISH command 124
PubSub
  implementing, with Redis 121-125
push method 140
PUT
  files, uploading via 44-46
putty
  URL 333
PUT upload stream example
  creating 321

Q

qop attribute 253
query method 95
querystring module
  parsing 11, 12

R

randomBytes method 249
rcpt variable 289
Read-Eval-Print-Loop (REPL) 40
read method 130-133
read's size argument
  using 130-132
readStream method 53, 55
ready variable 128
realm variable 254
real-time widget
  creating 171-177
Redis
  data, retrieving with 118-121
  data, storing with 118-121
  securing, from external connections 125

Redis authentication 125
remote add command 345
remote connections
  CouchDB HTTP interface, exposing to 115
Remote Procedure Calls. *See* RPC
request module
  URL 160
require function 181
respawn limit violation
  detecting 339, 340
respawn variable 339
response.end method 10
response.finished property 10
response parameter 117
res.render method 195, 197
res.resume method 133
res.sid function 277
REST architecture
  URL 275
rest parameter 206, 207
result parameter 103
results
  receiving, from MySQL server 98
resumes
  enabling, from broken downloads 57
reusable streams
  making 141, 142
rootName property 65
route
  handling 234, 235
router
  setting up 7-12
routes/index.js
  loading 186
route validation 193
routing modules 12
routing modules, Node
  URL 12
RPC
  used, with Socket.IO 167-170
  using, with SockJS 169, 170

S

safeMix function 229, 237
scalability
  preparing for 175, 176

screen
  using 335
scripts object 181
scripts.test property 348
secureShare function 296
security risk anti-patterns
  identifying 28-32
Send button 156, 165
sendfile method 247
sendmail
  used, as alternative transport 272, 273
sendMail method 272
sendSms method 277
serialized data
  sending, from client to server 75-79
serve method 293
Server Name Indication. *See* SNI
server property 157
server tier environments
  managing 187-191
session
  initializing 211-220
  using 211-220
set command 191
setx command 191
should.js
  unit tests, using with 304, 305
should methods
  URL 305
sides parameter 206
Simple API for XML (SAX) 66
Simple Mail Transfer Protocol (SMTP) 270
site-wide session management
  custom middleware, used for 215-217
size parameter 140
size property 25
slice method 56
SMS
  sending 274-279
SMTP server
  creating 285-290
smtp variable 290
SNI 295-297
Socket.IO
  Cross-browser real-time logic, using
    with 162-166
  RPC, using with 167-170

URL 163
socket.join method 175
socket parameter 157
socket.send method 157
SockJS
  about 169
  RPC, using with 169
sort
  updating 103-105
spawnInstance method 317
SQL
  connecting, to MySQL server 94-98
  sending, to MySQL server 94-98
SSH protocol
  URL 332
SSL/TLS
  Basic Authentication, securing with 259
  URL 242
start property 181
stat
  and statStream, merging 322, 323
stat function
  adding, to initialized mp3dat object 315, 316
static files
  serving 13-17
stat method 308, 313, 314
stats object 301, 306, 325
statStream
  and stat, merging 322, 323
statStream method 318, 320, 321
STDIN stream example
  creating 321
store parameter 143
stream chunk buffers
  processing 147-149
streaming
  performance, optimizing with 22-28
stream interfaces
  making 137-144
stream.pipe method 23, 24
stream property 320
streams
  about 127
  chaining 136
  consuming 128-134
  filtering 136
  URL 128

streamStat method 322
String.replace method 62
Styles 238
subdomain property
  URL 350
superagent
  URL 48
supervisor module
  URL 8

T

TCP
  communicating with 280-285
  streaming over 150, 151
TCP traffic
  watching, pcap used 284, 285
TDD
  URL 300
template engines
  URL 195
template engines, comparisons
  URL 195
test-driven development. *See* **TDD**
test-driven module specification
  creating 300-305
testFile variable 301
text nodes
  generating 67, 68
this object 323
throttle function 55
timeProcessor function 309, 312
timestamp property 27
toString method 279
transform function 93
transform method 92
transform stream 143, 144
transport.close method 272
trending tweets
  fetching 79-87
trends property 86
tweetPath method 87
Twilio account
  URL 275
Twilio dashboard
  URL 275
Twilio Markup Language (TwiML) 278

Twilio numbers account section
 URL 276
TwimlResponse method 278
Twitter tweets
 Google Hot Trends, cross referencing with 85-87

U

Uniform Resource Identifier (URI) 7
unique hashes
 making, with HMAC 249
unit tests
 used, with should.js 304, 305
updateProfiles function 79
Upstart
 URL 338
uRealm property 255
uri attribute 253
urlOpts variable 49
url.parse method 11
user input
 cleaning 97, 98
 using 97, 98
username attribute 253
username parameter 255
user property 214, 215
users variable 290

V

validate function 219
validOpts variable 320
views 235, 236
virtual hosting
 Express apps 293-295
 implementing 291-297
 SNI 295-297
Virtual Private Servers (VPS) 331
visitTag method 266

W

WebSockets
 used, as development tool 176, 177
WebSocket server
 creating 154-162
WebSocket stream 158-162
whitelisting 31
writable._write method 139
writeStream function 289
ws module
 URL 154

X

XML
 object, converting to 64-70
XML attributes
 generating 67, 68

Thank you for buying
Node Cookbook *Second Edition*

About Packt Publishing

Packt, pronounced 'packed', published its first book "*Mastering phpMyAdmin for Effective MySQL Management*" in April 2004 and subsequently continued to specialize in publishing highly focused books on specific technologies and solutions.

Our books and publications share the experiences of your fellow IT professionals in adapting and customizing today's systems, applications, and frameworks. Our solution based books give you the knowledge and power to customize the software and technologies you're using to get the job done. Packt books are more specific and less general than the IT books you have seen in the past. Our unique business model allows us to bring you more focused information, giving you more of what you need to know, and less of what you don't.

Packt is a modern, yet unique publishing company, which focuses on producing quality, cutting-edge books for communities of developers, administrators, and newbies alike. For more information, please visit our website: `www.packtpub.com`.

About Packt Open Source

In 2010, Packt launched two new brands, Packt Open Source and Packt Enterprise, in order to continue its focus on specialization. This book is part of the Packt Open Source brand, home to books published on software built around Open Source licences, and offering information to anybody from advanced developers to budding web designers. The Open Source brand also runs Packt's Open Source Royalty Scheme, by which Packt gives a royalty to each Open Source project about whose software a book is sold.

Writing for Packt

We welcome all inquiries from people who are interested in authoring. Book proposals should be sent to `author@packtpub.com`. If your book idea is still at an early stage and you would like to discuss it first before writing a formal book proposal, contact us; one of our commissioning editors will get in touch with you.

We're not just looking for published authors; if you have strong technical skills but no writing experience, our experienced editors can help you develop a writing career, or simply get some additional reward for your expertise.

[PACKT] open source
community experience distilled
PUBLISHING

Node Web Development
Second Edition

ISBN: 978-1-78216-330-5   Paperback: 248 pages

A practical introduction to Node.js, an exciting server-side JavaScript web development stack

1. Learn about server-side JavaScript with Node.js and Node modules.
2. Website development both with and without the Connect/Express web application framework.
3. Developing both HTTP server and client applications.

CoffeeScript Programming with jQuery, Rails, and Node.js

ISBN: 978-1-84951-958-8   Paperback: 140 pages

Learn CoffeeScript programming with the three most popular web technologies around

1. Learn CoffeeScript, a small and elegant language that compiles to JavaScript and will make your life as a web developer better.
2. Explore the syntax of the language and see how it improves and enhances JavaScript.
3. Build three example applications in CoffeeScript step by step.

Please check www.PacktPub.com for information on our titles

[PACKT] open source
community experience distilled

Using Node.js for UI Testing
ISBN: 978-1-78216-052-6   Paperback: 146 pages

Learn how to easily automate testing of your web apps using Node.js, Zombie.js and Mocha

1. Use automated tests to keep your web app rock solid and bug-free while you code.
2. Use a headless browser to quickly test your web application every time you make a small change to it.
3. Use Mocha to describe and test the capabilities of your web app.

Socket.IO Real-time Web Application Development
ISBN: 978-1-78216-078-6   Paperback: 140 pages

Build modern real-time web applications powered by Socket.IO

1. Understand the usage of various socket.io features such as rooms, namespaces, and sessions.
2. Secure the socket.io communication.
3. Deploy and scale your socket.io and Node.js applications in production.

Please check **www.PacktPub.com** for information on our titles

Printed in Great Britain
by Amazon.co.uk, Ltd.,
Marston Gate.